Data Governance Tools

Sunil Soares

MC Press Online, LLC

Boise, ID 83703 USA

Data Governance Tools: Evaluation Criteria, Big Data Governance, and Alignment with Enterprise Data Management
Sunil Soares

First Edition
© Copyright 2014 Sunil Soares. All rights reserved.

Every attempt has been made to provide correct information. However, the publisher and the author do not guarantee the accuracy of the book and do not assume responsibility for information included in or omitted from it.

Ab Initio is a registered trademark of Ab Initio Software Corporation. Activiti is a registered trademark of Alfresco Software, Inc. ADABAS is a registered trademark of Software AG. Adaptive is a trademark or registered trademark of Adaptive Computing Enterprises, Inc. Adobe, Acrobat, and Reader are registered trademarks of Adobe Systems Incorporated in the United States and/or other countries. Amazon, DynamoDB, EC2, Elastic Compute Cloud, and Redshift are trademarks of Amazon.com, Inc., or its affiliates. Apache, Cassandra, CouchDB, Flume, Hadoop, HBase, Hive, Oozie, Pig, and Sqoop are trademarks of The Apache Software Foundation. ASG, ASG-becubic, ASG-metaGlossary, ASG-MyInfoAssist, and ASG-Rochade are trademarks or registered trademarks of ASG. Remedy is a registered trademark or trademark of BMC Software, Inc. ERwin is a registered trademark of CA, Inc. Clarabridge is a trademark of Clarabridge, Inc. Cloudera and Cloudera Impala are trademarks of Cloudera, Inc. Collibra is a registered trademark of Collibra Corporation. Concur is a registered trademark of Concur Technologies, Inc. Constant Contact is a registered trademark of Constant Contact in the United States and other countries. Couchbase is a registered trademark of Couchbase, Inc. ActiveLinx and MetaCenter are trademarks of Data Advantage Group, Inc. Denodo is a registered trademark of Denodo Technologies. Diaku and Diaku Axon are the trademarks of Diaku Ltd. Eclipse is a trademark of Eclipse Foundation, Inc. Eloqua is a trademark of Eloqua Corporation. Embarcadero and all other Embarcadero Technologies product or service names are trademarks, service marks, and/or registered trademarks of Embarcadero Technologies, Inc. EMC, Archer, Documentum, Greenplum, Pivotal, RSA, and SourceOne are trademarks or registered trademarks of EMC Corporation in the United States and/or other countries. Facebook and the Facebook logo are registered trademarks of Facebook, Inc. Financial Industry Business Ontology (FIBO) is a trademark of the EDM Council. Force.com, Salesforce, and Salesforce.com are registered trademarks of salesforce.com. Google, Maps, and Search Appliance are trademarks or registered trademarks of Google, Inc. EnCase and Guidance Software are registered trademarks or trademarks owned by Guidance Software in the United States and other jurisdictions. Hortonworks is a trademark of Hortonworks Inc. HP and HP Vertica are trademarks of Hewlett-Packard Development Company, L.P. IBM, AS/400, BigInsights, CICS, Cognos, DataStage, DB2, Domino, Guardium, IMS, InfoSphere, MQSeries, Notes, OpenPages, Optim, QualityStage, PureData, and SPSS are trademarks of International Business Machines Corporation, registered in many jurisdictions worldwide. Imperva is a registered trademark of Imperva. Informatica, AddressDoctor, Informatica Cloud, and PowerCenter are trademarks or registered trademarks of Informatica Corporation in the United States and in foreign countries. InfoTrellis is a trademark or registered trademark of InfoTrellis, Inc., in Canada and other countries. JIRA is a trademark of Atlassian. MapR is a registered trademark of MapR Technologies, Inc., in the United States and other countries. Marketo is a trademark of Marketo, Inc. Microsoft, Azure, Excel, Exchange, Outlook, SharePoint, SQL Server, Visual Basic, and Word are either registered trademarks or trademarks of Microsoft Corporation in the United States and/or other countries. MongoDB is a registered trademark of MongoDB, Inc. Netezza is a registered trademark of IBM International Group B.V., an IBM Company. NetSuite is a registered trademark of NetSuite, Inc. All Nuix trademarks are the property of Nuix Pty Ltd. OpenText is a trademark or registered trademark of Open Text SA and/or Open Text ULC. Oracle, Endeca, Exalytics, Java and all Java-based trademarks and logos, and MySQL are trademarks or registered trademarks of Oracle and/or its affiliates. Orchestra Networks is a registered trademark of Orchestra Networks in France and in jurisdictions throughout the world. Pega is a registered trademark of Pegasystems, Inc. Pentaho is a registered trademark of Pentaho, Inc. Protegrity is a registered trademark of Protegrity Corporation. QlikView is a registered trademark of Qlik Technologies, Inc., or its subsidiaries in the United States, other countries, or both. Recommind and Axcelerate are trademarks or registered trademarks of Recommind or its subsidiaries in the United States and other countries. Riak is a registered trademark of Basho Technologies, Inc. Sage is a registered trademark of Sage Software, Inc. SAP, BusinessObjects, HANA, NetWeaver, PowerDesigner, and Sybase are trademarks and registered trademarks of SAP SE in Germany and other countries. SAS is a registered trademark of the SAS Institute, Inc. Semarchy and Convergence are trademarks or registered trademarks of Semarchy. Symantec and Enterprise Vault are trade-marks or registered trademarks of Symantec Corporation or its affiliates in the United States and other countries. Tableau is a registered trademark of Tableau Software. Talend and Talend ESB are trademarks of Talend, Inc. Teradata and Aster are registered trademarks of Teradata Corporation and/or its affiliates in the United States and worldwide. TIBCO and StreamBase are trademarks or registered trade-marks of TIBCO Software, Inc., or its subsidiaries in the United States and/or other countries. Trillium Software, The Trillium Software System, and/or other Trillium Software, A Harte Hanks Company products referenced herein are either registered trademarks or trademark of Trillium Software, A Harte Hanks Company Corporation in the United States and/or other countries. Twitter and the Twitter logo are registered trademarks of Twitter, Inc. Yahoo! is a registered trademark of Yahoo, Inc., in the United States, other countries, or both. ZyLAB is a registered trademark of ZyLAB North America. Other company, product, or service names may be trademarks or service marks of others.

MC Press offers excellent discounts on this book when ordered in quantity for bulk purchases or special sales, which may include custo¬ covers and content particular to your business, training goals, marketing focus, and branding interest.

MC Press Online, LLC 3695 W. Quail Heights Court, Boise, ID 83703-3861 USA • (208) 629-7275
service@mcpressonline.com • www.mcpressonline.com • www.mc-store.com

ISBN: 978-1-58347-844-8

Dedicated to my beautiful daughters, Maya and Lizzie.

Many thanks to my wife Helena, who came up with the idea for this book.

A big thanks to my parents Cecilia and Hubert for their prayers and guidance.

I also want to acknowledge the Information Asset team, including Jatin Bhoir, Michelle D'Sa, Royson Mendonca, Yanxin Shi, and Dorothy Xavier. The Enterprise Data Management lab is a critical success factor in our client engagements and in the development of this book.

ABOUT THE AUTHOR

Sunil Soares is the founder and managing partner of Information Asset, a consulting firm that specializes in data governance. Prior to this role, Sunil was director of information governance at IBM, where he worked with clients across six continents and multiple industries. Before joining IBM, Sunil consulted with major financial institutions at the Financial Services Strategy Consulting Practice of Booz Allen & Hamilton in New York.

Sunil's first book, *The IBM Data Governance Unified Process* (MC Press, 2010), details the almost 100 steps to implement a data governance program. This book has been used by several organizations as the blueprint for their data governance programs and has been translated into Chinese. Sunil's second book, *Selling Information Governance to the Business: Best Practices by Industry and Job Function* (MC Press, 2011), reviews the best practices to approach information governance by industry and function. His third book, *Big Data Governance (MC Press, 2012)*, addresses the specific issues associated with the governance of big data.

Sunil lives in New Jersey and holds an MBA in Finance and Marketing from the University of Chicago Booth School of Business.

CONTENTS

FOREWORD

by Aditya Kongara

Enterprise Data Management (EDM) over the past few years has quickly become an important discipline as organizations look to establish governance over their information assets. Effective data management needs the three pillars of people, process, and technology to be mature and well-functioning.

I have spent the majority of my career in large financial services organizations and working with Big Four consulting firms setting up data management and governance programs. In my opinion, the technology pillar of EDM is as important as the other two pillars.

Assume you are the data governance lead at a large bank that has to pass a data audit from the regulators. The bank's systems consist of hundreds of thousands of data elements spread over hundreds of databases and schemas. How do you demonstrate data lineage to the regulators without a metadata tool? Are you able to convince the Chief Information Security Officer that all instances of sensitive data have been discovered? Can you do that without a data discovery tool? Are your SQL queries robust and automated enough to produce data quality scorecards on a regular basis? For these reasons and others listed in the book, I feel that companies will increasingly have to rely on data management tools to automate various manual tasks.

I have known Sunil Soares for many years in a variety of job roles. I am excited by his knowledge and passion for data governance and for his thought leadership around tools. This book is a great read for any practitioner who wants to be successful in the data management and governance field.

Aditya Kongara
Head of Enterprise Data Management
American Family Mutual Insurance Company

FOREWORD

by John R. Talburt

This book on data governance tools could not have come at a better time for the field of information quality. I say this having been in the most fortunate position to observe the explosive growth and evolution of information and data quality over the past three decades, from both a practitioner and academic perspective. Given this perspective, let me start by giving a bit of background that I think explains why this book is so timely.

Deeply rooted in practice, the emerging field of information quality had its genesis in the seemingly endless data cleaning efforts that were necessary to launch the data warehousing movement of the 1980s. From cleaning and correcting data, it started to mature, first embracing root cause analysis, then later fully adopting and incorporating the principles of TQM (Total Quality Management). Having embraced the concept of managing information as product, it continued to develop and mature. In its current incarnation, information quality goes far beyond just repairing things gone wrong, to having a seat at the table for information architecture planning and design, and now is an integral part of information policy and strategy in the role of data governance.

Like data warehousing, data governance is one of those new ideas that in retrospect seems so obvious. Why wouldn't any enterprise want to have a clear policy around and a shared understanding of its information assets? But like data warehousing, it has taken some time to "iron out the wrinkles" and make data governance really work. Now that we know that it does work, the competitive advantage imparted by a well-defined data governance program has elevated it to an essential part of corporate strategy.

Accepting data governance as essential is one thing, but making it work is another. In the early years of information quality, everyone had to develop their own tools to try and get the job done. It was not long before the demand for easier tools with more functionality created a market demand that was addressed by the many data quality tool vendors we see today. Now we see a repeat of this cycle with data governance. Many vendors now offer various tools and suites of tools to help organizations implement data governance programs. However, one difference is that data governance programs are more diverse because the reasons for adopting them and their goals are often quite different.

This comes to the point of why this book is so timely and important. In one source, the reader can have an overview of the various categories of data governance tools and their key components. This book also gives a clear description of how and where these tools integrate into the data management strategy of the enterprise. Moreover, it is written by someone with extensive experience in data governance implementation, someone who has been there and knows how it works. This experience is reflected in the large amount of detail and concrete examples given in the book.

One really invaluable section of this book is the survey of data governance tools offered by the leading vendors. The overview will be a tremendous help to those still on the sidelines and getting ready to start a data governance program, as well as those who have started on their own, but now see the potential value in adopting a third-party system.

Another very helpful section is on big data governance tools. It contains a great discussion on the use of Hadoop MapReduce and NoSQL tools to gain insights into data. There are also sections explaining approaches to streaming computing and text analytics.

All in all, *Data Governance Tools* is a comprehensive, detailed guide to the landscape of data governance tools that will be valuable to everyone involved with enterprise data management, both from business and IT. I hope that everyone will take advantage of the wealth of information that it provides.

John R. Talburt, PhD, IQCP
Director of the Information Quality Graduate Program
University of Arkansas at Little Rock

FOREWORD
by Aaron Zornes

While Sunil's prior books represented a Rosetta Stone for IT professionals to map their traditional IT experiences (MDM, RDM, data governance, etc.) to big data, at last we now have a "Domesday Book" to categorize and better understand the vast menagerie of solutions that comprise the data governance software market. There is quite a lot more beyond Microsoft Excel and SharePoint, and Sunil's "reference architecture" provides the foundational touchstone.

Given the synergy and codependence between MDM and data governance, Sunil's latest book is a must read for any MDM practitioner who is charged with establishing or upgrading the data governance processes inherently necessary for enterprise MDM or RDM programs. Among other benefits, it provides a much appreciated reference architecture and set of evaluation criteria, as well as examples illustrating the practical application of these tools.

In my consultancy practice and experience, MDM and RDM mandate the application of data governance (not just people and processes, but also software tools) to be effective and sustainable. Clearly, data governance for MDM is moving beyond simple stewardship to convergence of task management, workflow, policy management, and enforcement. Moreover, it is now time for MDM vendors to instantiate their data governance marketing claims and finally move from "passive-aggressive" mode to "proactive" data governance mode. The evaluation criteria provided in this book is proof that MDM vendors have recently begun to deliver (especially IBM, Informatica, Orchestra Networks, and SAP).

Data Governance Tools is the plenary source that can successfully tutor and guide you into becoming a "data governance professional." Moreover, it is a key asset that I'll be sharing with the 3,000+ annual attendees of my MDM & Data Governance Summit series.

Aaron Zornes
Chief Research Officer, The MDM Institute
Conference Chairman, The MDM & Data Governance Summit
(London, New York City, San Francisco, Shanghai, Singapore, Sydney, Tokyo, Toronto)

Data governance is the formulation of policy to optimize, secure, and leverage information as an enterprise asset by aligning the objectives of multiple functions. Data governance programs have traditionally focused on people and process. Cost has historically been a key consideration because data governance programs have often started from scratch, with little to no funding. As a result, Microsoft Excel and SharePoint have been the tools of choice to document and share data governance artifacts. While the marginal cost of these tools is zero, they are often missing critical functionality. Meanwhile, vendors have matured their data governance offerings to the extent that organizations need to consider tools as a critical component of their data governance programs.

It is not always clear, however, what "data governance tools" really mean. In this book, I review a reference architecture for data governance software tools. I seek to define the category called "data governance," as well as lay out evaluation criteria for software tools, the vendor landscape, and the alignment with big data.

This book consists of the following sections:

1. *Introduction*

    The chapters in this section provide an introduction to data governance and the Enterprise Data Management (EDM) reference architecture.

2. *Categories of Data Governance Tools*

    These chapters discuss key data governance tasks that can be automated by tools for business glossaries, metadata management, data profiling, data quality management, master data management, reference data management, and information policy management.

3. *The Integration Between Enterprise Data Management and Data Governance Tools*

    This section is an overview of the integration points between EDM tools and data governance. EDM tools relate to data modeling, data integration, analytics and reporting, business process management, data security and privacy, and information lifecycle management.

4. *Big Data Governance Tools*

    The chapters in this section provide an overview of how data governance tools interact with big data technologies, including Hadoop, NoSQL, stream computing, and text analytics.

5. *Evaluation Criteria and the Vendor Landscape*

    This section is a review of the overall evaluation criteria for data governance tools. This section also provides an overview of key vendor platforms, including ASG, Collibra, Global IDs, IBM, Informatica, Orchestra Networks, SAP, and Talend.

This book is geared toward business users and is relatively nontechnical. Sample roles who might be interested in this book include the following:

- Chief Information Officer
- Chief Data Officer
- Data Governance Lead
- Business Intelligence Lead
- Data Warehousing Lead
- Enterprise Data Management Lead
- Chief Information Security Officer
- Chief Privacy Officer
- Chief Medical Information Officer

All the best, and happy reading.

PART ONE

INTRODUCTION

1

AN INTRODUCTION TO DATA GOVERNANCE

We are in the middle of a major shift in the market. Scarcely a day goes by without a company restating earnings or a bank having to set aside more capital to deal with unforeseen losses. A lot of these issues can be traced back to poor data governance. The rise of big data makes data governance even more important. After all, companies need to trust their big data before they invest huge sums of money in analyzing it. The marketplace is gradually coalescing around data governance as a separate and unique discipline. A search on LinkedIn produces thousands of hits for "data governance." Vendors such as ASG, Collibra, Informatica, IBM, and Talend have released offerings to support data governance.

Definition

Data governance can be defined as follows:

Data governance is the formulation of policy to optimize, secure, and leverage information as an enterprise asset by aligning the objectives of multiple functions.

By decomposing this definition, we lay out the essential prerequisites[1] of data governance:

- *Formulate policy*—Policy includes the written or unwritten declarations of how people should behave in a given situation. For example, data governance might institute a "search before create" policy that requires customer service agents to avoid duplicates by searching for an existing customer record before creating a new one.
- *Optimize information*—Consider how organizations might apply the principles of the physical world to their information. Companies have well-defined enterprise asset management programs to care for their machinery, aircraft, vehicles, and other physical assets. Over the past decade, companies have seen an explosion in the volume of this information. With the onset of big data, it is nearly impossible for companies to know where all this information is located. Similar to cataloging physical assets, organizations need to build inventories of their existing information. We refer to this process as "data profiling" or "data discovery," and cover it later in this book. In addition, all companies have routine preventive maintenance programs for their physical assets. Companies need to institute similar maintenance programs around the information about their customers, vendors, products, and assets. We refer to this process as "data quality management," also covered later in this book.
- *Secure information*—Organizations need to secure business-critical data within their enterprise applications from unauthorized access, since this can affect the integrity of their financial reporting, as well as the quality and reliability of daily business decisions. They must also protect sensitive customer information such as credit card numbers as well as intellectual property such as customer lists, product designs, and proprietary algorithms from both internal and external threats.
- *Leverage information*—Organizations need to get the maximum value out of their information to support broader initiatives that grow revenues, reduce costs, and manage risk.
- *Treat information as an enterprise asset*—Traditional accounting rules do not allow companies to treat information as a financial asset on their balance sheets unless it is purchased from external sources. Despite this conservative accounting treatment, organizations now recognize that they should treat information as an asset.

---

1 This list of prerequisites includes modified content from *Selling Information Governance to the Business*, Sunil Soares (MC Press, 2011).

- *Align the objectives of multiple functions*—Because multiple functions leverage the same information, their objectives need to be reconciled as part of a data governance program. For example, ownership of customer data is typically an issue when different departments use that information for different purposes. This can result in challenges such as inconsistent definitions for the term "customer."

Case Study

Let's review a situation that shows the impact of poor data governance on people's lives. Case Study 1.1 details the unfortunate events surrounding the Mars Climate Orbiter.[2]

Case Study 1.1: Data governance and the Mars Climate Orbiter[3,4,5]

Any effort to launch objects into space requires immense amounts of data. The ill-fated mission by the United States National Aeronautics and Space Administration (NASA) to launch the Mars Climate Orbiter is a good example of the lack of data governance.

In 1999, just before orbital insertion, a navigation error sent the satellite into an orbit 170 kilometers lower than the intended altitude above Mars. One of the most expensive measurement incompatibilities in space exploration history caused this error. NASA's engineers used English units (pounds) instead of NASA-specified metric units (newtons). This incompatibility in the design units resulted in small errors being introduced in the trajectory estimate over the course of the nine-month journey and culminated in a huge miscalculation in orbital altitude. Ultimately, the orbiter could not sustain the atmospheric friction at low altitude. It plummeted through the Martian atmosphere and burned up.

This relatively minor mistake resulted in the loss of $328 million for the orbiter and lander and set space exploration back by several years in the United States.

The Pillars of Data Governance

Most business initiatives rest on the three pillars of people, process, and technology. Data governance programs have traditionally focused on people and process. Because data governance programs have often started from scratch with little or no funding, technology

---

2   This case study was originally published in *Big Data Governance*, Sunil Soares (MC Press, 2012).

3   http://en.wikipedia.org/wiki/Mars_Climate_Orbiter.

4   "Mars Climate Orbiter Fact Sheet," http://mars.jpl.nasa.gov/msp98/orbiter/fact.html.

5   "Mars Climate Orbiter Mishap Investigation Board Phase I Report," November 1999.

has historically not been a key consideration. The remainder of this book focuses on the technology pillar of data governance programs.

Summary

In this chapter, we defined data governance as the formulation of policy to optimize, secure, and leverage information as an enterprise asset by aligning the objectives of multiple functions. While traditional data governance programs have focused on people and process, this book focuses on technology.

2

ENTERPRISE DATA MANAGEMENT REFERENCE ARCHITECTURE

E nterprise Data Management (EDM) refers to the ability of an organization to precisely define, easily integrate, and effectively retrieve data for both internal applications and external communication.[1]

Like data governance, EDM involves the three pillars of people, process, and technology. Also like data governance, there has been a historical emphasis in EDM on the people and process pillars. However, the technology pillar is at least as important as the other two because it makes data governance tangible in the eyes of business users. The EDM reference architecture includes 20 categories, as shown in Figure 2.1.

---

1   http://en.wikipedia.org/wiki/Enterprise_data_management.

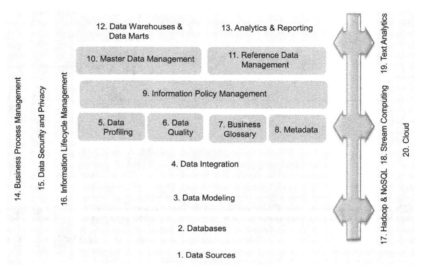

Figure 2.1: The EDM reference architecture.

EDM Categories

EDM consists of a number of categories. Some of these categories are more closely tied to data governance than others. In addition, these categories are interrelated in several important aspects. A high-level description of the 20 categories of EDM follows; the rest of the book goes into more detail:

1. *Data Sources*—At the very bottom, we have the data sources that need to be governed. These data sources may be internal or external to the organization. Internal data sources include enterprise applications such as SAP, Oracle, and Salesforce. External data sources include social media, sensor data, and information purchased from data brokers.

2. *Databases*—Databases fall into a few different categories:
   - *In-Memory*—In-memory database management systems rely on main memory for data storage. Compared to traditional database management systems that store data to disk, in-memory databases are optimized for speed. SAP HANA, Oracle TimesTen In-Memory Database, and IBM solidDB are all examples of in-memory databases.
   - *Relational*—Relational database management systems (RDBMSs) rely on relational data and are at the heart of most distributed computing platforms

today. IBM DB2, Oracle Database 12c, and Microsoft SQL Server are all examples of RDBMS solutions.

- *Legacy*—Legacy database management systems such as IBM Information Management System (IMS) rely on non-relational approaches to database management.

3. *Data Modeling*—Data modeling is a critical exercise to develop an understanding of an organization's data artifacts. Data modeling tools include Embarcadero ERwin Data Modeler, SAP PowerDesigner, Embarcadero ER/Studio, and IBM InfoSphere Data Architect.

4. *Data Integration*—Data integration tools fall into a few different categories:

- *Bulk Data Movement*—Bulk data movement includes technologies such as Extract, Transform, and Load (ETL) to extract data from one or more data sources, transform the data, and load the data into a target database. Tools include IBM InfoSphere Data Stage and Informatica PowerCenter.

- *Data Replication*—According to *Information Management Magazine*, data replication is the process of copying a portion of a database from one environment to another and keeping the subsequent copies of the data in sync with the original source. Changes made to the original source are propagated to copies of the data in other environments.[2] Replication technologies such as change data capture (CDC) allow the capture of only change data and transfer it from publisher to subscriber systems. Replication tools include IBM InfoSphere Data Replication, Oracle GoldenGate, Informatica Fast Clone, and Informatica Data Replication.

- *Data Virtualization*—Data virtualization is also known as data federation. According to *Information Management Magazine*, data federation is the method of linking data from two or more physically different locations and making the access/linkage appear transparent, as if the data were co-located. This approach is in contrast to the data warehouse method of housing data in one place and accessing data from that single location.[3] Data virtualization allows an application to issue SQL queries against a virtual view of data in heterogeneous sources such as in relational databases, XML documents, and on the mainframe. Offerings include IBM InfoSphere Federation Server, Informatica Data Services, and Denodo.

---

2   http://www.information-management.com/glossary/d.html.

3   *Ibid.*

5. *Data Profiling*—Data profiling is the process of understanding the data in a system, where it is located, and how it relates to other systems. This includes developing a statistical analysis of the data, such as data type, null percentages, and uniqueness. While there might be some nuances that distinguish data profiling from data discovery, we will use the terms synonymously in this book.

   In the absence of tools, data analysts have historically resorted to the use of SQL queries to discover and profile data. Offerings include IBM InfoSphere Information Analyzer, Informatica Data Quality, Oracle Enterprise Data Quality, SAP Information Steward, SAS Data Management, and Trillium Software TS Discovery. These tools support a variety of data sources, including Hadoop.

6. *Data Quality*—Data quality management is a discipline that includes the methods to measure and improve the quality and integrity of an organization's data. While data profiling uncovers issues with the data, data quality actually remediates those issues. Offerings include IBM InfoSphere QualityStage, Informatica Data Quality, Oracle Enterprise Data Quality, SAP Information Steward, SAS Data Management, and Trillium Software TS Quality.

7. *Business Glossary*—A business glossary is a repository of key terms that brings together common definitions across business and IT. Offerings include Adaptive Business Glossary Manager, ASG-metaGlossary, Collibra Business Glossary, Embarcadero CONNECT, IBM InfoSphere Business Glossary, Informatica Business Glossary, and SAS Data Management.

8. *Metadata*—Metadata is information that describes the characteristics of any data artifact, such as its name, location, perceived importance, quality, or value to the enterprise, and its relationships to other data artifacts that the enterprise deems worth managing. Offerings include Adaptive Metadata Manager, ASG-Rochade, Data Advantage Group MetaCenter, IBM InfoSphere Metadata Workbench, and Informatica Metadata Manager.

9. *Information Policy Management*—Most business glossary vendors also support the management of information policies. In addition, Governance, Risk, and Compliance (GRC) platforms such as EMC RSA Archer GRC and IBM OpenPages GRC also offer capabilities to manage broader policies, including those relating to information.

10. *Master Data Management*—Master Data Management (MDM) refers to the discipline associated with establishing a single version of the truth for critical data domains such as customer, vendor, product, location, asset, employee, and chart of

accounts. MDM vendors include IBM, Informatica, Oracle, Orchestra Networks, Riversand, SAP, SAS, Semarchy, Stibo Systems, and Talend.

11. *Reference Data Management*—Reference data is relatively static and may be placed in lookup tables for reference by other applications. Reference data is sometimes referred to as code tables, code lists, code sets, and lists of values. Examples of reference data include country codes, state codes, and province codes. Tools include Collibra Data Governance Center, IBM InfoSphere Master Data Management Reference Data Management Hub, Oracle Data Relationship Management, and Orchestra Networks EBX.

12. *Data Warehouses and Data Marts*—Organizations have large investments in data warehouses and data marts that might be based on the following:
    - Relational databases such as Oracle Database 12c and IBM DB2
    - Columnar databases such as SAP Sybase IQ and HP Vertica, which are geared toward big data analytics
    - Data warehousing appliances such as Oracle Exalytics In-Memory Machine, IBM PureData System for Analytics, SAP HANA, EMC Pivotal Greenplum, and Teradata Aster

13. *Analytics and Reporting*—At the end of the day, organizations need to analyze their data needs to make business decisions. A number of open source and proprietary tools can support big data analytics and reporting. These tools include SAS Business Intelligence, SAS Analytics, IBM Cognos, IBM SPSS, SAP BusinessObjects, Tableau, QlikView, R, and Pentaho.

14. *Business Process Management*—Business process management (BPM) is a holistic management approach to aligning an organization's business processes with the wants and needs of clients.[4] BPM tools include IBM Business Process Manager and Pega Business Process Management. In addition, the Eclipse open-source framework includes a plug-in for Business Process Model and Notation (BPMN).

15. *Data Security and Privacy*—This category includes a number of subcategories, including data masking, data tokenization, database encryption, and database monitoring. Offerings include IBM InfoSphere Guardium, IBM InfoSphere Optim Data Privacy, Imperva, Informatica Data Masking, and Protegrity.

16. *Information Lifecycle Management*—Information lifecycle management (ILM) is a process and methodology for managing information through its lifecycle, from creation through disposal, including compliance with legal, regulatory, and privacy

---

4 http://en.wikipedia.org/wiki/Business_process_management.

requirements. ILM programs should enable the efficient disposition of information at the end of its usefulness to the business, and in accordance with legal and regulatory obligations. ILM includes a number of sub-categories, including information archiving, records and retention management, legal holds and evidence collection (eDiscovery), and test data management. Vendors include Symantec, IBM, Informatica, EMC, HP, and OpenText.

17. *Hadoop and NoSQL*—Apache Hadoop is an open source software library that supports the distributed processing of large data sets across thousands of computers based on commodity hardware. The Apache Hadoop project grew out of pioneering work at Yahoo! and Google, where researchers worked with huge volumes of data across large clusters of computers. As with other open source software, Apache Hadoop does not come with product support for things like bug fixes. To address these shortcomings, a number of vendors have released their own distributions of Hadoop, which have undergone release testing. These vendors bundle product support and offer training for an additional fee. Most enterprises that have deployed Hadoop for commercial use have selected one of the Hadoop distributions. Offerings include Cloudera, MapR, Hortonworks, IBM InfoSphere BigInsights, Amazon Elastic MapReduce, and EMC Pivotal Greenplum HD.

NoSQL ("Not Only SQL") databases are a category of database management systems that do not use SQL as their primary query language. These databases may not require fixed table schemas, and they do not support join operations. They are optimized for highly scalable read-write operations, rather than for consistency. Offerings include Apache HBase, Apache Cassandra, MongoDB, Apache CouchDB, Couchbase, Riak, and Amazon DynamoDB.

18. *Stream Computing*—Stream computing refers to a class of technologies that leverage massively parallel processing capabilities to analyze data in motion, as opposed to landing large volumes of structured, unstructured, and semi-structured data on disk. There are a number of open source and vendor-proprietary tools in this space. These tools include Apache Flume, IBM InfoSphere Streams, TIBCO StreamBase, and SAP Sybase Event Stream Processor.

19. *Text Analytics*—Text analytics is a method for extracting usable knowledge from unstructured text data through the identification of core concepts, sentiments, and trends, and then using this knowledge to support decision-making. Text analytics results can then be incorporated into models used for predictive analytics. Offerings

include SAS Text Miner, Oracle Endeca Information Discovery, IBM text analytics solutions, and Clarabridge.

20. *Cloud*—Organizations are turning to the cloud because of perceived flexibility, faster time-to-deployment, and reduced capital expenditure requirements. A number of vendors offer data governance platforms in the cloud, including the following:

   - Data brokers such as Acxiom, Reed Elsevier, Thomson Reuters, and literally thousands of others that specialize by dataset or industry. These companies offer many types of data enrichment and validation services to organizations.
   - Collibra Data Governance Center includes Business Glossary, Reference Data Accelerator, and Data Stewardship Manager as a cloud offering with a monthly fee.
   - Harte-Hanks Trillium Software TS Quality on Demand provides data validation, cleansing, and enrichment of names, email addresses, and street addresses as a service.
   - Informatica Cloud provides data loading, synchronization, profiling, and quality services for Salesforce and other cloud applications.

Big Data

Big data is generally referred to in the context of the three *V*s—volume, velocity, and variety. Let's consider each of these terms:

- *Volume (data at rest)*—Big data is generally large. Enterprises are awash with data, easily amassing terabytes and petabytes of information, and even zettabytes in the future. Category 17 (Hadoop and NoSQL) of the EDM reference architecture is most closely tied to this aspect of big data.
- *Velocity (data in motion)*—Often time-sensitive, streaming data must be analyzed with millisecond response times to bolster real-time decisions. Category 18 (stream computing) of the EDM reference architecture is most closely tied to this aspect of big data.
- *Variety (data in many formats)*—Big data includes structured, semi-structured and unstructured data, such as email, audio, video, clickstreams, log files, and biometrics. Category 19 (text analytics) of the EDM reference architecture is most closely tied to this aspect of big data, although there is significant crossover with Hadoop and NoSQL.

Data Governance Tools

There is limited consensus in the marketplace in terms of what constitutes "data governance tools." However, our experience is that the following seven categories are most closely tied with data governance (the grey boxes in Figure 2.1):

- Data profiling
- Data quality
- Business glossary
- Metadata
- Information policy management
- Master data management
- Reference data management

Summary

In this chapter, we reviewed the different components of the EDM reference architecture. These components include data sources, databases, data modeling, data integration, data profiling, data quality, business glossary, metadata, information policy management, master data management, reference data management, data warehouses and data marts, analytics and reporting, business process management, data security and privacy, information lifecycle management, Hadoop and NoSQL, stream computing, text analytics, and cloud.

PART TWO

CATEGORIES OF DATA GOVERNANCE TOOLS

CHAPTER 3

THE BUSINESS GLOSSARY

A business glossary is a repository of key terms that brings together common definitions across business and IT. A business glossary is often maintained separately from data dictionaries, which contain the descriptions of key columns and tables. However, business glossaries and data dictionaries need to be integrated. For example, suppose the business glossary contains the definition for the term "customer identifier," the data dictionary for Application A contains a description for the CYSTOID column, and the data dictionary for Application B contains a description for the CLIENT_ NUM column. These three artifacts should be linked to each other.

In the remainder of this chapter, we will review critical data governance tasks that can be automated using business glossary tools.

Bulk-Load Business Terms in Excel, CSV, or XML Format

Most organizations already have business terms embedded in manuals, spreadsheets, PDF files, and other repositories. For example, Figure 3.1 shows an Excel file with business terms relating to the Dodd-Frank banking legislation in the United States.

term	definition
affiliate	Section 2 of the Bank Holding Company ActFor purposes of this Act the term "affiliate" means any com
agency	Section 1 of the International Banking Act"Agency" means any office or any place of business of a forei
bank	Section 3 of the Federal Deposit Insurance Act.The term "bank"-- (A) means any national bank and Sta
bank holding company	Section 2 of the Bank Holding Company Act(a)(1) Except as provided in paragraph (5) of this subsectior
branch	Section 1 of the International Banking Act "branch" means any office or any place of business of a forei
commercial firm	Section 602 of Dodd FrankA company is a "commercial firm" if the annual gross revenues derived by tl
company	Section 2 of the Bank Holding Company Act"Company" means any corporation, partnership, business t
control	Section 2 of the Bank Holding Company Act (2) Any company has control over a bank or over any comp
credit	Section 103 of the Truth in Lending ActThe term "credit" means the right granted by a creditor to a deb
credit card	Section 103 of the Truth in Lending ActThe term "credit card" means any card, plate, coupon book or ot
debit card	Section 920 of the Electronic Funds Transfer ActThe term "debit card"-- (A) means any card, or other pi
deposit	Section 3 of the Federal Deposit Insurance ActThe term "deposit" means-- (1) the unpaid balance of m
depository institution	Section 3 of the Federal Deposit Insurance Act.The term "depository institution" means any bank or sa
depository institution holding con	Section 3 of the Federal Deposit Insurance Act.The term "depository institution holding company" mei
discount	Section 920 of the Electronic Funds Transfer ActThe term "discount"-- (A) means a reduction made fro
dormancy fee	Section 915 of the Electronic Funds Transfer ActThe term "dormancy fee" means a fee, charge, or pena
electronic debit transaction	Section 920 of the Electronic Funds Transfer ActThe term "electronic debit transaction" means a transa
exposure	Section 23 of the Federal Reserve ActAn insured depository institution's "exposure" to another deposi
federal agency	Section 1 of the International Banking Act "Federal agency" means an agency of a foreign bank establis
federal branch	Section 1 of the International Banking Act"Federal branch" means a branch of a foreign bank establishe
federal depository institution	Section 3 of the Federal Deposit Insurance Act.The term "Federal depository institution" means any ne
federal savings association	Section 3 of the Federal Deposit Insurance Act.The term "Federal savings association" means any Fede
foreign bank	Section 1 of the International Banking Act"foreign bank" means any company organized under the law:
foreign country	Section 1 of the International Banking Act"foreign country" means any country other than the United S

Figure 3.1: This Excel spreadsheet contains business terms relating to Dodd-Frank legislation.

Organizations can accelerate the implementation of their business glossaries by bulk-loading terms in Excel, CSV, or XML format. Figure 3.2 shows the Excel Import wizard in Collibra Data Governance Center. The wizard allows users to map Collibra attribute names to Excel column names. For example, the "Name" attribute in Collibra maps to the term "column" in Excel. Similarly, the "Definition" attribute in Collibra maps to the "definition" column in Excel.

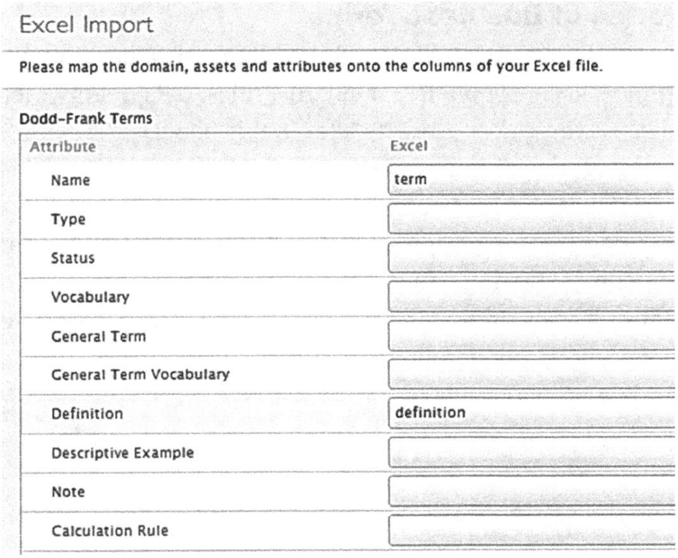

Figure 3.2: The Excel Import wizard for business terms in Collibra Data Governance Center.

In Figure 3.3, we see that the user has created a preferred view of the Dodd-Frank business terms in Collibra. The view shows the name, definition, steward, and status of the business term.

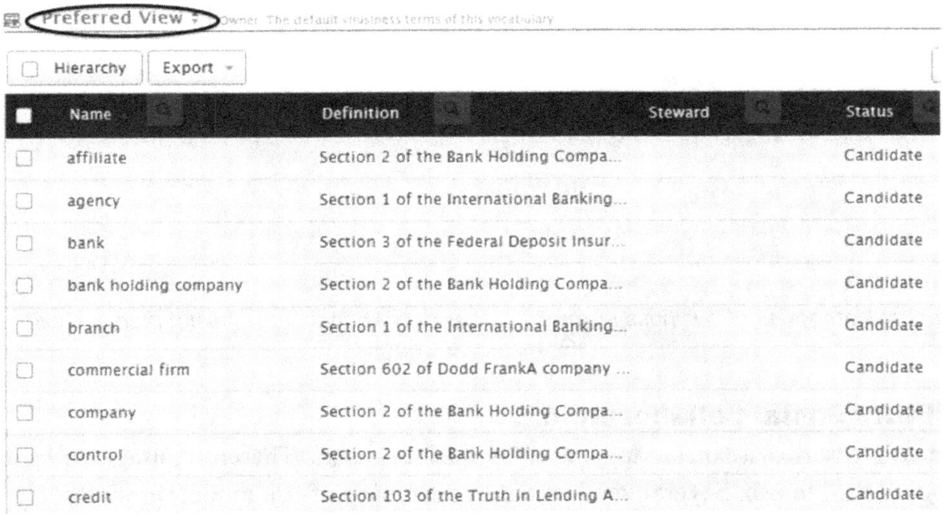

Figure 3.3: A preferred view of Dodd-Frank business terms in Collibra Data Governance Center.

Create Categories of Business Terms

Business glossaries should support the creation of categories that contain business terms and other data artifacts such as policies, standards, rules, data quality metrics and code values. We will discuss these data artifacts later in this book.

Figure 3.4 lists categories of business terms and other data artifacts in Collibra Data Governance Center. A health plan (an insurer) has created a number of communities, or categories, representing logical groupings of data artifacts. These groupings including Network Management, Marketing, Underwriting, Health Services, Medicaid, Informatics, Medical Informatics, Privacy, Member Services, Exchanges, Medicare, and Actuarial.

Figure 3.4: Categories of business terms and other data artifacts for a health plan in Collibra Data Governance Center.

Facilitate Social Collaboration

Business glossaries are meant to be used by business users. Therefore, usage will suffer if the tool is hard to use. Several vendors have added ease-of-use to their products' features. For example, the vendors Informatica and Embarcadero Technologies have adopted a

"Facebook-style" user interface and social collaboration features to improve the usability of the business glossary. Figure 3.5 shows the Facebook-style user interface and social collaboration features within Embarcadero CONNECT.

Topic	Started By	New Discussion
✚ FIFO and LIFO Methods	Sam	
✚ Changes to Accounting Estimate	Sam	
━ Importing current terms	Sarah	

My team would like our current spreadsheet of terms imported in to this Glossary

John I shall action this. I did this to the Business Glossary last week and it was very easy.
Aug 20, 2013 12:37:51 PM   Delete

Write a reply...

Figure 3.5: Embarcadero CONNECT is a business glossary with a Facebook-style user interface and social collaboration features. (Image courtesy of Embarcadero Technologies.)

Automatically Hyperlink Embedded Business Terms

Business glossaries should also support the automatic hyperlinking of business terms that are embedded within the definitions of other business terms. Figure 3.6 shows the definition of "Cash" in Collibra Data Governance Center.

Figure 3.6: The definition of "Cash" in Collibra Data Governance Center.

In Figure 3.7, the definition of "Working Capital" in Collibra Data Governance Center includes the term "Cash," so it is hyperlinked. The user can click on the hyperlink to navigate directly to the term. This is a huge productivity benefit and allows data stewards to easily navigate the business glossary.

Figure 3.7: The definition of "Working Capital" in Collibra Data Governance Center.

Add Custom Attributes to Business Terms and Other Data Artifacts

Business glossary tools typically ship with out-of-the-box (OOTB) attributes such as Definition, Short Description, Long Description, and Example. However, business glossary tools should also allow administrators to create custom attributes, such as Security Classification and Critical Data Element. Figure 3.8 shows the Create New Custom Attribute wizard to create a custom attribute in IBM InfoSphere Business Glossary.

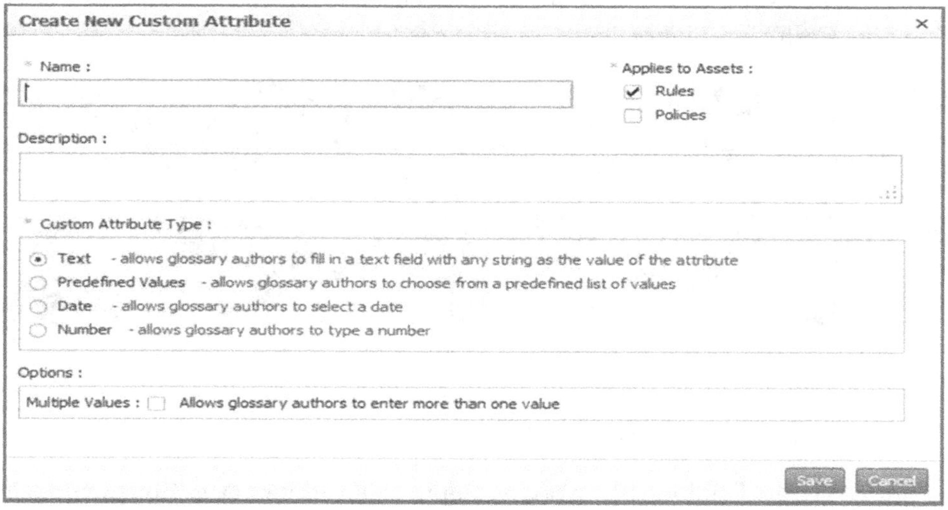

Figure 3.8: IBM InfoSphere Business Glossary allows administrators to create custom attributes.

Add Custom Relationships to Business Terms and Other Data Artifacts

Most business glossaries ship with OOTB relationships between business terms and other business terms, policies, standards, rules, and other data artifacts. As shown in Figure 3.9, Collibra Data Governance Center contains a number of OOTB relations, including Definition, Descriptive Example, Note, Synonym, Synonym Of, Acronym, Code Value, Groups Business Asset, Grouped by Business Asset, Represents Data Asset, and Allowed Value. Once again, the business glossary tool should allow administrators to add custom relations.

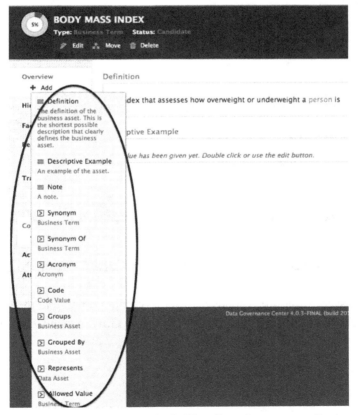

Figure 3.9: OOTB relations in Collibra Data Governance Center.

Add Custom Roles to Business Terms and Other Data Artifacts

Data governance tools typically ship with OOTB roles such as Steward. However, every organization has its own data governance vernacular. Accordingly, data governance tools should also support custom roles, such as Data Owner, Data Executive, Data Sponsor, Stakeholder, Subject Matter Expert, Responsible, Accountable, Consulted, and Informed. Figure 3.10 shows the definition for a business term called "State" in Data Advantage Group MetaCenter. This figure also shows the custom roles Data Executive, Managing Data Steward, Consulted, and Informed.

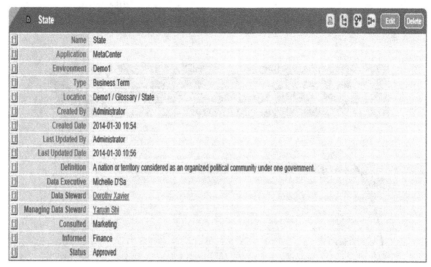

Figure 3.10: Data Advantage Group MetaCenter manages custom roles for the business term "State."

Link Business Terms and Column Names to the Associated Reference Data

The business glossary should link a business term or column name to the underlying reference data. As shown in Figure 3.11, Collibra Data Governance Center links the term "Bangladesh" with the code value BD.

Figure 3.11: Collibra Data Governance Center links the business term "Bangladesh" with the code value BD.

Link Business Terms to Technical Metadata

The business glossary should also link a business term to the associated technical metadata. As shown in Figure 3.12, Data Advantage Group MetaCenter links the business term "State" to the STATE_ABBRV attribute in the logical model in ER/Studio and to the codelist "US and Canadian States" in MetaCenter.

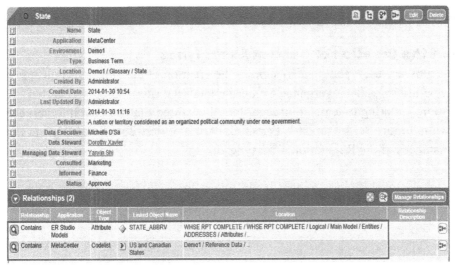

Figure 3.12: Data Advantage Group MetaCenter links the business term "State" to the logical model and the codelist.

Figure 3.13 shows the results of clicking the STATE_ABBRV attribute to uncover additional information about this object stored in the MetaCenter metadata repository. We can see that STATE_ABBRV is part of a logical model for ADDRESSES that is stored in ER/Studio. The data type is VARCHAR(10), and nulls are allowed.

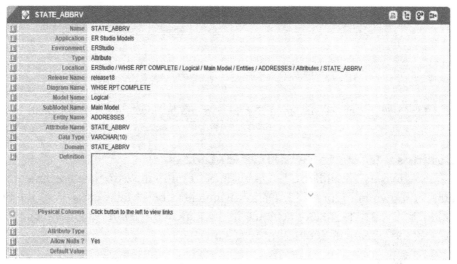

Figure 3.13: Detailed information about STATE_ABBRV in Data Advantage Group MetaCenter.

Support the Creation of Custom Asset Types

Business glossary tools should also support the creation of custom asset types. For example, Collibra Data Governance Center includes a custom asset type called "Regulation," relating to legislation regarding the United States Federal Reserve system. As shown in Figure 3.14, Part-201, Part-202, Part-203, Part-204, Part-205, and Part-228 are all instances of the Regulation asset type.

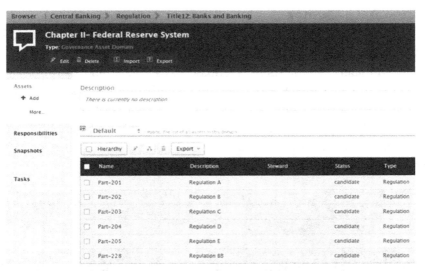

Figure 3.14: The Regulation asset type within Collibra Data Governance Center.

In Figure 3.15, Regulation Part-201 has a "regulates" relation with multiple business terms in Collibra Data Governance Center. These business terms include "Appropriate Federal Banking Agency" and "Critically undercapitalized insured depository institution." This allows users to view all the business terms associated with a given regulation.

Regulates

Name	Definition	Descriptive Example	Domain
Appropriate Federal Banking Agency	Section 3 of the Federal Deposi...		Extensions of Credit by Federal Reserve Banks
Critically undercapitalized insured depository institution	section 3 of the Federal Deposi...		Extensions of Credit by Federal Reserve Banks
Depository Institution	(1)Section 3 of the Federal Dep...		Extensions of Credit by Federal Reserve Banks
Nonpersonal time deposit	(1) The term means (i) A time d...		Extensions of Credit by Federal Reserve Banks
Transaction Account	A deposit or account from whic...		Extensions of Credit by Federal Reserve Banks
Undercapitalized insured depository institution	Section 3 of the Federal Deposi...		Extensions of Credit by Federal Reserve Banks
viable	The term "viable" with respect t...		Extensions of Credit by Federal Reserve Banks

Figure 3.15: Regulation Part-201 has a "regulates" relation with multiple business terms in Collibra Data Governance Center.

Flag Critical Data Elements

The business glossary tool should also allow users to flag Critical Data Elements (CDEs). A CDE is an element that has a significant impact on regulatory reporting, operational performance, and business intelligence. CDEs should generally constitute not more than five to ten percent of the total number of attributes. As shown in Figure 3.16, EMAIL_ADDRESS has been flagged as a CDE in Collibra Data Governance Center. The administrator has created a custom asset type called "Critical Data Element." Alternatively, the administrator could have created a custom attribute called "Critical Data Element" and set the flag to "Yes."

Figure 3.16: EMAIL_ADDRESS is flagged as a Critical Data Element in Collibra Data Governance Center.

Provide OOTB and Custom Workflows to Manage Business Terms and Other Data Artifacts

In this section, we use Data Advantage Group MetaCenter to discuss how workflows manage changes to business terms and other data artifacts. For the sake of brevity, we have only included screenshots of key stages in the workflow.

Users can assign a workflow to any user-defined type in MetaCenter. Users can either propose changes to an existing object or propose the creation of a new object. Let's say an administrator has assigned a workflow to a custom object, "System." This causes the workflow to run for all objects of type "System" in MetaCenter. As shown in Figure 3.17, the user clicks the **Propose** button to start the workflow for the Life System.

Figure 3.17: A user proposes a change to an existing object of type "System" in Data Advantage Group MetaCenter.

Once the workflow has started, the form shown in Figure 3.18 appears. This form contains a list of attributes that the user can change as needed. In this case, the user is interested in changing the attribute "Data Executive" of the object "Life System" from "John Smith" to "Yanxin Shi." After making the necessary changes, the user clicks the **Propose** button again to save the proposed changes.

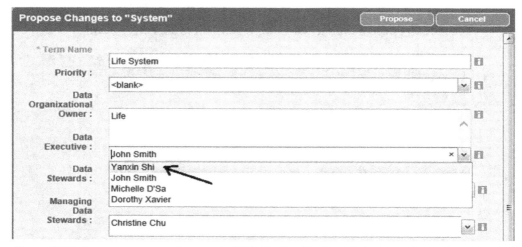

Figure 3.18: A user proposes changes to "Life System" in Data Advantage Group MetaCenter.

As shown in Figure 3.19, the user then provides a reason for proposing the change and clicks **OK**.

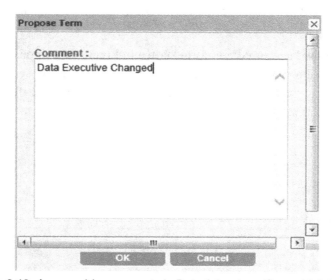

Figure 3.19: A user adds comments in Data Advantage Group MetaCenter.

MetaCenter then displays all the proposed object changes in a task list, as shown in Figure 3.20. MetaCenter sends an email notification only if any proposed changes require the user's review or vote. The task notification in the menu bar also indicates that the user has one open task. The user can double-click a row in the **Task List** table to enter a comment or edit the name or attributes of the object. An object will stay in the review stage until it is submitted for a vote or the review is finalized.

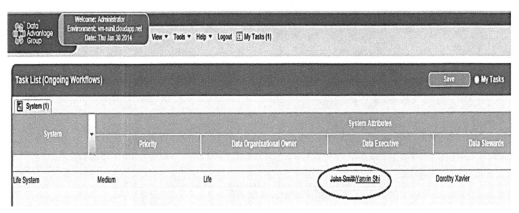

Figure 3.20: A user reviews the task list in Data Advantage Group MetaCenter.

As shown in Fig 3.21, the user comments "Good" on the proposed change and submits the change for voting.

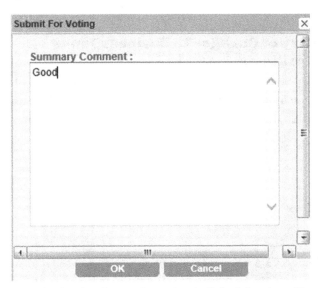

Figure 3.21: A user submits the change for voting in Data Advantage Group MetaCenter.

Once the object has gone through the voting process, the user receives the Force Outcome form shown in Figure 3.22. This finalizes the changes to "Life System."

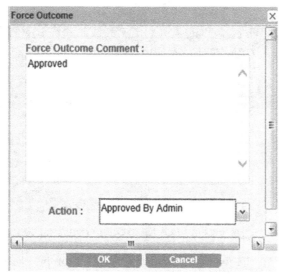

Figure 3.22: A user finalizes the task by approving the proposed change in Data Advantage Group MetaCenter.

Review the History of Changes to Business Terms and Other Data Artifacts

The business glossary should carry an audit trail with the history of changes to business terms and other data artifacts. Continuing with the example in the previous section, Data Advantage MetaCenter shows the history for the "Life System" term in Figure 3.23.

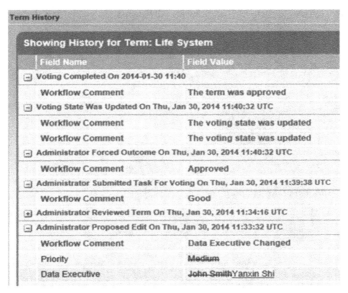

Figure 3.23: Data Advantage Group MetaCenter contains a history for the "Life System" term.

Allow Business Users to Link to the Glossary Directly from Reporting Tools

Business understanding is critical, yet time pressures often keep business users from leveraging available resources. For example, you might read an email or white paper and come across a term or phrase that seems ambiguous. You are not sure how it is being defined or used in your organization. You know you can find it in your company's online glossary by simply opening a web browser, but that would require you to pause in your current task. Instead, you postpone looking up the term until later. By then, you might have forgotten about it, missing some important information.[1]

The business glossary should be integrated with any application on the user's desktop, including Microsoft Excel, Microsoft Word, Adobe PDF, IBM Cognos, Tableau, and Microsoft Outlook. Business glossary tools provide client-side widgets with a small footprint that can be installed on user desktops or laptops. Depending on the configuration, a user can simply highlight the term and press **Shift+F5**, and the term's definition will pop up instantly from the business glossary.

In Figure 3.24, the user has installed a client widget called IBM InfoSphere Business Glossary Anywhere on her desktop. The user then highlights the business term "Liquidity

---

1 Soares, Sunil. *Selling Information Governance to the Business*. MC Press, 2011.

coverage ratio" in Adobe Reader, clicks **Shift+F5**, and pulls up the definition that is stored in IBM InfoSphere Business Glossary.

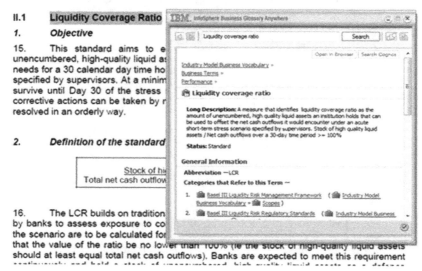

Figure 3.24: Using IBM InfoSphere Business Glossary Anywhere to look up the definition of "Liquidity coverage ratio" within Adobe Reader.

Search for Business Terms

Users should also be able to search for business terms in the glossary using fuzzy matching. In Figure 3.25, a user types "Customer" in the search box of the Metapedia module within SAP Information Steward. The search results include not only the "Customer," but also terms like "Business Partner" and "Cost Center," which have the term "Customer" embedded in their definitions.

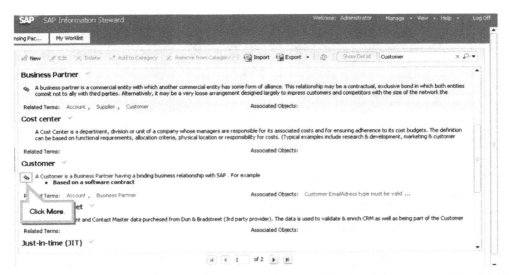

Figure 3.25: A user types "Customer" in the search box within the Metapedia module of SAP Information Steward. (Image courtesy of SAP Community Network.)

Integrate Business Terms with Associated Unstructured Data

The business glossary should also support the linkage of business terms with additional information that may be in an unstructured format. For example, in Figure 3.26, IBM InfoSphere Business Glossary contains the definition for the term "customer." At the bottom of the screen, we can also view the search results for artifacts within the organization's Intranet that contain the word "customer." These search results were produced by IBM InfoSphere Data Explorer. Other organizations may use a search engine like the Google Search Appliance to integrate unstructured content with the business glossary.

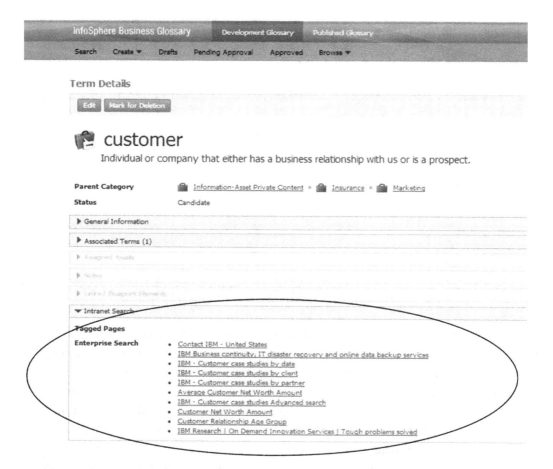

Figure 3.26: IBM InfoSphere Business Glossary shows the business term "customer," along with search results from IBM InfoSphere Data Explorer.

Summary

In this chapter, we learned that business glossaries need to be user-friendly and support custom attributes, relationships, roles, and asset types. Business glossaries also need to integrate with technical metadata and reference data. They should also support workflow management, history, search, and unstructured data.

CHAPTER 4

METADATA MANAGEMENT

M etadata is information that describes the characteristics of any data artifact, such as its name, location, perceived importance, quality, or value to the enterprise, and its relationships to other data artifacts that the enterprise deems worth managing. For the purposes of this book, there are two types of metadata:

- *Business metadata* involves the definition of business terms, along with the relations between these terms, the associated business rules, and reference data. We covered this topic in the previous chapter.
- *Technical metadata* is information that describes the assets, models, and process elements used in IT systems. This is the focus of this chapter.

Metadata tools can automate a number of manual tasks relating to data governance.

Pull Logical Models from Data Modeling Tools

Metadata repositories need to pull in logical models from data modeling tools such as CA ERwin Data Modeler, SAP PowerDesigner, Embarcadero ER/Studio, and IBM InfoSphere Data Architect. As shown in Figure 4.1, IBM InfoSphere Metadata Workbench contains a logical model for EWS Warehouse. This model contains the logical entities Manufacture Plant, Production, Product Unit, and Sales Transaction. The logical model is implemented by the physical EWS Warehouse Model.

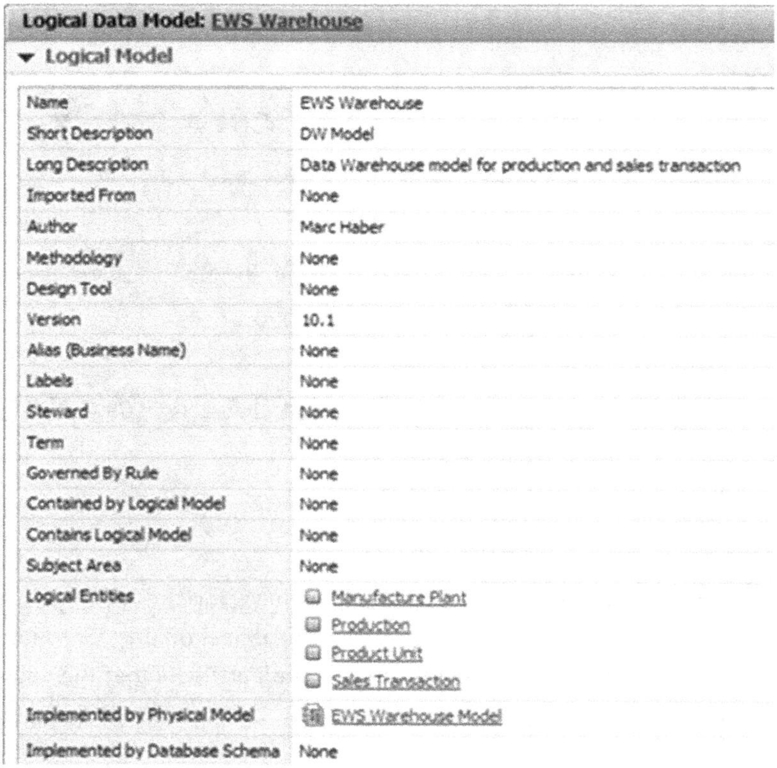

Figure 4.1: The logical model of EWS Warehouse in IBM InfoSphere Metadata Workbench.

Pull Physical Models from Data Modeling Tools

Metadata repositories also need to pull in physical models from data modeling tools. As shown in Figure 4.2, IBM InfoSphere Metadata Workbench also contains the physical data model for EWS Warehouse Model. We can see that the physical model relates to the Manufacture Plant, Production, Product Unit, and Sales Transaction tables in the PRODUCT database schema. We can also see that the model implements the EWS Warehouse logical model.

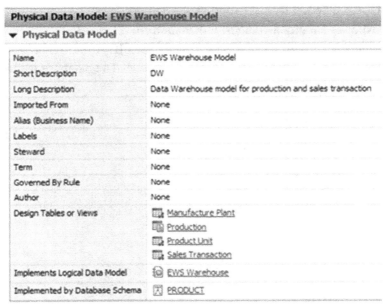

Figure 4.2: The physical model of EWS Warehouse Model in IBM InfoSphere Metadata Workbench.

Figure 4.3 presents a graph view of the EWS Warehouse Model physical model in IBM InfoSphere Metadata Workbench.

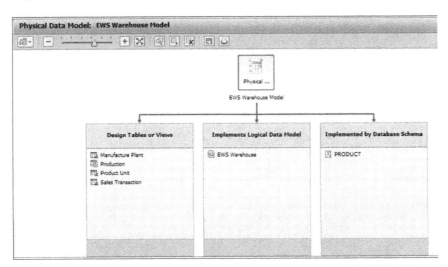

Figure 4.3: A graph view of EWS Warehouse Model's physical model in IBM InfoSphere Metadata Workbench.

Ingest Metadata from Relational Databases

Metadata repositories should also ingest metadata from relational databases. Figure 4.4 shows the metadata relating to the SALES database in IBM InfoSphere Metadata Workbench. Jackie Smith is the steward for the database. The database is implemented in DB2 and the SCHEMA1 database schema.

Database: SALES	
▼ Database	
Database Name	SALES
Imported From	None
Alias (Business Name)	None
Short Description	None
Long Description	None
Included in Business Lineage	True
Location	None
DBMS	DB2
DBMS Server Instance	localhost
DBMS Vendor	None
DBMS Version	10.10.0000
Data Connection	SALES
Labels	Corporate Division
Steward	Jackie Smith
Term	Customer
Governed By Rule	Data quality rules for customer address
Host	Data Server
Database Schemas	SCHEMA1
▸ Attributes	
▼ Database Design Information	
Written by Job (Design)	None
Read by Job (Design)	EWS_SalesLookup

Figure 4.4: The metadata for the SALES database in IBM InfoSphere Metadata Workbench.

Figure 4.5 shows the SCHEMA1 database schema from the SALES database in IBM InfoSphere Metadata Workbench. The schema contains the SLS_LOOKUP database table.

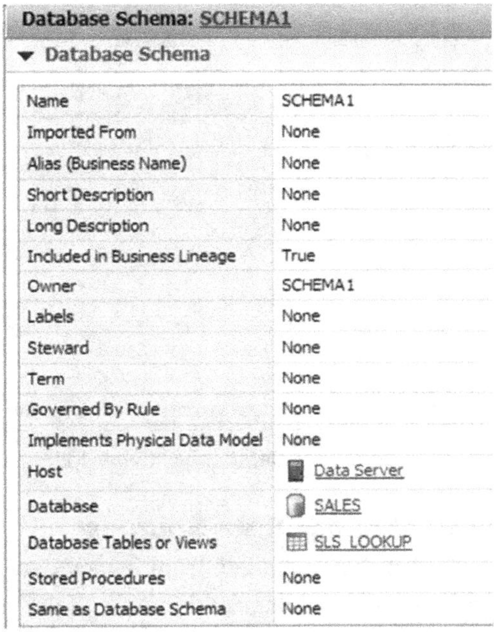

Database Schema: SCHEMA1	
▼ Database Schema	
Name	SCHEMA1
Imported From	None
Alias (Business Name)	None
Short Description	None
Long Description	None
Included in Business Lineage	True
Owner	SCHEMA1
Labels	None
Steward	None
Term	None
Governed By Rule	None
Implements Physical Data Model	None
Host	▤ Data Server
Database	▤ SALES
Database Tables or Views	▦ SLS_LOOKUP
Stored Procedures	None
Same as Database Schema	None

Figure 4.5: The SCHEMA1 database schema in IBM InfoSphere Metadata Workbench.

Pull in Metadata from Data Warehouse Appliances

Metadata repositories should also scan metadata from data warehouse appliances like Teradata, IBM PureData System for Analytics (formerly Netezza), and EMC Pivotal Greenplum Database. Figure 4.6 shows the Global IDs Database Crawler for Greenplum.

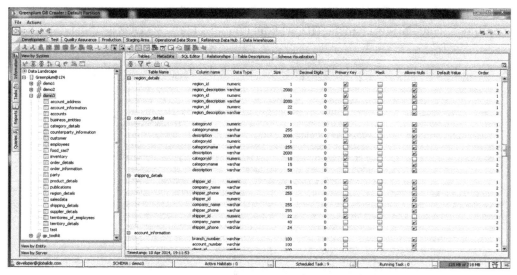

Figure 4.6: The Global IDs Database Crawler for Greenplum.

Integrate Metadata from Legacy Data Sources

Metadata repositories should also scan metadata from legacy data sources, which may contain large volumes of mission-critical data. In Figure 4.7, the Global IDs Cobol Copybook Scanner has profiled a mainframe-based entity called Ams-Vendor with fields that include Brand, Location-Number, Location-Type, Location-Name, and Address-1. The bottom of the screen provides a view of the actual data.

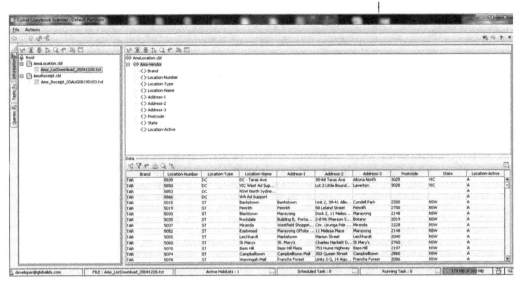

Figure 4.7: The Global IDs COBOL Copybook Scanner.

Pull Metadata from ETL Tools

ETL tools often include thousands of transformations and mappings between sources and targets. As a result, integration with ETL tools is often the trickiest part of any metadata implementation. Popular ETL tools include Ab Initio, IBM InfoSphere DataStage, Informatica PowerCenter, Oracle Data Integrator, and Talend Data Integration. Most metadata tools include pre-built scanners to integrate ETL into the metadata repository. In Figure 4.8, IBM InfoSphere Metadata Workbench displays metadata relating to DataStage jobs beginning with "EWS."

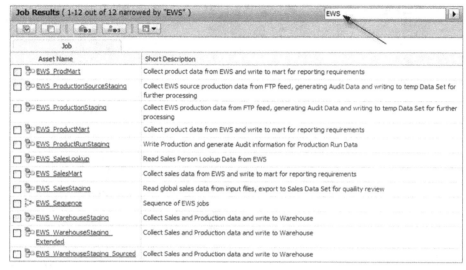

Figure 4.8: IBM InfoSphere Metadata Workbench displays metadata relating to DataStage jobs beginning with "EWS."

Pull Metadata from Reporting Tools

Users also need metadata relating to business intelligence and reporting tools. Figure 4.9 shows the Transaction Report imported from IBM Cognos BI Reporting into IBM InfoSphere Metadata Workbench. Jackie Smith is the steward for this report. The report contains the 6511 Central Banking and Average Number of Customers terms. It relates to the Query1 and Query2 business intelligence queries. The report also relates to the INDV_ NM and PLANT business intelligence query members.

Figure 4.9: A Transaction Report from IBM Cognos BI Reporting reflected in IBM InfoSphere Metadata Workbench.

Reflect Custom Code in the Metadata Tool

The metadata tool also needs to reflect data transformations that may be embedded in programming languages like Java and Visual Basic. Figure 4.10 provides a conceptual view of data flows at a retail bank. The conceptual view shows three applications: C# (C Sharp), Front End, and Retail Web Services. The C# application uses data from Microsoft SQL Server. The Front End application uses Java business logic that invokes COBOL business logic and data from DB2.

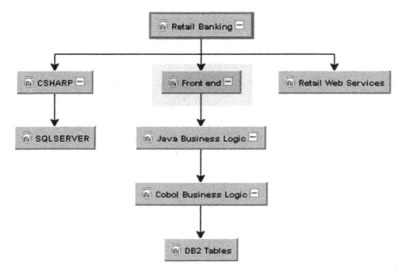

Figure 4.10: A conceptual view of data flows at a retail bank.

In Figure 4.11, ASG-becubic provides a more detailed view of the data flows from the Java Server Pages (JSPs), to the Java programs, to the COBOL programs and the DB2 tables. These flows can then be pulled into a broader data lineage within ASG-Rochade.

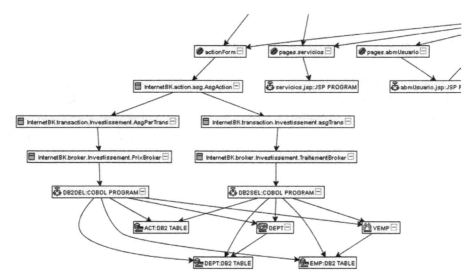

Figure 4.11: ASG-Rochade and ASG-becubic show data lineage encompassing Java programs, COBOL, and DB2.

Pull Metadata from Analytics Tools

Metadata tools also need to scan metadata from analytics tools. Figure 4.12 shows the SAS scanner within ASG-Rochade. The SAS scanner has the following three components:

- The scanner component analyzes the SAS Data Sets and returns the extracted metadata in an XML file.
- The XML Import component imports the analyzed metadata into a subject area of the ASG-Rochade database.
- The scanner then analyzes the SAS Libraries, Data Sets, Views, and Fields.

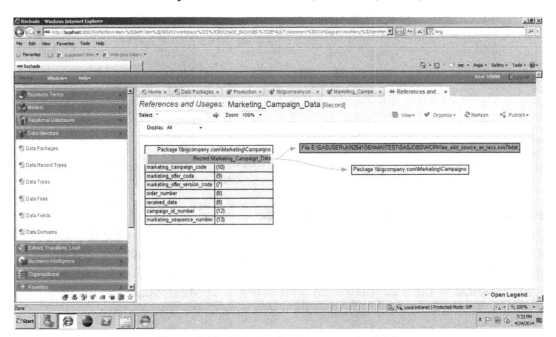

Figure 4.12: ASG-Rochade scanner for SAS.

Link Business Terms with Column Names

The metadata repository should support the linkage of business terms to logical names, physical names, or both. In Figure 4.13, the "Customer Name" term is associated with the LastName and FirstName columns from the Customer table in the AdventureWorksLT database within SAP ERP Central Component. The term is also associated with the NAME1 column from the MDM_DW_Customer Master Data Management hub.

Figure 4.13: "Customer Name" is associated with objects within the Metapedia module of SAP Information Steward. (Image courtesy of SAP Community Network.)

Pull Metadata from Data Quality Tools

Metadata tools should also pull metadata from data quality rules. As shown in Figure 4.14, IBM InfoSphere Business Glossary contains an Information Governance Rule relating to the data quality for customer address. This Information Governance Rule is implemented by the Data Rule called "CityExists" in IBM InfoSphere Information Analyzer. The Information Governance Rule also governs the business term "city."

Information Governance Rule Details

Data quality rules for customer address

Customer address information needs to be complete

Long Description	Undefined
Referencing Policies (0)	Undefined
Labels (0)	Undefined
Steward	Undefined

▼ General Information

Owner	Undefined
System	Undefined
Created By	Mr. Sunil Soares
Created On	Jan 27, 2013 4:42:50 PM
Last Modified By	Mr. Sunil Soares
Last Modified On	Jan 27, 2013 5:07:57 PM

▶ Related Rules (0)

▼ Implemented By (1)

Implemented by Assets (1)	CityExists
Implemented by External Assets (0)	Undefined

▼ Governs (1)

Governs Assets (1)	city / Information-Asset Private Content » Utilities » Customer Service
Governs External Assets (0)	Undefined

Figure 4.14: This Information Governance Rule links to the Data Rule "CityExists" and the business term "city" in IBM InfoSphere Business Glossary.

If we click the **CityExists** link in Figure 4.14, we can view details of the Data Rule in IBM InfoSphere Metadata Workbench, as shown in Figure 4.15. The Data Rule is a null and blank value check. It was originally created in IBM InfoSphere Information Analyzer and then pulled into IBM InfoSphere Metadata Workbench.

Data Rule Definition Details

CityExists
City Exists; null and blank value check

Labels (0)	Undefined
Status	ACCEPTED
Steward	Undefined
Assigned To Terms (0)	Undefined
Implements Rule (1)	Data quality rules for customer address

▼ General Information (0)

Included by Data Rule Set Definitions (0)	Undefined
Published	True
Publication Date	Oct 31, 2012 8:00:49 AM
Rule Logic	City EXISTS AND len(trim(City)) <> 0
Created By	Sam Watson
Created On	Oct 31, 2012 8:00:49 AM
Last Modified By	Sam Watson
Last Modified On	Oct 31, 2012 8:00:49 AM

▶ Notes (0)

Figure 4.15: Drilling down into the IBM InfoSphere Information Analyzer Data Rule called "CityExists" stored in IBM InfoSphere Metadata Workbench.

Pull Metadata from Big Data Sources

Big data expands the volume, velocity, and variety of information, while adding new challenges in building and maintaining a coherent metadata infrastructure. As organizations store more of their data within Hadoop, they will need to address data lineage and impact analysis within this environment as well. Figure 4.16 shows an example of a Hadoop ActiveLinx within Data Advantage Group MetaCenter. An ActiveLinx is a scanner or connector that allows MetaCenter to pull metadata from a Hadoop data repository.

Figure 4.16: An ActiveLinx for Hadoop within Data Advantage Group MetaCenter.

Figure 4.17 shows how Talend can extract metadata from Hadoop data sources and services including HBase, Hive, HDFS, HCatalog, and Oozie. We discuss this topic in greater detail in chapter 16, on Hadoop and NoSQL.

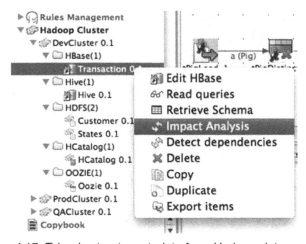

Figure 4.17: Talend extracts metadata from Hadoop data sources.

Provide Detailed Views on Data Lineage

Business users often have to answer questions like these:

- Where did this data come from?
- Where is it going?
- What happens to it along the way?
- What is the impact if we drop this column?

Organizations need a strong metadata foundation to be able to answer these questions. Once metadata tools have ingested technical metadata from a variety of data sources, they should be able to address these questions. Figure 4.18 shows an example of a data lineage report in IBM InfoSphere Metadata Workbench.

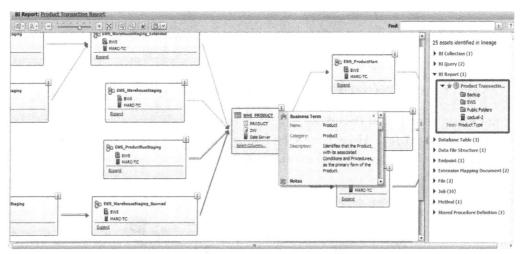

Figure 4.18: A data lineage report in IBM InfoSphere Metadata Workbench.

Customize Data Lineage Reporting

Data lineage views can be quite complex when there are thousands of data artifacts. Metadata tools should allow users to customize views so they can view only a subset of the data lineage. Figure 4.19 shows a High-Level Forward Lineage of the CUSTOMERS table in ASG-Rochade. The lineage report shows the "table only" view from the operational source system to the data warehouse and to the Total Revenue by Country Report-Schema.

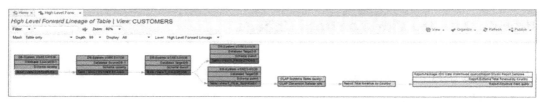

Figure 4.19: A High-Level Forward Lineage using the Table view in ASG-Rochade.

Figure 4.20 shows a Detailed Forward Lineage of the "column only" view of the CUSTOMERS table in ASG-Rochade.

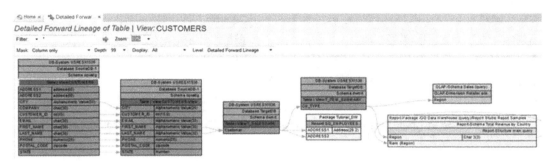

Figure 4.20: A Detailed Forward Lineage using the Column view in ASG-Rochade.

In Figure 4.21, we can see the more detailed Map level, which shows the Extract-Transform-Load (ETL) steps as diamonds between the columns or fields. A filled diamond indicates that a transformation occurs within a step, rather than just moving data from source to target.

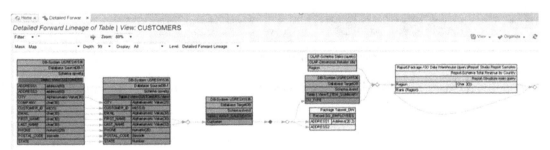

Figure 4.21: A Detailed Forward Lineage using the Map view in ASG-Rochade.

In Figure 4.22, a user highlights the way that Region was built in the Total Revenue by Country Report Schema in ASG-Rochade.

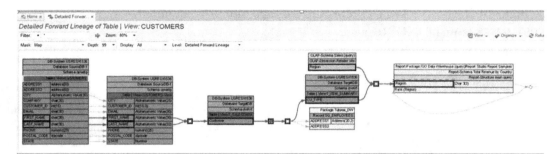

Figure 4.22: Highlighting the way Region was built in the Total Revenue by Country Report Schema.

In Figure 4.23, the user further customizes the view to show only the highlighted boxes in ASG-Rochade.

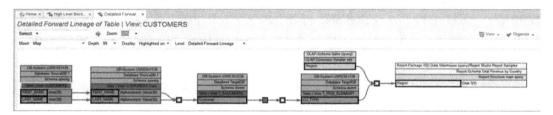

Figure 4.23: Further customizing the view to show only highlighted boxes in ASG-Rochade.

Finally, the user can also view a one-hop source to target lineage at the column level, as shown in Figure 4.24.

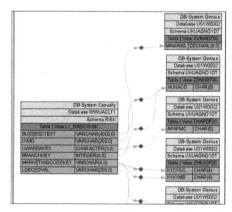

Figure 4.24: Viewing a one-hop source to target lineage at the column level in ASG-Rochade.

Manage Permissions in the Metadata Repository

Administrators need to set up permissions to control access to the metadata repository. Permissions determine the privileges assigned to the users of the metadata repository. For example, IBM InfoSphere Information Server centralizes core administrative tasks across various repositories such as IBM InfoSphere Business Glossary, IBM InfoSphere Metadata Workbench, and IBM InfoSphere Metadata Asset Manager.

Users are created in the Administration console of IBM InfoSphere Information Server. The administrator can then assign suite roles to the users. These roles grant top-level and administrative access to IBM InfoSphere Information Server. The suite component contains a list of roles to be assigned to the users of the metadata repository. As shown in Figure 4.25, the user named "Dorothy" is assigned a number of roles, including the Business Glossary Administrator and Business Glossary Author roles within the suite component. As a result, Dorothy has administration rights for IBM InfoSphere Business Glossary and can create, update, and delete assets.

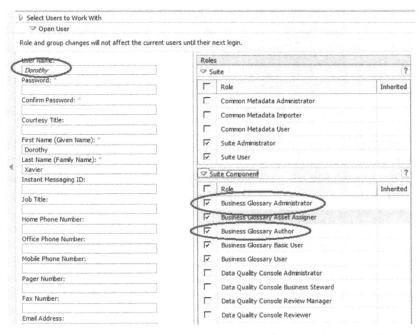

Figure 4.25: Assigning roles to a user in IBM InfoSphere Information Server.

Business Glossary Administrators should also be able to restrict specific users from accessing certain glossary content. Figure 4.26 shows how IBM InfoSphere Business Glossary manages the Published Glossary permissions for Jackie Smith with the security role Business Glossary User. Only Jackie has the right to view the contents of the Information Asset category.

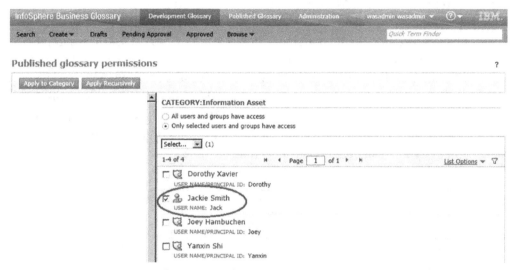

Figure 4.26: Published Glossary permissions in IBM InfoSphere Business Glossary.

As shown in Figure 4.27, Data Advantage Group MetaCenter maintains metadata permissions at the group level. The Data Steward group has the Manage Repository, Dashboard–Manage, Dashboard–Templating, and Dashboard–View permissions. The remaining permissions are set to inherit from their parents.

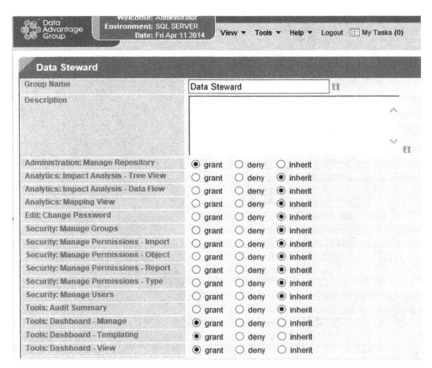

Figure 4.27: Establishing privileges for the Data Steward Group in Data Advantage Group MetaCenter.

Support the Search for Assets in the Metadata Repository

The metadata repository should also support complex and fuzzy search. For example, Figure 4.28 shows the results for a search for "Customer" within the Global IDs metadata repository. The search returns the CustomerID column from the ORDER_INFORMATION table, the Customer_Code column from the CUSTOMER table, the Customer_Name column from the SALESDATA table, the CUSTOMER table from the CRM schema, and the Customer_Code column from the CONTACTS table.

Figure 4.28: Searching for "Customer" within the Global IDs metadata repository.

Summary

In this chapter, we learned that metadata repositories need to integrate with key enterprise data repositories. These include logical models, physical models, relational databases, data warehouse appliances, legacy data sources, custom code, ETL tools, reporting tools, analytic engines, data quality tools, and Hadoop. Metadata hubs need to support critical functionality such as data lineage reporting, managing permissions, and searching.

CHAPTER 5

DATA PROFILING

Data profiling is the process of understanding the data in a system, where it is located, and how it relates to other systems. This process includes developing a statistical analysis of the data such as data type, null percentages, and uniqueness. While there might be some nuances, we will use the terms "data profiling" and "data discovery" synonymously. In the absence of tools, data analysts have historically resorted to the use of SQL queries to discover and profile data. Data profiling tools can automate a number of tasks associated with data governance.

Conduct Column Analysis

The first step in any data profiling exercise is to conduct an analysis of the columns. In Figure 5.1, IBM InfoSphere Discovery displays a column analysis for the HQ_EMP table. The column analysis displays basic metadata about each column, as discussed below (not all metadata is shown in the screenshot):

- #—The sequence number of the column.
- *Column Name*—The name of the column as shown in the database table.
- *Data Type*—The data type, such as NumberString, Varchar, and DateTime. For example, the data type for the EMPLOYEE_ID column in Figure 5.1 is NumberString.
- *Length*—The defined length of the column. For example, the length of EMPLOYEE_ID is seven characters.

- *Precision*—The maximum number of digits that can be present in a number. For example, EMPLOYEE_ID can have a maximum of 31 digits.
- *Scale*—The maximum number of decimals after the decimal point. For example, EMPLOYEE_ID has zero digits after the decimal point.
- *Cardinality*—The number of unique values in a column. For example, FNAME and LNAME have 228 and 219 unique values, respectively.
- *Selectivity*—The degree of uniqueness of the values (including nulls) in the column, calculated as *Cardinality / (Row Count – Null Count)*. Selectivity is calculated on each column individually and is not the result of comparison to another column. This value is never greater than one.
- *Min*—The smallest or lowest value in the column, calculated numerically for numeric columns and alphabetically for other columns.
- *Max*—The largest or greatest value in the column, calculated numerically for numeric columns and alphabetically for other columns.
- *Mode*—The most common value in the column, not including null values. This value is calculated only if a particular value is displayed in more than five percent of the rows. In Figure 5.1, the mode for STATE is TX.
- *Mode%*—The number of times the mode (the most common value) is displayed in this column, as a percentage of all values in the column. For example, TX appears eight percent of the time in STATE.
- *Sparse*—Indicates whether the column is sparse, based on the Mode %. A sparse column contains mostly the same value except for a few exceptions.
- *Null Count*—The number of rows where the column value is null.
- *Blank Count*—The number of rows in the column that are blank (empty).

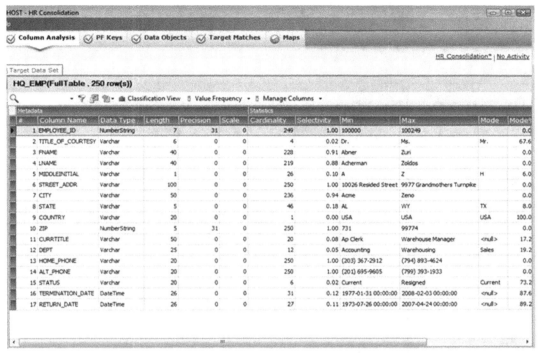

Figure 5.1: IBM InfoSphere Discovery displays the column analysis for the HQ_EMP table.[1]

Discover the Values Distribution of a Column

Data discovery tools should also display the most frequent values of a specific column. As shown in Figure 5.2, Trillium TS Discovery displays the Values Distribution, which shows the top five values for the Name column. The names "Michelle," "Dorothy," "Joey," "Royson," and "Sunil" appear 28.571%, 14.286%, 14.286%, 14.286%, and 14.286% of the time, respectively.

---

1   From the IBM Redbook *Metadata Management with IBM InfoSphere Information Server*, October 2011, Jackie Zhu et al.

Figure 5.2: The Values Distribution for the Name column in Trillium TS Discovery.

Discover the Patterns Distribution of a Column

Data discovery tools should also display the patterns distribution of a specific column. As shown in Figure 5.3, Trillium TS Discovery displays the Patterns Distribution, which shows the top five patterns for the Name column. The most common patterns are alphanumeric six characters and alphanumeric eight characters, each with 28.571% of the records. These are followed by alphanumeric four, alphanumeric five, and alphanumeric seven, each with 14.286% of the records.

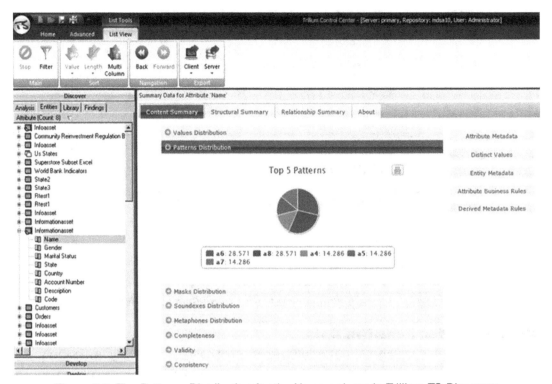

Figure 5.3: The Patterns Distribution for the Name column in Trillium TS Discovery.

Discover the Length Frequencies of a Column

Data discovery should also display the length frequencies of columns. In Figure 5.4, IBM InfoSphere Discovery displays the length frequencies for CHECKING.ACCOUNT_ BALANCE. For example, values with a length of eight and seven occur 559 and 337 times, respectively. The bottom of the screen shows a preview of the rows where the length of CHECKING.ACCOUNT_BALANCE is seven.

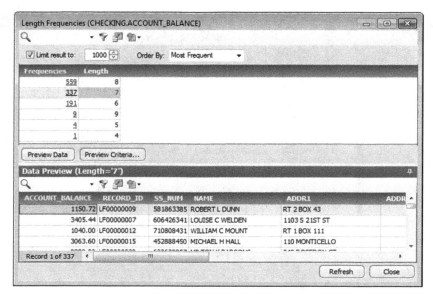

Figure 5.4: Length frequencies in IBM InfoSphere Discovery.[2]

Discover Hidden Sensitive Data

Data discovery tools can also discover hidden sensitive data, which is a specific form of pattern matching. The sensitive nature of the data might not be reflected in column or table names. For example, U.S. Social Security numbers might be hidden in a field called EMP_NUM. Figure 5.5 shows that credit card numbers have been discovered by the Global IDs Profiler within the CoffeeChainSheet.txt, MedSpan2.5_DataSample.txt, and customer_sample_value.csv data sources.

2   From the IBM Redbook *Metadata Management with IBM InfoSphere Information Server*, October 2011, Jackie Zhu et al.

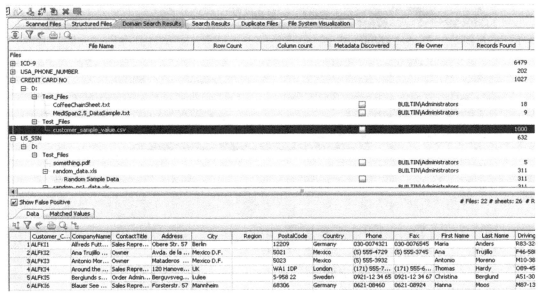

Figure 5.5: The Global IDs Profiler discovers credit card numbers within multiple data sources.

Discover Values with Similar Sounds in a Column

The data discovery tool should also discover column values with similar sounds. As shown in Figure 5.6, the Soundexes Distribution in Trillium TS Discovery shows the Name values with a similar sound that are grouped together as soundexes when the data is analyzed. The soundex is based on the first four values of every attribute. Trillium TS Discovery also checks for the Metaphone, which is based on the entire attribute value, helping to check for misspellings and data discrepancies.

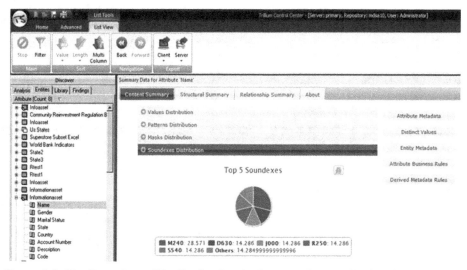

Figure 5.6: The Soundexes Distribution for the Name column in Trillium TS Discovery.

Agree on the Data Quality Dimensions for the Data Governance Program

According to DAMA UK in "The Six Primary Dimensions for Data Quality Assessment" (October 2013), a data quality dimension is a recognized term used by data management professionals to describe a characteristic, attribute, or facet of data that can be measured or assessed against defined standards in order to determine the quality of data. The next step is to select the data quality dimensions that need to be measured in the scorecard. Although there are no industry-standard definitions for data quality dimensions, Table 5.1 lists some data quality dimensions and the way they are used in business rules.

Table 5.1: Data Quality Dimensions		
Data Quality Dimension	**Definition**	**Sample Business Rule**
1. Completeness	The degree to which data elements are populated	Customer phone number should not be null or blank.
2. Conformity	The degree to which data elements correspond to expected formats or valid values or ranges of values	State should be from the agreed upon list of code values for state. Phone number should be in the format NNN-NNN-NNNN. Further, "000-000-0000," "111-111-1111," and "999-999-9999" are not allowed.

Table 5.1: Data Quality Dimensions (continued)		
Data Quality Dimension	Definition	Sample Business Rule
3. Consistency	The degree of relational integrity between data elements and other data elements	Minors should have guardians. The insurance policy expiration date should be greater than or equal to the policy effective date.
4. Synchronization	The degree to which data elements are consistent from one data store to the next	The transaction database should only contain orders for customer records that already exist in the master data hub. A student's date of birth has the same value and format in the school register as that stored within the student database.[3]
5. Uniqueness	The degree to which data elements are unique within a data store	U.S. Social Security numbers should not be repeated in the customer database. Employee IDs should not be repeated in the employee database.
6. Timeliness	The degree to which data is available on a timely basis	Emergency contacts should be entered into the system within two days of being provided by the employee. For example, Tina Jones provides details of an updated emergency contact number on June 1, 2013, which is then entered into the student database by the administration team on June 4, 2013. This indicates a delay of three days.[3]
7. Accuracy	The degree to which data elements are accurate	Email addresses should be validated by customer service every six months. Mail items should not be returned by the United States Postal Service as undeliverable.

Develop Business Rules Relating to the Data Quality Dimensions

The data governance team should document business rules in the business glossary. These business rules should relate to only one data quality dimension. This is important because

---

3 From the IBM Redbook *Metadata Management with IBM InfoSphere Information Server*, October 2011, Jackie Zhu et al.

the data profiling results for each business rule will roll up by data quality dimension and ultimately for a data entity such as customer. We will discuss this topic in the context of data quality scorecards in the next chapter.

Figure 5.7 shows seven business rules in Collibra Data Governance Center:

1. *Completeness*—The customer code should not be null.
2. *Conformity*—The customer name should consist of six alphanumeric characters.
3. *Consistency*—The shipped date must be greater than or equal to the order date.
4. *Synchronization*—The sales database must only contain customers numbers that already exist in the data warehouse.
5. *Uniqueness*—Each customer record should have a unique name and country combination.
6. *Timeliness*—A police report should be loaded into the claims system within 30 days of the effective date of the report.
7. *Accuracy*—Customer service representatives should validate email addresses when talking to the customer.

Each of these business rule relates to a data profiling rule discussed in the sections that follow.

☐ Name
☐ Customer Code should not be null
☐ Customer Name should consist of six alphanumeric characters.
☐ Customer Service Representatives should validate email addresses when talking to the customer.
☐ Customer records should have a unique name and country combination.
☐ Police reports should be loaded into the claims system within 30 days of the effective date of the police report.
☐ Sales database must contain only customer numbers that already exist in the data warehouse
☐ Shipped Date must be greater than or equal to Order Date.

Figure 5.7: Business rules in Collibra Data Governance Center.

Profile Data Relating to the Completeness Dimension of Data Quality

Data profiling tools should highlight the null and space values in columnar data. In Figure 5.8, Trillium TS Discovery shows that the Code column has one empty data row for Joey. This results in "null count = 1," which accounts for 14.286% of the number of records.

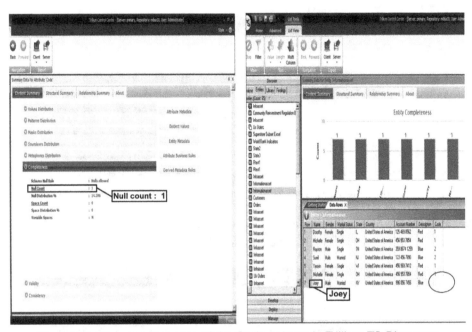

Figure 5.8: The completeness of the Code column in Trillium TS Discovery.

Profile Data Relating to the Conformity Dimension of Data Quality

The conformity dimension of data quality should be tested based on attribute business rules. Examples of an attribute business rule might be a null check that tests for the existence of null values within a column. In Figure 5.9, we set the expression for the Patterns Check attribute business rule to "Customer Name pattern equals a6." This means that the business rule will pass only if all the data rows for the attribute called Customer Name are six characters long. We also set the Passing Fraction to 100 percent, so that the rule will fail unless all rows are compliant. The business rule failed because not all the data rows are six characters in length. The Passing Fraction turned out to be only 75 percent.

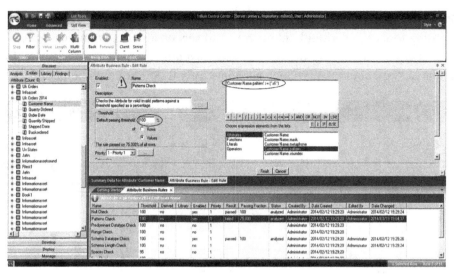

Figure 5.9: The Patterns Check attribute business rule within Trillium TS Discovery.

We can drill down to view the failing rows, as shown in Figure 5.10. These are all the rows where Customer Name is not six characters long.

Figure 5.10: Drilling down into rows where Customer Name is not six characters long.

Profile Data Relating to the Consistency Dimension of Data Quality

Data profiling tools should also test business rules relating to the consistency dimension of data quality. Trillium TS Discovery supports business rules that are created at the entity level to run against multiple attributes in that entity. Figure 5.11 shows the Validate Shipped Date business rule in Trillium TS Discovery. The expression for this business rule states that Shipped Date must be greater than or equal to Order Date. The passing threshold for this business rule is 100 percent. At the bottom of the screenshot, you can see that the business rule has passed, indicating that the rows are 100 percent compliant.

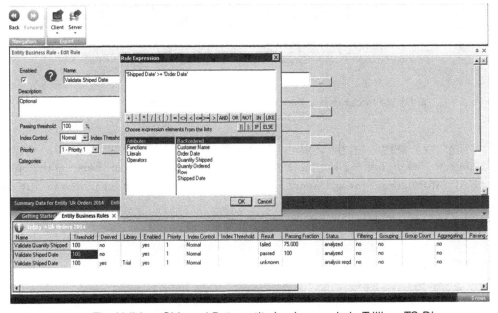

Figure 5.11: The Validate Shipped Date entity business rule in Trillium TS Discovery.

Profile Data Relating to the Synchronization Dimension of Data Quality

In the synchronization dimension of profiling, we check whether values in one or more columns also occur in another set of columns. Figure 5.12 shows the Define Redundancy Task in the Data Insight module within SAP Information Steward. This task compares the customer numbers in two data sources. We will check that values in the CustomerID column in the Views.US_Customers sales database also exist in the CUSTOMER_NR column in the MDM_DW_Customer.dbo.CUSTOMER data warehouse. If the sales database contains customer numbers that don't already exist in the data warehouse, we have a problem.

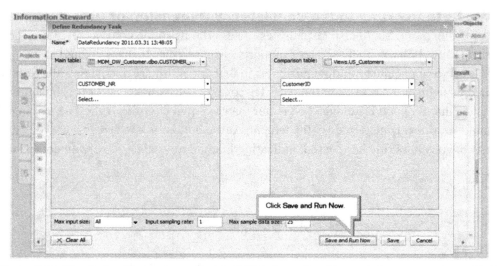

Figure 5.12: The Define Redundancy Task in SAP Information Steward. (Image courtesy of SAP Community Network.)

As shown in Figure 5.13, the profiling shows that there are nine customer IDs in the sales database that do not exist in the data warehouse. The details are shown at the bottom of the SAP Information Steward screen. These anomalies need to be explored in further detail.

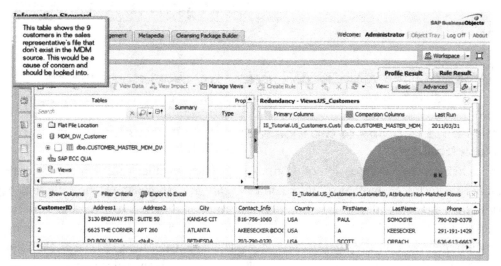

Figure 5.13: The Redundancy view in SAP Information Steward. (Image courtesy of SAP Community Network.)

Profile Data Relating to the Uniqueness Dimension of Data Quality

The data profiling tool should also discover the uniqueness of the values in a given column or set of columns. In this section, we will explore how the Data Insight module within SAP Information Steward can uncover the number of customer records with the same name and country combination. As shown in Figure 5.14, we define a uniqueness task within the Data Insight module of SAP Information Steward. For the MDM_DW_Customer.dbo.CUSTOMER_MASTER_MDM_DW table, we select the COUNTRY and NAME1 columns.

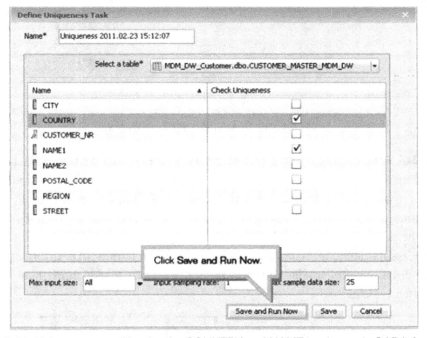

Figure 5.14: Uniqueness profiling for the COUNTRY and NAME1 columns in SAP Information Steward. (Image courtesy of SAP Community Network.)

In Figure 5.15, SAP Information Steward produces a pie chart with the results of the uniqueness profiling. The pie chart shows that 74.27 percent of the customer records had unique combinations of country and name. On the other hand, 25.73 percent of the customer records had non-unique combinations of country and name. The user can drill down to view sample records.

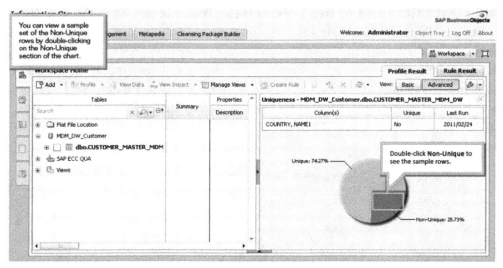

Figure 5.15: SAP Information Steward produces the results of the uniqueness profiling. (Image courtesy of SAP Community Network.)

Profile Data Relating to the Timeliness Dimension of Data Quality

Data profiling tools should also test against the timeliness dimension of data quality. For example, suppose an insurance carrier has a standard that police reports should be loaded into the claims system within 30 days of the effective date of a report. In many instances, however, the police report is not obtained in a timely manner, resulting in delays in claims processing due to non-availability of the report. In Figure 5.16, Informatica PowerCenter has a simple mapping to flag all police reports loaded more than 30 days after the effective date:

```
POL_REPORT_LOAD_DATE - POL_REPORT_EFF_DATE > 30
```

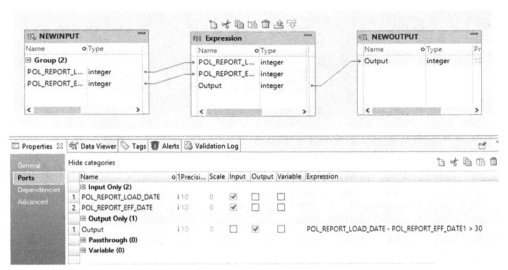

Figure 5.16: Informatica PowerCenter tests the timeliness dimension for police reports within an insurance claims process.

Profile Data Relating to the Accuracy Dimension of Data Quality

The accuracy dimension of data quality is generally the most difficult to measure and requires some creativity. For example, suppose an insurance carrier wants to measure the accuracy of its customer email addresses. The carrier institutes a policy that requires customer service representatives to validate email addresses when on the phone with a customer.

In Figure 5.17, Informatica PowerCenter includes an expression to flag all email addresses where the email validation date is less than 180 days ago. This metric is a good proxy for the accuracy of email addresses. In other words, if an email address has not been validated in the previous 180 days, its accuracy is suspect.

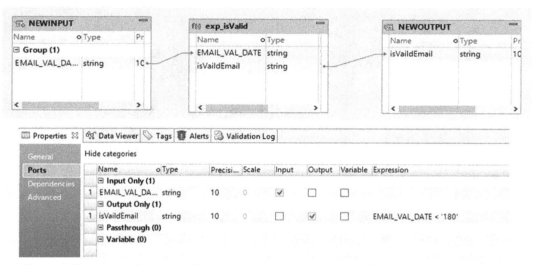

Figure 5.17: Informatica PowerCenter tests the accuracy of email addresses based on the validation date.

Discover Data Overlaps Across Columns

Data discovery tools should also discover overlapping data across columns within the same data source or across data sources. Figure 5.18 shows the overlap analysis in IBM InfoSphere Discovery. IBM InfoSphere Discovery looks at the values of the columns (not just the column names) to produce this cross-domain analysis. We can see that the Community, Region, and CRM data sets each have three tables. These tables have 31, 31, and 33 columns, respectively. The analysis also shows that the CRM data set has three columns that have been flagged as Critical Data Elements (CDEs). Based on an analysis of the column values, it appears that the Community data set has 20 overlapping columns and 11 exclusive (non-overlapping) columns.

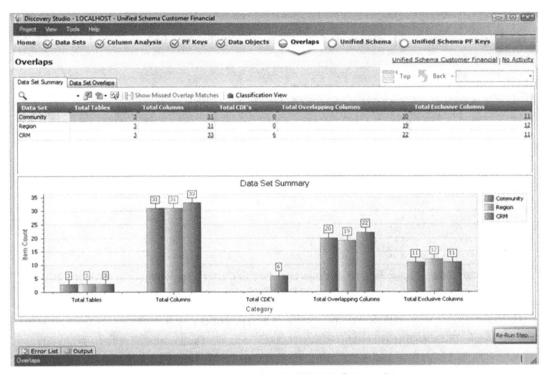

Figure 5.18: Overlap analysis with IBM InfoSphere Discovery.

Figure 5.19 shows the results of drilling down further to view the overlaps for the Community data set. In this example, the COMMUNITY_BRCH.F_NAME column has overlaps with the Region and CRM data sets, as shown in the right panel. On a left-to-right basis, 50 percent, or 25 unique values, in the COMMUNITY_BRCH.F_NAME overlap with Region. On a right-to-left basis, 51 percent, or 25 unique values, in Region overlap with COMMUNITY_BRCH.F_NAME.

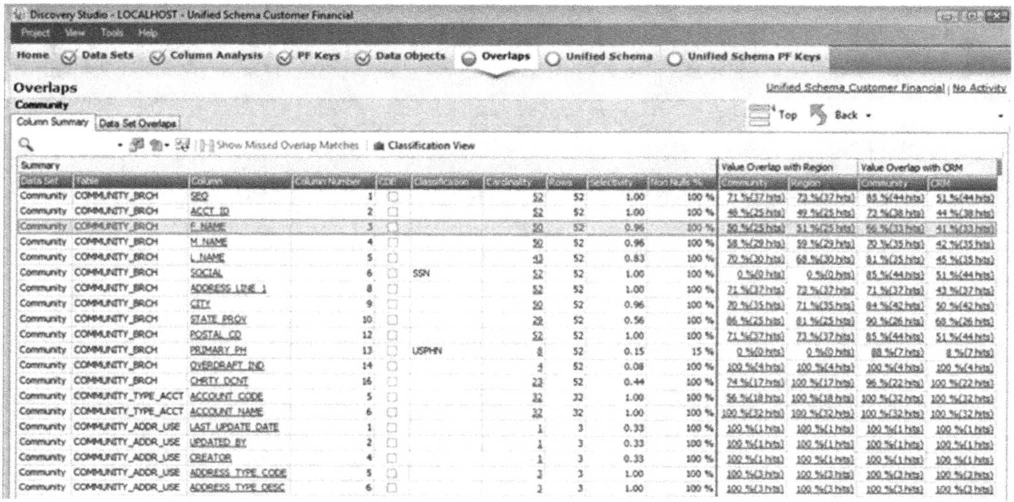

Figure 5.19: Drilling down to view the overlaps for the Community data set in IBM InfoSphere Discovery.

In Figure 5.20, the drill-down shows the overlaps for the COMMUNITY_BRCH.F_NAME column with REGION_BRCH.FN and REGION_BRCH.MI. On the right, the left-to-right row hit rate is 52% (27/72). This means that 52 percent, or 27 out of 52 rows in COMMUNITY_BRCH.F_NAME, overlap with REGION_BRCH.FN. Similarly, the right-to-left hit rate is 53% (27/51). This means that 53 percent, or 27 out of 51 rows in REGION_BRCH.FN, overlap with COMMUNITY_BRCH.F_NAME. The value hit rate focuses on unique values. As a result, 50 percent, or 25 out of 50 values from COMMUNITY_BRCH.F_NAME, overlap with REGION_BRCH.FN on a left-to-right basis.

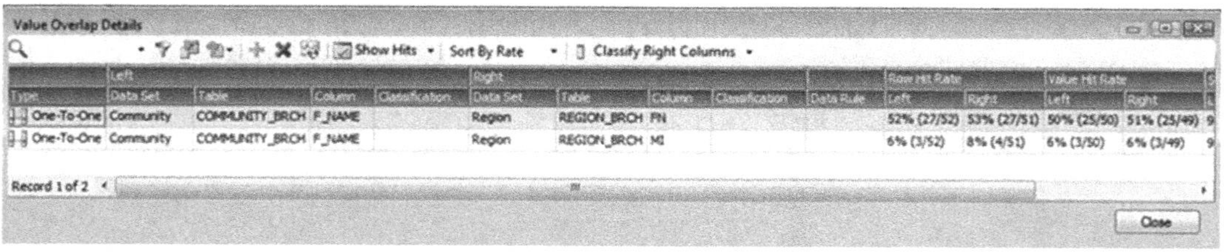

Figure 5.20: Drilling down further to view the overlaps for the COMMUNITY_BRCH.F_NAME column in IBM InfoSphere Discovery.

Figure 5.21 shows the actual overlapping values between COMMUNITY_BRCH.F_NAME and REGION_BRCH.FN. For example, the first three rows show overlapping values for ADABELL, CARL, and CARMEL.

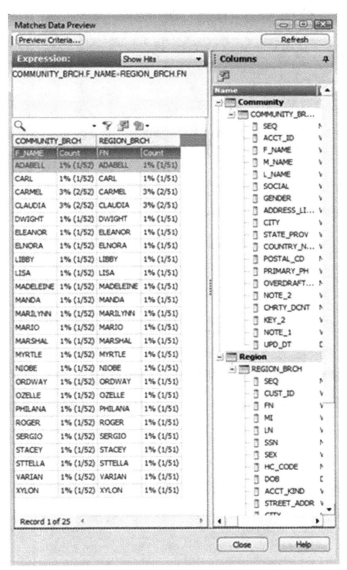

Figure 5.21: Drilling down further to view the actual overlapping values between COMMUNITY_ BRCH.F_NAME AND REGION_BRCH.FN in IBM InfoSphere Discovery.

Discover Hidden Relationships Between Columns

Data discovery tools can also discover hidden relationships that can then be formally reflected in enterprise data modeling tools. Figure 5.22 shows a basic column analysis of the OPTIM_CUSTOMERS table using IBM InfoSphere Discovery.

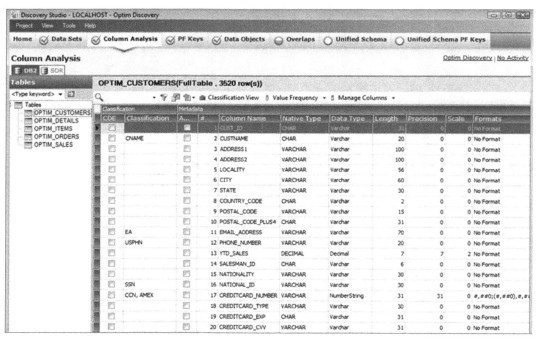

Figure 5.22: A column analysis of the OPTIM_CUSTOMERS table using IBM InfoSphere Discovery.

In Figure 5.23, a Primary-Foreign Key diagram shows discovered relationships with IBM InfoSphere Discovery.

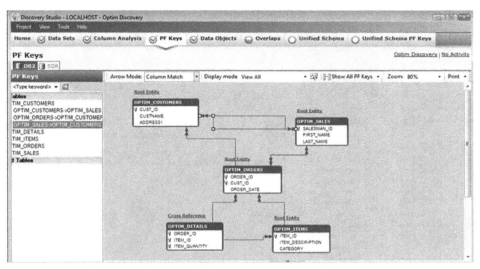

Figure 5.23: Primary-Foreign Key diagram showing discovered relationships in IBM InfoSphere Discovery.

These newly discovered relationships can also be represented in tabular format, as shown in Figure 5.24. For example, OPTIM_SALES.SALESMAN_ID is the primary key, while OPTIM_CUSTOMERS.SALESMAN_ID is the foreign key.

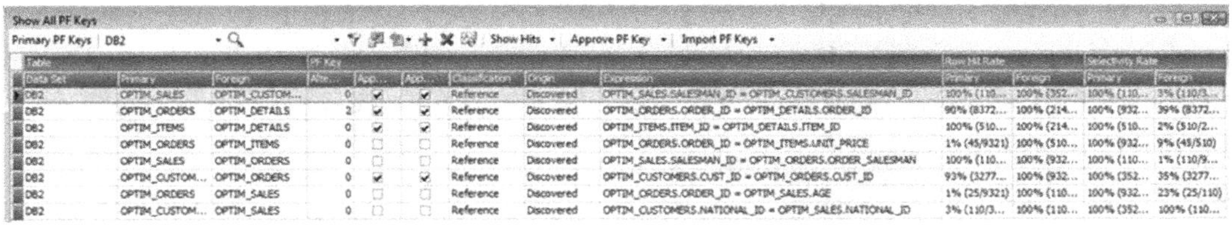

Figure 5.24: A tabular view of the relationship between primary and foreign keys in IBM InfoSphere Discovery.

Discover Dependencies

Data discovery tools should uncover dependencies among multiple columns within the same data source, or among multiple columns across multiple data sources. This section shows how the Data Insight module within SAP Information Steward can be used to uncover customers with missing region information in SAP ERP Central Component (ECC).

In Figure 5.25, the user selects QUA.KNA1.LAND1 as the primary column because it contains the country key. The user also selects QUA.KNA1.REGIO as the dependent column because it contains the region (state, province, or county).

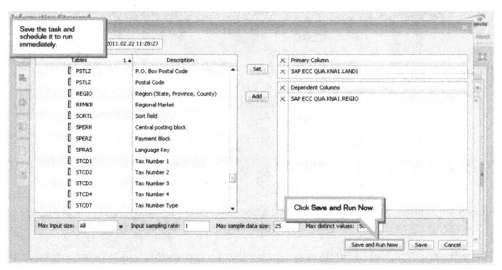

Figure 5.25: Selecting the primary and dependent columns in SAP Information Steward. (Image courtesy of SAP Community Network.)

The user views the results in Figure 5.26. SAP Information Steward organizes the entries for a region as dependent on the country. There are 48 regions for the United States, 17 for Germany, and 9 for Great Britain. Almost 97 percent of the customers are located in these three countries.

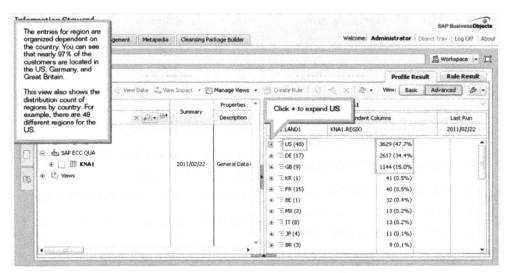

Figure 5.26: SAP Information Steward organizes the entries for region dependent on country. (Image courtesy of SAP Community Network.)

In Figure 5.27, the user drills down further into SAP Information Steward to view the number of customers by U.S. state. We can see that 924 customers are located in Illinois. In addition, 162 customers have no state assigned.

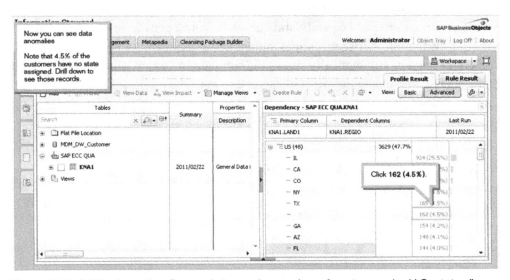

Figure 5.27: SAP Information Steward shows the number of customers by U.S. state. (Image courtesy of SAP Community Network.)

In Figure 5.28, the user drills down in SAP Information Steward to view the customer records with missing region information.

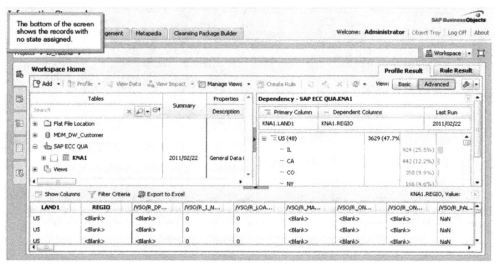

Figure 5.28: SAP Information Steward shows a detailed view of customers with missing region information. (Image courtesy of SAP Community Network.)

Discover Data Transformations

As part of data migration and consolidation projects, data discovery tools should also identify transformations between sources and targets. As shown in Figure 5.29, IBM InfoSphere Discovery automatically shows the summary of a map from the HQ_LOC and HQ_DEPT source columns to the WDPT01 target column. The map shows the join and binding conditions.

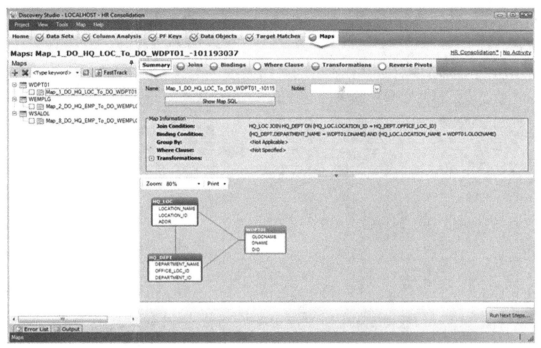

Figure 5.29: IBM InfoSphere Discovery automatically discovers the join and binding conditions
between the source and target columns.

As shown in Figure 5.30, IBM InfoSphere Discovery automatically discovers the
following CASE statement that reflects the transformation between the HQ_EMP (source)
column and the WEMPLG (target) column:

```
CASE WHEN HQ_EMP.STATUS in ( 'Current',  'Fired',  'Resigned')  or
HQ_EMP.STATUS is null THEN HQ_EMP.TERMINATION_DATE ELSE HQ_EMP.RETURN_DATE END
```

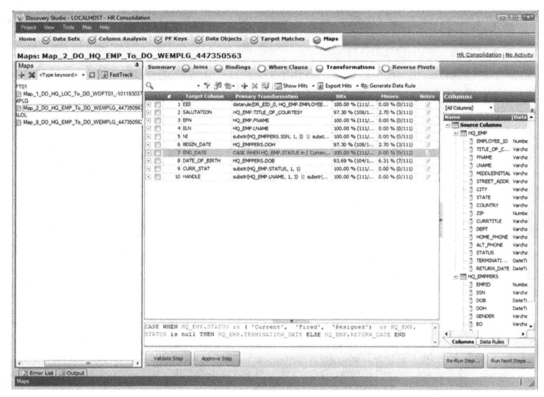

Figure 5.30: IBM InfoSphere Discovery automatically discovers the CASE statement that reflects the transformation between the source and target column.

Create Virtual Joins or Logical Data Objects That Can Be Profiled

Data profiling tools should be able to operate on data from multiple sources simultaneously. For example, IBM InfoSphere Information Analyzer creates a virtual table that filters the number of rows and columns to produce a much smaller and more focused table on which analysis and rules can be applied.

Figure 5.31 shows the virtual table definition pane in IBM InfoSphere Information Analyzer. The base table, Overdue_Reporting_GRM_Credit_units.txt, is too large, and its analysis would consume too much processing power. The data analyst creates a virtual table to look at customers with high outstanding amounts. The analyst selects only the RATING TYPE, RATING AGENCY, YEAR END, CREDIT OFFICER, and Outstandings CAD columns. In the right panel, the analyst also applies a filter to select only rows where the Outstandings are greater than CAD 1,000.

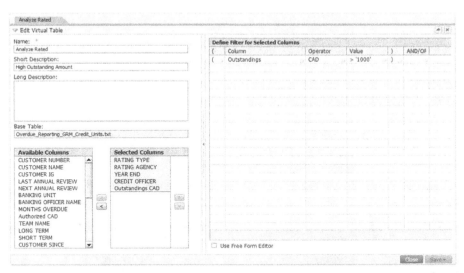

Figure 5.31: The virtual table definition pane in IBM InfoSphere Information Analyzer.[4]

Informatica has the concept of a logical data object (LDO) that describes a logical entity in an enterprise. A logical data object mapping associated with the LDO can integrate data from multiple sources and formats into a standardized view. Consider a scenario where the enterprise data model requires a standardized view of customer data. This is to be accomplished by creating an LDO. In Figure 5.32, Informatica Developer contains an LDO for the Customer entity based on Read_Boston_Customers and Read_LA_ Customers.

---

4   From the IBM Redbook *Metadata Management with IBM InfoSphere Information Server*, October 2011, Jackie Zhu et al.

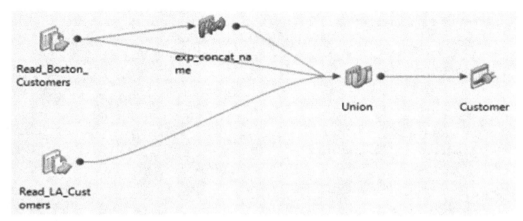

Figure 5.32: A logical data object for Customer in Informatica Developer. (Image courtesy of Informatica Community.)

Summary

In this chapter, we learned about the seven dimensions of data quality: completeness, conformity, consistency, synchronization, uniqueness, timeliness, and accuracy. We also reviewed certain critical functionality in data profiling tools, including column analysis and virtual tables. Finally, we discussed data discovery functionality such as sensitive data, overlaps, transformations, dependencies, and hidden relationships.

CHAPTER 6

DATA QUALITY MANAGEMENT

Data quality management is a discipline that includes the methods to measure and improve the quality and integrity of an organization's data. While data profiling uncovers issues with the data, data quality actually remediates those issues. Data quality tools support the automation of key data governance processes.

Transform Data into a Standardized Format

Data quality tools need to standardize data that might be in multiple formats. For example, the addresses in Figure 6.1 are not in a standardized format. One of the issues is that they include street names with "Ave."

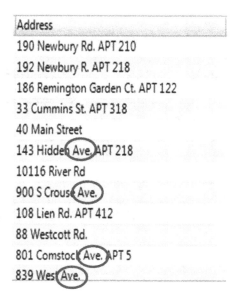

Figure 6.1: These non-standardized addresses contain street names with "Ave."

Figure 6.2 shows the expression in Informatica Data Quality to standardize the "Ave." and "Ave" to "Avenue." The replace_Ave_with_Avenue mapping on the left accepts the raw addresses in the inAddress field and outputs cleansed addresses in the outAddress field. The replace_Avenuenue_with_Avenue mapping on the right accepts the outAddress from the previous mapping as the inAddress and outputs the results as outAddress.

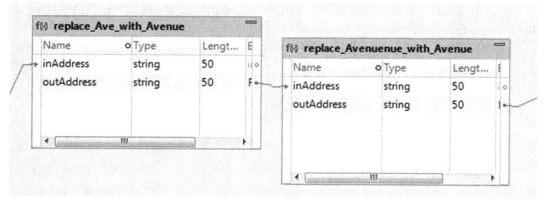

Figure 6.2: Informatica Data Quality mappings.

Let's drill down into the expression for the replace_Ave_with_Avenue mapping. As shown in Figure 6.3, it replaces variations of "ave" with "Avenue."

Figure 6.3: The expression for replace_Ave_with_Avenue in Informatica Data Quality.

However, we have one last issue. The expression in Figure 6.3 will replace "Avenue" with "Avenuenue." The expression in Figure 6.4 fixes this issue.

Figure 6.4: The expression for replace_Avenuenue_with_Avenue in Informatica Data Quality.

Figure 6.5 shows the standardized addresses.

	outAddress
1	190 Newbury Rd. APT 210
2	192 Newbury R. APT 218
3	186 Remington Garden Ct. APT 122
4	33 Cummins St. APT 318
5	40 Main Street
6	143 Hidden Avenue APT 218
7	10116 River Rd
8	900 S Crouse Avenue
9	108 Lien Rd. APT 412
10	88 Westcott Rd.
11	801 Comstock Avenue APT 5
12	839 West Avenue

Figure 6.5: The standardized street addresses contain street names with "Avenue."

Similarly, Informatica Data Quality standardizes phone numbers in the (XXX)XXX-XXXX format, as shown in Figure 6.6. The actual expression is shown in the middle.

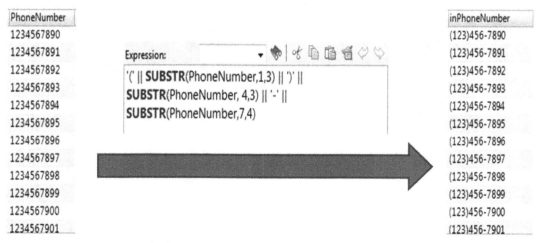

Figure 6.6: Standardization of phone numbers using Informatica Data Quality.

Improve the Quality of Address Data

Addresses are critical data that need to be the focus of a data quality program. For example, the customer service department at a large North American utility saved $20,000 a day by implementing a data stewardship program around ZIP+4 information for U.S. postal codes. This resulted in higher discounts from the U.S. Postal Service. In addition, the billing department improved cash flow by receiving payments faster. Finally, the utility was able to dramatically reduce complaints that occurred when it sent a bill to the wrong customer.[1]

The first step to improve the quality of address data is to conduct address profiling. In this section, we use the Data Insight module of SAP Information Steward to determine the percentage of address data that is valid, correctable, or invalid. Valid addresses can be delivered by the U.S. Postal Service. Correctable addresses can be automatically corrected by using the Address Transform function in SAP Data Services. Invalid addresses are undeliverable and cannot be automatically corrected by SAP Data Services.

Figure 6.7 shows the results of an address profiling exercise in the Data Insight module of SAP Information Steward. The address profiling exercise was conducted on the US_Customers table, focusing on the Address1, City, State, PostalCode, and Country columns. The pie chart shows that 40 percent of the addresses are valid, 8.96 percent are invalid, and the remaining are correctable by SAP Data Services.

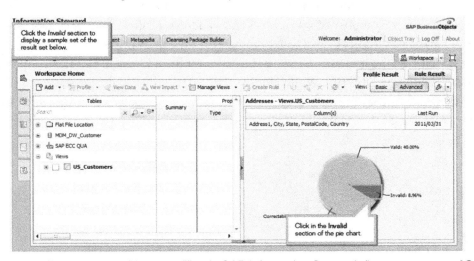

Figure 6.7: The result of address profiling in SAP Information Steward. (Image courtesy of SAP Community Network.)

1   Soares, Sunil. *Selling Information Governance to the Business*. MC Press, 2011.

In Figure 6.8, we drill down into the explanation for why the addresses are not correctable.

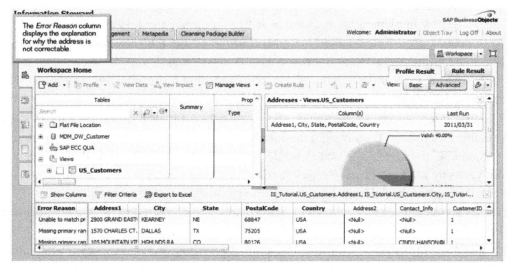

Figure 6.8: SAP Information Steward supports drilling down into the reasons why the addresses are not correctable. (Image courtesy of SAP Community Network.)

Many third-party vendors such as Acxiom, Experian, Informatica AddressDoctor, and PitneyBowes offer a number of services, such as address verification, geocoding, and National Change of Address (NCOA). Figure 6.9 shows an example using Informatica AddressDoctor. In the Input panel, we manually enter the address "1600 Pennsylvania Avenue, Washington DC" (the White House). The Suggestions panel provides the fully formatted address, and the Result panel shows that AddressDoctor has a high level of certainty regarding this address.

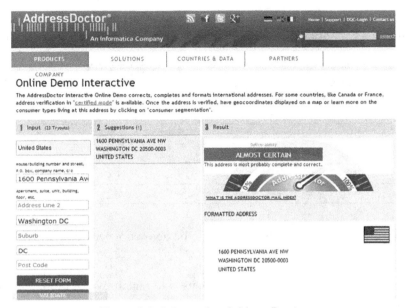

Figure 6.9: Informatica AddressDoctor.

Match and Merge Duplicate Records

Data quality tools also need to automate the process of discovering duplicate records. In Figure 6.10, Talend Studio automates the process of discovering duplicate customer records. At the bottom of the screen, Talend displays potential duplicate records for FLAGG BROS. SHOES from SFDC and CRM. The records have the same values for name, city, and state.

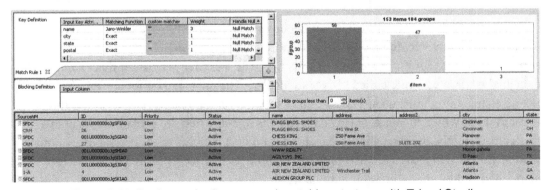

Figure 6.10: Design and refine a record-matching strategy with Talend Studio.

We drill down further to see that there are five matching attributes, as shown in Table 6.1. (Only the first four attributes are visible in the top left panel of Figure 6.10.)

Table 6.1: Matching Attributes in Talend Studio		
Matching Attribute	Matching Function	Confidence Weight
name	Jaro–Winkler	3
city	Exact	1
state	Exact	1
postal	Exact	1
contactPhone	Jaro–Winkler	2

There are a few important terms that need to be defined when dealing with duplicate records:

- *Matching attribute*—An attribute that is used to match two or more records as duplicates.
- *Matching function*—The specific algorithm that is deployed to match two or more records. In this case, Talend Studio deploys either the Jaro–Winkler or Exact matching function.
- *Jaro–Winkler*—A measure of similarity between two strings. The higher the Jaro–Winkler distance, the more similar the strings are. The Jaro–Winkler distance metric is best suited for short strings such as customer names. The score is normalized such that zero equates to no similarity, and one is an exact match.[2]
- *Exact*—A matching algorithm that requires two strings to be exactly the same.

In Figure 6.11, the Match Rule Settings in Talend Studio allows the data analyst to define rules that decide whether two or more data records match, and to configure survivorship rules for the matching records to create a golden record. In this example, the data analyst creates a rule called "MyMatchRule." The data analyst identifies lname and fname as matching attributes. The matching function is set to Jaro–Winkler. The threshold is set to 0.75, which means that two data records match when the probability is above this value. Finally, the data analyst assigns confidence weights to each attribute. In other words, Talend will assign a much higher weighting if two records have the same last name than if they share the same first name.

---

2   http://en.wikipedia.org/wiki/Jaro-Winkler_distance.

Figure 6.11: The Match Rule Settings feature in Talend Studio.

As shown in Figure 6.12, Talend Data Quality helps find the best fit for de-duplication at design time. Talend does this by visually highlighting the potential false positive and false negative until the matching algorithm is fine-tuned.

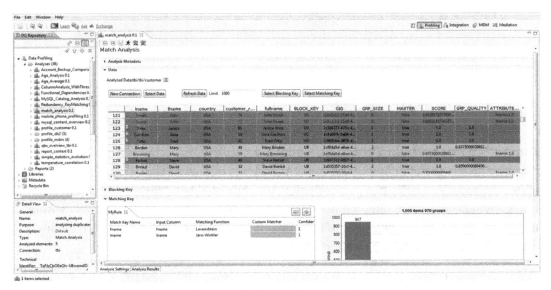

Figure 6.12: Talend Data Quality.

Create a Data Quality Scorecard

Practitioners can use data quality tools to produce scorecards or dashboards. In this section, we use the Data Insight module in SAP Information Steward to create a data quality scorecard for customer data. The steps to create a data quality scorecard are documented in the sections that follow.

Select the Data Domain or Entity

Figure 6.13 shows an input box within SAP Information Steward. We type **Customer Master**, which is the data domain for which we want to create a data quality scorecard.

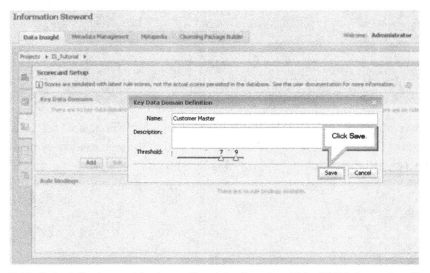

Figure 6.13: Select Customer Master as the data domain within SAP Information Steward. (Image courtesy of SAP Community Network.)

Define the Acceptable Thresholds of Data Quality

The next step is to define lower and upper thresholds of data quality. Data quality scores above the threshold will "pass," those below the threshold will "fail," and those in the middle will be subject to ongoing review. SAP Information Steward flags scores within these tiers as green, red, and yellow, respectively. In Figure 6.13, we configure the lower and upper thresholds to be **7** and **9**, respectively.

Select the Data Quality Dimensions to Be Measured for the Specific Data Domain or Entity

The next step is to select a subset of data quality dimensions to be measured for the specific data domain or entity. In Figure 6.14, we select the **Completeness**, **Conformity**, and **Consistency** dimensions for Customer Master within SAP Information Steward.

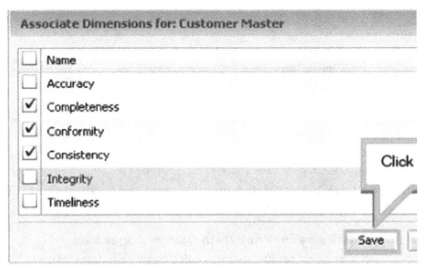

Figure 6.14: Select the data quality dimensions in SAP Information Steward. (Image courtesy of SAP Community Network.)

Select the Weights for Each Data Quality Dimension

The next step is to calculate the weights to be assigned to each data quality dimension. In Figure 6.15, we assign the weights **34** percent, **33** percent, and **33** percent to Completeness, Conformity, and Consistency, respectively.

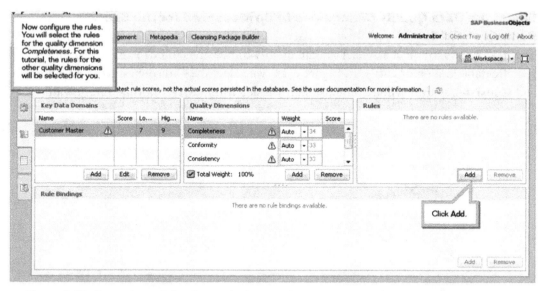

Figure 6.15: Enter the weights for each data quality dimension in SAP Information Steward. (Image courtesy of SAP Community Network.)

Select the Business Rules for Each Data Quality Dimension

In the next step, we have to select the business rules from each data quality dimension. In Figure 6.16, we select **Customer Country Exists** and **Customer Region Exists** from the Completeness dimension for Customer Master. These business rules were already created earlier and assigned to the Completeness dimension.

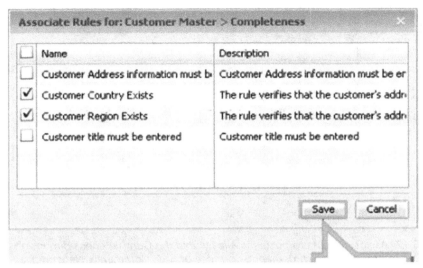

Figure 6.16: Select the business rules for the completeness dimension in SAP Information Steward. (Image courtesy of SAP Community Network.)

Assign Weights to Each Business Rule in a Given Data Quality Dimension

The next step is to assign weights to each business rule within a given data quality dimension. In Figure 6.17, we assign **50** percent weights to the Customer Country Exists and Customer Region Exists business rules within the Completeness dimension of the Customer Master.

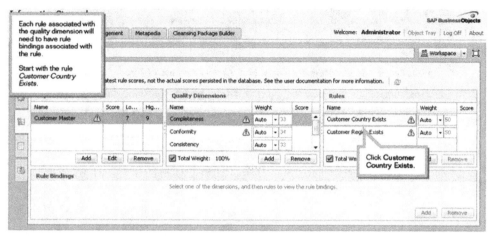

Figure 6.17: Assign weights to business rules within the Completeness dimension in SAP Information Steward. (Image courtesy of SAP Community Network.)

Bind the Business Rules to the Relevant Columns

The final step is to bind the business rules to the relevant columns that contain the actual data values. In Figure 6.18, we bind the business rule **Customer Region Exists** to the REGION and REGIO columns, each with a **50** percent weighting. The scorecard has now been fully set up. The next section discusses how to view data quality scorecards.

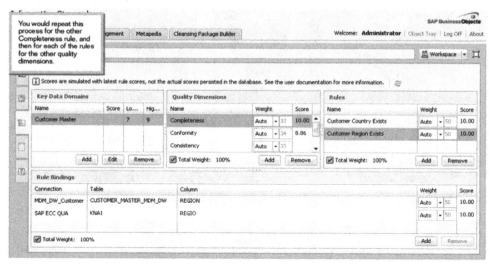

Figure 6.18: Bind business rules to columns in SAP Information Steward. (Image courtesy of SAP Community Network.)

View the Data Quality Scorecard

Data governance tools should also expose data quality results in the form of a dashboard. As shown in Figure 6.19, Collibra Data Governance Center produces a data quality scorecard for a business term called "Customer." Trillium TS Discovery is used to profile the source Customer data consisting of 32,636 rows. The results were then passed from Trillium to Collibra using an application programming interface (API). The weighted average score for Customer data is 90.6 percent. This score can be decomposed into Accuracy (94.2 percent), Conformity (99.5 percent), Completeness (98.5 percent), and Consistency (57.5 percent).

In Figure 6.19, Accuracy, Conformity, and Completeness have upward-pointing arrows, indicating that they have exceeded the acceptable threshold. On the other hand, the overall Customer score and the Consistency dimension have downward-pointing arrows, indicating that they are below the acceptable threshold. The scorecard also allows a drill-down for the data quality score for each data quality dimension and business rule. For example, 8,840 rows out of 10,000 passed the Date of Birth Verification business rule, which resulted in a data quality score of 88.40%.

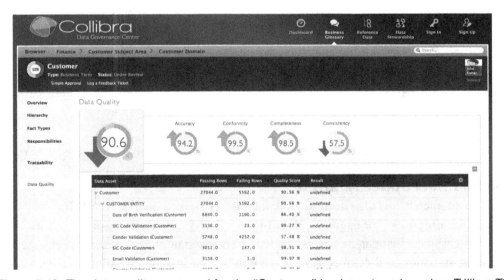

Figure 6.19: The data quality scorecard for the "Customer" business term based on Trillium TS Discovery and Collibra Data Governance Center.

Highlight the Financial Impact Associated with Poor Data Quality

Data governance tools should highlight the cost and business benefits associated with poor data quality. Figure 6.20 shows how SAP Information Steward displays the financial impact associated with the poor quality of email addresses. Based on assumptions, the tool estimates the total cost of poor customer data at $468,000. Of this, the accuracy dimension accounts for $242,000, of which invalid email addresses result in losses of $103,000, while incorrect countries result in an additional $139,000. In addition, the completeness dimension accounts for losses of $44,300, which is largely due to missing addresses.

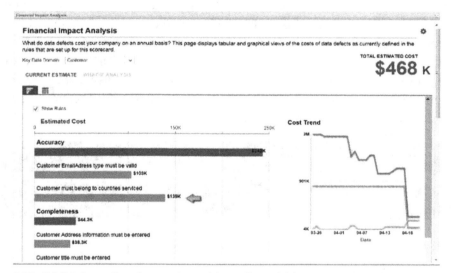

Figure 6.20: SAP Information Steward provides a financial impact analysis for customer data.

Conduct Time Series Analysis

Data governance teams also need to view the history of data quality results for comparison purposes. For example, IBM Information Analyzer stores data rules as executable objects that can be run as needed or on schedule. Each object generates a set of results, statistics, and detailed results recorded in the InfoSphere Analyzer Database, which is a special database workspace designated for storing analysis and data rules execution results. Because these objects run repeatedly, they create a time series of events that can be tracked, reported, and trended over time.

InfoSphere Information Analyzer's presents the current results, as shown in Figure 6.21. On the right, each red icon with an *X* indicates a down or worsening trend, while each green icon with a check mark indicates an improving trend.

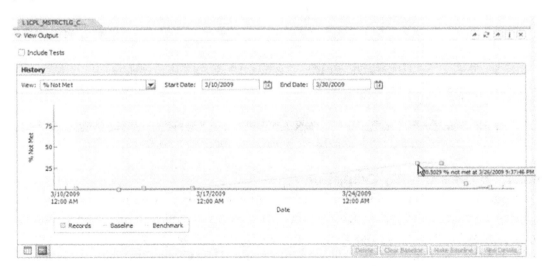

Figure 6.21: The data quality alert report in IBM InfoSphere Information Analyzer.[3]

As shown in Figure 6.22, the data analyst can view a longer history of results in a graphical format for a given data rule.

Figure 6.22: IBM InfoSphere Information Analyzer shows the trend for a business rule.

3   From the IBM Redbook *Metadata Management with IBM InfoSphere Information Server*, October 2011, Jackie Zhu et al.

Data analysts should be able to gather data quality results in intervals such as hours, days, weeks, and months. Users should also be able to specify a start date and time, an end date and time, and the frequency. As shown in Figure 6.23, Trillium TS Discovery supports the creation of a new entity after every interval.

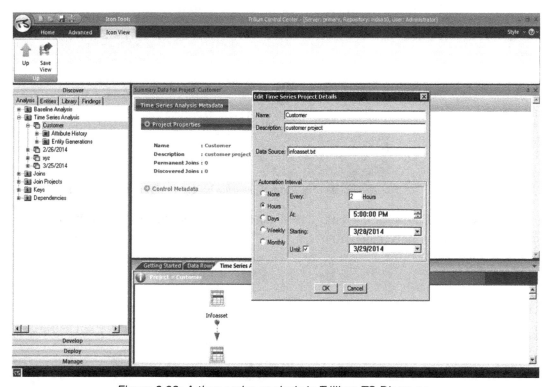

Figure 6.23: A time series analysis in Trillium TS Discovery.

Manage Data Quality Exceptions

Data quality tools also need to support an exception handling process with data stewards. This means that human tasks such as manual data cleansing and de-duplication should be integrated with automated tasks such as auto-matching and data standardization. Figure 6.24 shows a schematic of a workflow in Informatica Data Quality that includes both automated and human tasks.

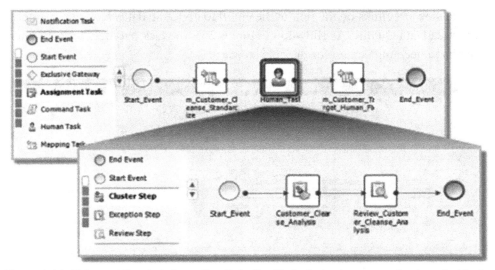

Figure 6.24: This workflow in Informatica Data Quality includes human and automated tasks.

As shown in Table 6.2, the data governance team establishes upper and lower thresholds for match probability within Informatica Data Quality. As a result, records with a match probability above 80 percent will be auto-matched. Records with a match probability below 60 percent will be auto-rejected. Finally, Informatica Data Quality initiates a human workflow for records with a match probability between 60 percent and 80 percent. As part of this workflow, Informatica sends an email to the appropriate data steward with a link to the data stewardship interface.

Table 6.2: A Triage of Duplicates in Informatica Data Quality		
Tier	**Match Probability**	**Action**
Lower	0%–60%	Informatica Data Quality automatically rejects the records as matches.
Middle	60%–80%	Informatica Data Quality initiates a human workflow and sends the data steward an email with a link to the data stewardship interface.
Upper	80%–100%	Informatica Data Quality automatically accepts the records as matches.

The data steward clicks on the link in the email to go to the data stewardship interface in Informatica Data Quality. As shown in Figure 6.245, the task list includes a number of tasks that have been queued up for the data steward.

Figure 6.25: Data stewardship interface in Informatica Data Quality.

Summary

In this chapter, we discussed how tools can support an overall data quality management program. We discussed data standardization, address cleansing, duplicates, scorecards, time series analysis, data stewardship, and linkage to financial benefits.

CHAPTER 7

MASTER DATA MANAGEMENT

Master data management (MDM) refers to the discipline associated with establishing a single version of the truth for multiple data domains, such as customer, vendor, product, location, asset, employee, and chart of accounts. MDM vendors include IBM, Informatica, Oracle, Orchestra Networks, Riversand, SAP, SAS, Semarchy, Stibo Systems, and Talend. In this chapter, we review critical data governance tasks that are automated by MDM hubs.

Define Business Terms Consumed by the MDM Hub

MDM hubs consume critical data that needs to be defined. As shown in Figure 7.1, Semarchy Convergence for MDM lists the definition of "Customer" as "an individual or organization to whom we deliver goods or services for payment." The matching behavior for customer records has been set to Fuzzy Matching.

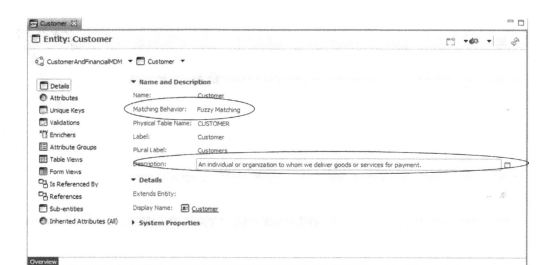

Figure 7.1: The definition of the term "Customer" in Semarchy Convergence for MDM.

Some organizations may elect to store key business terms in a separate tool such as IBM InfoSphere Business Glossary, Informatica Metadata Manager, or Collibra Data Governance Center. Figure 7.2 shows a similar definition for the business term "Customer" in Collibra Data Governance Center.

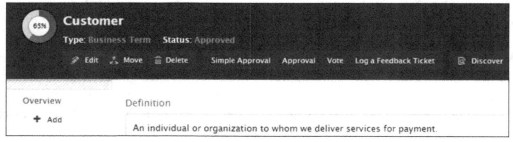

Figure 7.2: The definition of the term "Customer" in Collibra Data Governance Center.

Orchestra Networks EBX provides a unified platform for the business glossary, data modeling, MDM, and reference data management. In Figure 7.3, the left panel shows the EBX business glossary that is compliant with the ISO/IEC Metadata registry standard. The glossary includes a definition for NAICS code. This definition can then be reused within an EBX data model for MDM, as shown in the right panel. At the bottom of the screen, the definition for NAICS is also available as a tool tip when reviewing the industry classification for GE as provided by Dun & Bradstreet (D&B).

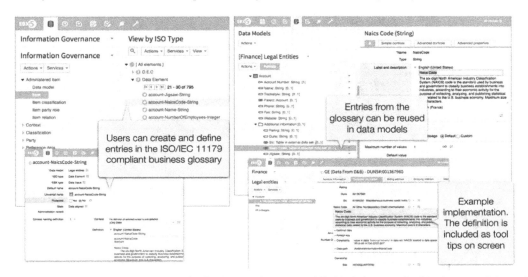

Figure 7.3: The business glossary in Orchestra Networks EBX is integrated with data models and MDM.

Manage Entity Relationships

Many MDM hubs also manage logical and physical relationships between data entities. Figure 7.4 shows a diagram view of a manufacturer's entities in Semarchy Convergence for MDM. The diagram view contains a logical view of the Customer, Employee, Contact, and CostCenter entities. The diagram also contains the attributes and data types for each entity. For example, Customer ID, Customer Name, Total Revenue, Input Address, Geocoded Address, and Account Manager are attributes of the Customer Entity. In addition, the diagram defines relationships between these entities. For example, Employees manage Customers in an Account Manager relationship. Some Employees manage other Employees as Managers. In addition, Contacts relate to individuals within Customers.

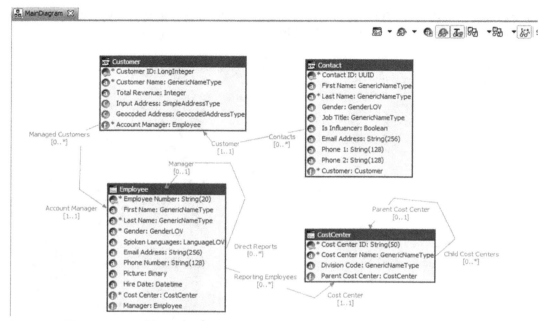

Figure 7.4: A diagram view of entity relationships in Semarchy Convergence for MDM.

Manage Master Data Enrichment Rules

Data enrichment rules add more context and richness to data. These rules are often not written down, or are in people's heads. In Figure 7.5, the data enrichment rule in Semarchy Convergence for MDM implements a plug-in for the Google Maps Enricher. The data enrichment rule accepts Address Line, City, Country, and Postal Code as basic input. The data enrichment rule then outputs a fully geocoded address, including east-bound longitude, north-bound longitude, south-bound longitude, west-bound longitude, and latitude.

As shown in Figure 7.6, the business rule to enrich "address" master data is documented in plain English in Collibra Data Governance Center.

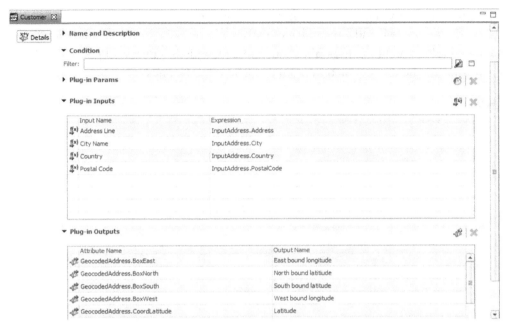

Figure 7.5: A master data enrichment rule for the customer address in Semarchy Convergence for MDM.

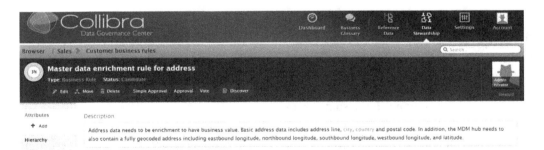

Figure 7.6: The business rule for master data enrichment of address data in Collibra Data Governance Center.

Manage Master Data Validation Rules

MDM hubs also need to contain rules to validate key master data. Figure 7.7 shows a sample MDM data validation rule that requires a source address to contain at least one address line and either a postal code or a city. The ValidateAddressCompleteness rule is written using a SQL-like script. In addition, the scope of the validation is pre-consolidation only. This means that the rule validates the records before they are matched, de-duplicated, and consolidated. Only valid records for these validations participate in the matching, de-duplication, and consolidation phase. Once again, this business rule can be documented in plain English in the business glossary.

Figure 7.7: An address data validation rule in Semarchy Convergence for MDM.

Manage Record Matching Rules

MDM hubs match records to capture duplicates. These record matching rules need to be properly managed and governed. In Figure 7.8, the record matching rules for customer data are as follows:

- The records belong to the same country.
- The records have a strong similarity based on their names. This similarity is greater than 65 percent using the Levenshtein distance algorithm. The Levenshtein distance is a string metric for measuring the difference between two sequences. The Levenshtein distance between two words is the minimum number of single-character edits (insertions, deletions or substitutions) required to change one word into the other.[1]
- The records have a strong similarity on their address lines and cities. This similarity is greater than 65 percent using the Levenshtein distance algorithm.

---

1   http://en.wikipedia.org/wiki/Levenshtein_distance.

Data stewards may document these plain English business rules in a business glossary. The business rules are then implemented in Semarchy Convergence for MDM. We first create a so-called "binning expression" by country, so that the matching algorithm only works for records within a given country. This speeds up the matching algorithm. We then create a SQL-like expression to implement the rest of the matching algorithm.

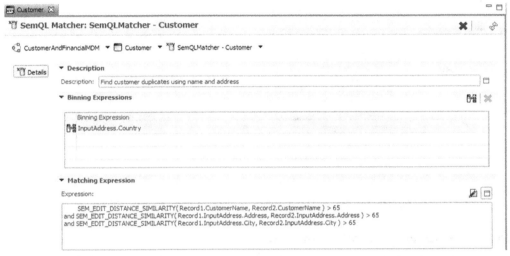

Figure 7.8: A record matching rule for customer data in Semarchy Convergence for MDM.

Figure 7.9 shows the matching policy for the Third Parties entity in Orchestra Networks EBX. EBX offers a wide range of out-of-the-box matching algorithms.

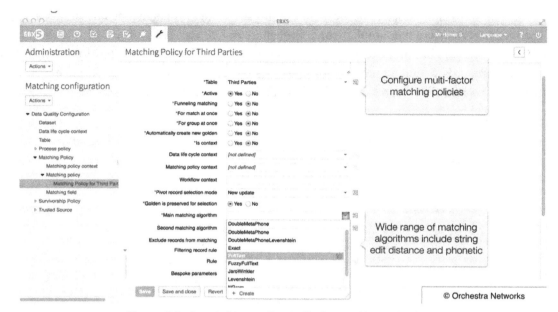

Figure 7.9: A matching policy in Orchestra Networks EBX.

Manage Record Consolidation Rules

Data stewards need to define rules to consolidate source records into a golden record. In Figure 7.10, the following record consolidation rules are implemented in Semarchy Convergence for MDM:

- The customer name in the golden record should be based on the most frequent value in the source records.
- The employee or account manager name follows a similar rule.
- The lines in the geocoded address use manual data entry, the CRM application, the Marketing application, the Finance application, and the HR application, in descending order of priority.

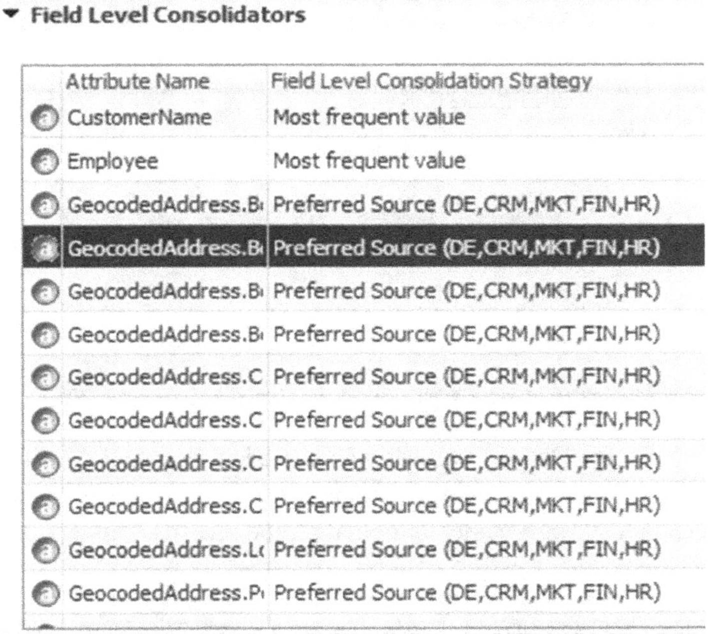

▼ Field Level Consolidators

	Attribute Name	Field Level Consolidation Strategy
⚙	CustomerName	Most frequent value
⚙	Employee	Most frequent value
⚙	GeocodedAddress.B	Preferred Source (DE,CRM,MKT,FIN,HR)
⚙	GeocodedAddress.B	Preferred Source (DE,CRM,MKT,FIN,HR)
⚙	GeocodedAddress.B	Preferred Source (DE,CRM,MKT,FIN,HR)
⚙	GeocodedAddress.B	Preferred Source (DE,CRM,MKT,FIN,HR)
⚙	GeocodedAddress.C	Preferred Source (DE,CRM,MKT,FIN,HR)
⚙	GeocodedAddress.C	Preferred Source (DE,CRM,MKT,FIN,HR)
⚙	GeocodedAddress.C	Preferred Source (DE,CRM,MKT,FIN,HR)
⚙	GeocodedAddress.C	Preferred Source (DE,CRM,MKT,FIN,HR)
⚙	GeocodedAddress.L	Preferred Source (DE,CRM,MKT,FIN,HR)
⚙	GeocodedAddress.P	Preferred Source (DE,CRM,MKT,FIN,HR)

Figure 7.10: A customer record consolidation rule in Semarchy Convergence for MDM.

View a List of Outstanding Data Stewardship Tasks

All the above-mentioned master data rules generate exception tasks that need to be handled manually by data stewards. The MDM hub needs to generate a list of outstanding data stewardship tasks, as shown in Figure 7.11.

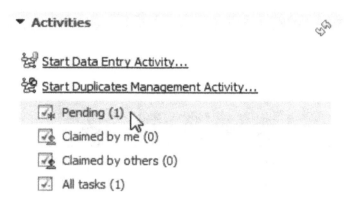

Figure 7.11: Data stewards can view a list of pending tasks in Semarchy Convergence for MDM.

Figure 7.12 shows the Data Stewardship Console in Talend MDM. The Talend Data Stewardship Console organizes the outstanding tasks associated with a data steward. In this example, the data steward wants to look at all the records that need a decision before de-duplication.

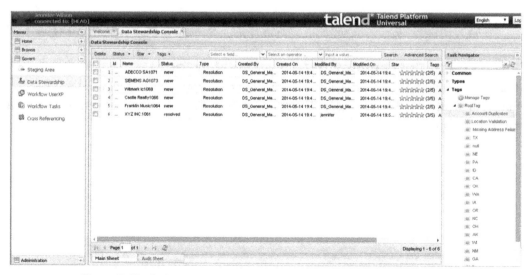

Figure 7.12: A data steward views outstanding tasks in Talend MDM.

Manage Duplicates

Human workflows enable business users to manage the data in the MDM hub via an application. When stewards want to manage the master data, they initiate an activity based on a human workflow. Figure 7.13 shows a duplicate management workflow in Semarchy Convergence for MDM. This is a simple workflow to allow data stewards to override the decisions taken by the automated matching rules in the MDM hub. Through these workflows, stewards can either manually match unmatched records or split duplicate groups that were incorrectly matched because they were false matches.

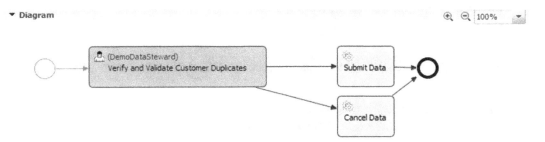

Figure 7.13: A duplicate management workflow in Semarchy Convergence for MDM.

In Figure 7.14, we drill further into how a data steward might manage duplicate records in Semarchy Convergence for MDM. For example, a data steward can view the golden record for a customer called "Gadgetron." He or she can also view the associated source records that were used to create the golden record. The consolidation rule is that the customer name should be the most frequent value in the group of matched records. As a result, Gadgetron is the consolidated name. The account manager is Matthew Weiss because the consolidation rule is also the most frequent value. However, total revenue in the golden record is $123,000 because the consolidation rule is the largest value in the group of matched records. Finally, the input address is the one that was manually entered by the steward, which has a higher priority than any other in the consolidation rule.

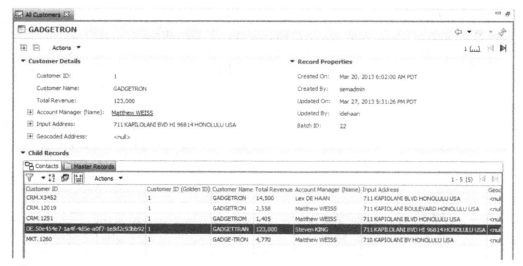

Figure 7.14: A data steward views a golden record based on consolidation rules in Semarchy Convergence for MDM.

On further inspection, the steward determines that the fourth record should actually be its own golden record. In other words, this record was incorrectly matched. As shown in Figure 7.15, the steward manually splits the fourth record into its own golden record. As a result, Customer ID 2 and Customer ID 101 represent separate golden records.

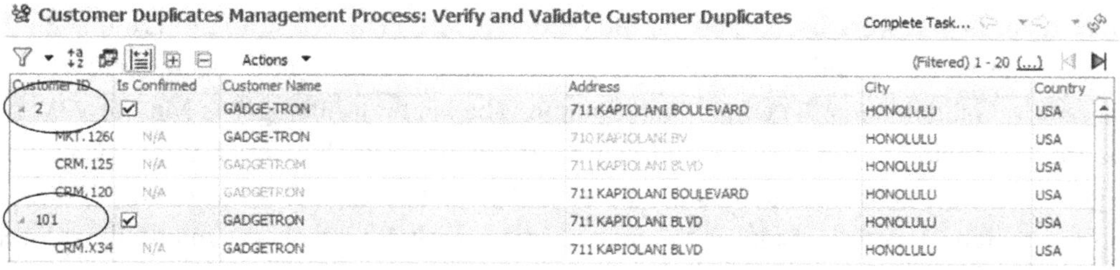

Figure 7.15: A data steward manually splits Customer ID 101 into its own golden record in Semarchy Convergence for MDM.

Figure 7.16 shows a manual de-duplication process within Talend MDM. The data steward views the record for CASTLE REALTY CO within the CRM and 1-A source applications. The data steward then creates the golden record manually from the three applications.

Figure 7.16: A data steward creates a golden record manually within Talend MDM.

View the Data Stewardship Dashboard

Data stewards need dashboards to highlight critical metrics relating to the MDM hub. As shown in the top left area of Figure 7.17, the Workflow Activities section of the Semarchy Convergence for MDM dashboard shows the number of activities pending for the user, claimed by the user or claimed by other users. Data Certification Jobs (top right) shows the status of the certification jobs in progress, queued, or completed. Data Location Statistics (lower section of the screen) shows key metrics for the entities in the hub.

The highlighted customer entity in Figure 7.17 shows that there are 81 golden records relating to a total of 96 master records or source records. The Selected Entity Details section also shows additional statistics relating to records with duplicates. Of the 25 master records with duplications, Semarchy created 10 golden records.

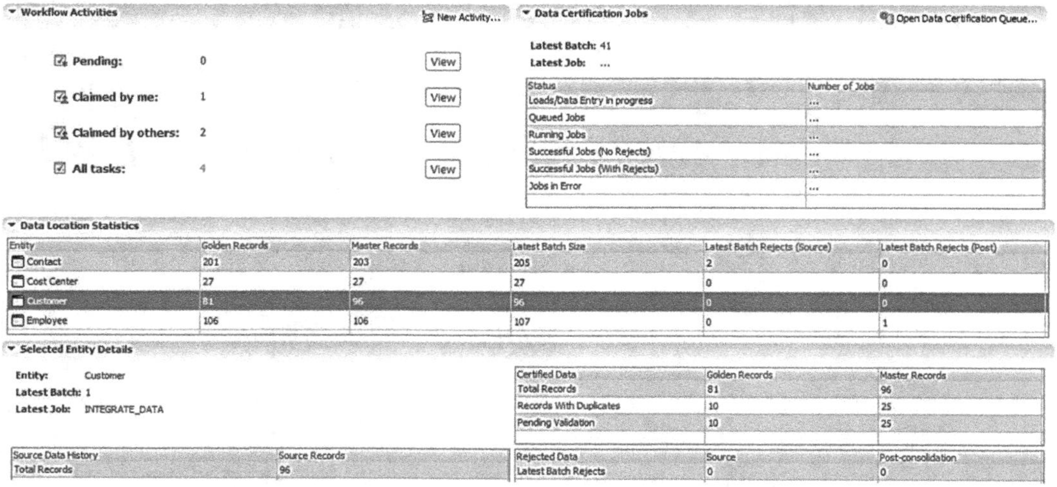

Figure 7.17: The data stewardship dashboard in Semarchy Convergence for MDM.

Manage Hierarchies

Hierarchy management is a key component of master data governance. In Figure 7.18, Orchestra Networks EBX maintains a legal entity hierarchy. For example, the D&B DUNS number for Advanced Services is associated with four DUNS numbers through a parent-child relationship. Hierarchy management features also allow authorized users to maintain the hierarchy. For example, a user can attach a child record to another parent, create a new record, duplicate an existing record, delete a record, or export the hierarchy as a CSV file.

Improve the Quality of Master Data

MDM vendors and third party providers offer tools to monitor the quality of data in the master data hubs. Figure 7.19 shows an example of a data quality dashboard for member (customer) master data at a health plan (insurer). The member data resides in IBM InfoSphere Master Data Management, but the dashboard is produced by InfoTrellis Veriscope. The dashboard provides charts on the quality issues backlog, issue discovery trends, issue resolution trends, and issue backlog trends. In addition, we can see that there are 7,930 high priority issues, 2,709 medium priority issues, and six low priority issues.

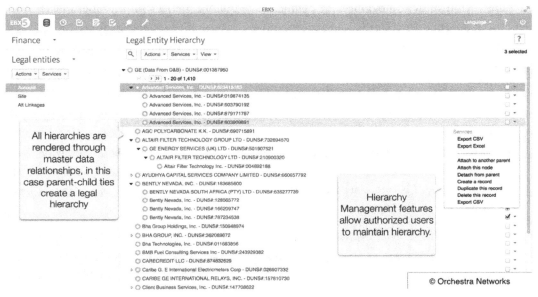

Figure 7.18: The legal entity hierarchy in Orchestra Networks EBX.

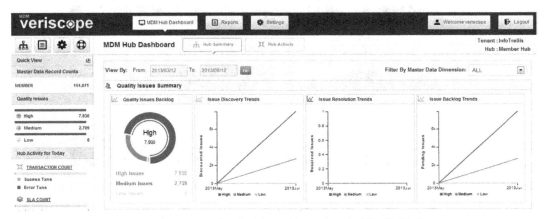

Figure 7.19: A data quality dashboard based on InfoTrellis Veriscope.

Figure 7.20 shows an example of detailed data quality metrics for member master data. In this figure, InfoTrellis Veriscope exposes data quality issues within IBM InfoSphere Master Data Management. Based on the report, we note the following high-severity issues:

- *Birth date*—There are 588 instances where the member is too old.
- *Social Security number*—There are 5,644 instances where the Social Security number is invalid.
- *Social Security number*—There are 1,697 instances where the Social Security number is missing.
- *Name*—There is one instance where the company name is stored as a person's last name.

Time Breakdown for Quality Issue and Resolution

Severity : High	Quality Issue : Birth Date: Invalid Value (too old)				Unit Cost : $0	
Time Dimension	Reported	%Change	Resolved	%Change	Total Outstanding	% Change
2013 Year-to-Date	588	-	0	-	588	-
Total	588		0		588	

Severity : High	Quality Issue : Identifier: SSN Invalid				Unit Cost : $0	
Time Dimension	Reported	%Change	Resolved	%Change	Total Outstanding	% Change
2013 Year-to-Date	5,644	-	0	-	5,644	-
Total	5,644		0		5,644	

Severity : High	Quality Issue : Identifier: SSN Missing				Unit Cost : $0	
Time Dimension	Reported	%Change	Resolved	%Change	Total Outstanding	% Change
2013 Year-to-Date	1,697	-	0	-	1,697	-
Total	1,697		0		1,697	

Severity : High	Quality Issue : Member: Company Stored as Member (last name)				Unit Cost : $0	
Time Dimension	Reported	%Change	Resolved	%Change	Total Outstanding	% Change
2013 Year-to-Date	1	-	0	-	1	-
Total	1		0		1	

Figure 7.20: InfoTrellis Veriscope exposes detailed data quality metrics for health plan member data within IBM InfoSphere Master Data Management.

Once master data quality issues have been identified, they need to be rectified. Figure 7.21 shows how the web user interface in Talend MDM allows the data steward to manually manipulate the data for XYZ ABC INC., provided he or she has the appropriate access rights.

Figure 7.21: The web user interface in Talend MDM.

Integrate Social Media with MDM

MDM hubs should enrich business insights by integrating social media. Informatica has been highlighting the integration of MDM with social media data. For example, Informatica has showcased the ability of a retailer to do the following:[2]

- Gain a customer's permission to leverage his or her Facebook data by offering the ability to participate in a VIP rewards program.
- Reconcile the customer's Facebook and MDM profiles based on the entity resolution and stewardship capabilities of Informatica MDM.
- Enrich the current MDM profile with additional relationships from the customer's Facebook profile.
- Discover additional linkages between the customer and other people in the network (for example, they shop at the same store and have the same concierge).
- Use this additional insight to make compelling offers to the customer.

As shown in Figure 7.22, Informatica Master Data Management includes a number of attributes about the customer, including address, telephone numbers, email address, products, transactions, names, wish list, and relationships, as well as his or her social profile from Facebook.

---

2 http://www.informatica.com/videos/demos/1826_socialmedia_mdm/default.htm.

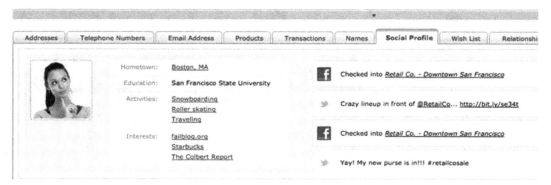

Figure 7.22: Informatica Master Data Management includes the customer's social profile from Facebook.

Manage Master Data Workflows

MDM tools should also support workflows to manage tasks such as de-duplication, data enrichment, and data cleansing. Figure 7.23 shows a data stewardship dashboard in Informatica Master Data Management. The dashboard includes a list of open tasks. It also integrates with pre-built workflows to allow the data steward to manage and reassign tasks.

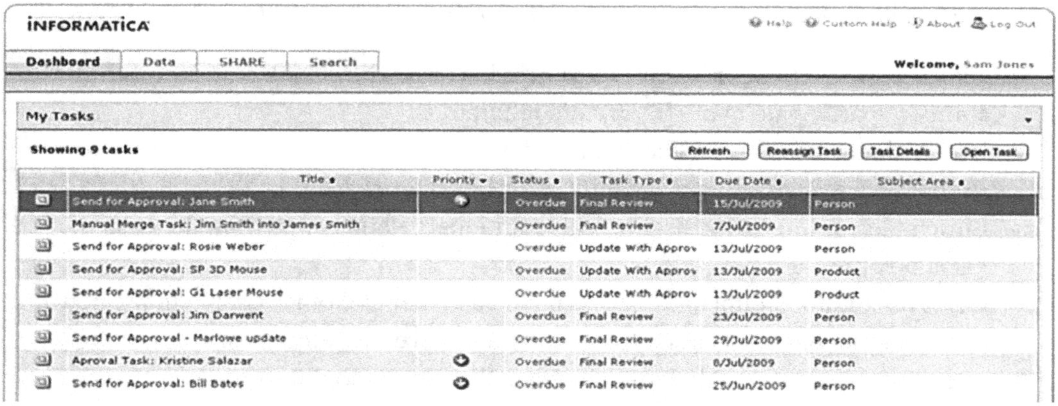

Figure 7.23: The data stewardship console in Informatica Master Data Management.

Figure 7.24 shows how Orchestra Networks supports collaborative workflow for new master data on-boarding and approval. As part of the Create Account xx78 workflow, BartS in Finance has a Create a Cost Center task. After this task is completed, the Link to the Hierarchy and Validate/Enrich the Account tasks need to be addressed.

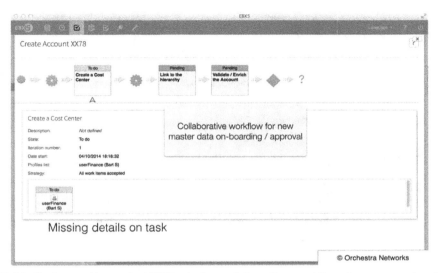

Figure 7.24: Orchestra Networks EBX includes collaborative workflow for new master data on-boarding and approval.

Compare Snapshots of Master Data

MDM hubs should support the creation of snapshots of master data. Figure 7.25 provides an example of data spaces and snapshots in the context of Orchestra Networks EBX. A data space allows an organization to make concurrent updates to a data repository. A snapshot is a type of data space that represents a static view of the data and relationships for a given set of records at a given point in time. A snapshot allows an organization to revert to a more stable version of the data. In the example, the organization has created a Finance data space, which represents a historical snapshot of customer data. The organization has also created a Q2 Changes data space, which has incorporated changes from the Finance data space. The data steward can now compare the two data spaces and determine which changes need to be merged back into the Finance data space.

Figure 7.25: Orchestra Networks MDM allows users to compare snapshots of master data.

Provide a History of Changes to Master Data

MDM hubs should also record a history of changes to master data in terms of who changed what record, when the change was made, and how the change was made. In Figure 7.26, Orchestra Networks EBX provides a history of changes to the master data for the Third Parties record. EBX provides critical data in terms of the audit trail, including the transaction ID, data space, transaction date, operation type, and user.

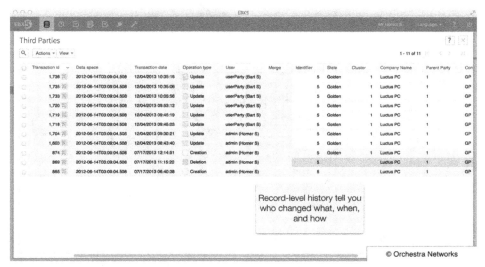

© Orchestra Networks

Figure 7.26: Orchestra Networks EBX provides a history of changes to individual master data records.

Offload MDM Tasks to Hadoop for Faster Processing

MDM hubs are increasingly required to deal with large datasets that may run into the millions of records. In these scenarios, MDM hubs should integrate with Hadoop to enable faster processing. (This topic is discussed in detail in chapter 16.)

Talend MDM supports de-duplication for very large datasets natively in Hadoop. As shown in Figure 7.27, Talend MDM generates a de-duplication job that executes natively in Hadoop.

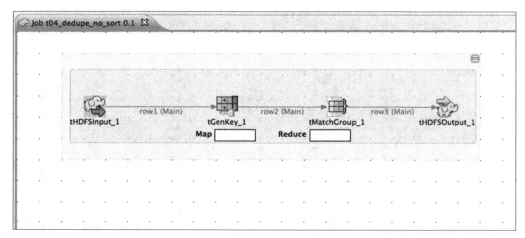

Figure 7.27: Talend MDM generates a data de-duplication job that executes natively in Hadoop.

Figure 7.28 shows a stub of the MapReduce code that is generated to support data de-duplication in Hadoop.

```
Job t04_dedupe_no_sort 0.1 🖾
2540
2541                    job.setInputFormat(row1StructInputFormat.class);
2542
2543                    /**
2544                     * [tHDFSInput_1 mrconfig ] stop
2545                     */
2546                    /**
2547                     * [tGenKey_1 mrconfig ] start
2548                     */
2549
2550                    ChainMapper.addMapper(job, tGenKey_1Mapper.class,
2551                            NullWritable.class, row1Struct.class,
2552                            NullWritable.class, row2Struct.class, true,
2553                            new JobConf(false));
2554                    /**
2555                     * [tGenKey_1 mrconfig ] stop
2556                     */
2557                    /**
2558                     * [tMatchGroup_1 mrconfig ] start
2559                     */
2560
2561                    ChainMapper.addMapper(job, tMatchGroup_1Mapper.class,
2562                            NullWritable.class, row2Struct.class,
2563                            mOutKey_tMatchGroup_1Struct.class,
2564                            row2Struct.class, true, new JobConf(false));
2565
2566                    ChainReducer.setReducer(job, tMatchGroup_1Reducer.class,
2567                            mOutKey_tMatchGroup_1Struct.class,
2568                            row2Struct.class, NullWritable.class,
2569                            row3Struct.class, true, new JobConf(false));
2570                    /**
2571                     * [tMatchGroup_1 mrconfig ] stop
2572                     */
```

Figure 7.28: Talend MDM automatically generates MapReduce code to support data de-duplication.

Summary

In this chapter, we discussed how MDM hubs can support data stewardship and governance. From a master data policy and rules perspective, we reviewed support for business terms, relationships, enrichment, validation, matching, and consolidation. From an operational master data perspective, we reviewed task management, stewardship consoles, duplicates, hierarchy, data quality management, workflows, snapshots, change history, social media, and Hadoop integration.

CHAPTER 8

REFERENCE DATA MANAGEMENT

R eference data is relatively static and may be placed in lookup tables for reference by other applications. Reference data is sometimes referred to as code tables, code lists, code sets, and lists of values. The following are good examples of reference data:

- Country codes
- State and province codes
- Zip or postal codes
- Currency codes
- Industry codes such as the North American Industry Classification System (NAICS)
- Country dialing codes
- Current Procedural Terminology (CPT) codes in healthcare
- Race and ethnicity codes
- Organizational unit codes
- Value Added Tax (VAT) codes

Let's consider a simple example that distinguishes master data from reference data. Table 8.1 is a small table with master data on customers. Mr. John Smith is a male, Ms. Jane Doe is a female, Dr. Jim Donahue is a male, and Ms. Susan McMahon is a female.

Table 8.1: Master Data for Customers			
Salutation	First Name	Last Name	Gender
Mr.	John	Smith	Male
Ms.	Jane	Doe	Female
Dr.	Jim	Donahoe	Male
Ms.	Susan	McMahon	Female

Table 8.2 includes the reference data values for salutation, which are Mr., Ms., and Dr..

Table 8.2: Reference Data for Salutation
Salutation
Mr.
Ms.
Dr.

Finally, Table 8.3 includes the reference data values for gender, which are Male and Female.

Table 8.3: Reference Data for Gender
Gender
Male
Female

Reference data management tools support the automation of key data governance processes.

Build an Inventory of Code Tables

Data governance teams should use tools to build an inventory of code tables. Figure 8.1 shows a catalog of code tables including Office Codes, Regions, and Sales Territories in Data Advantage Group MetaCenter.

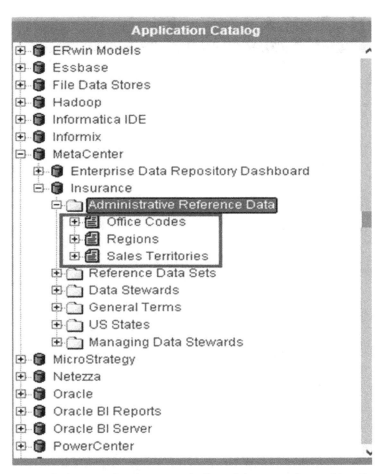

Figure 8.1: Reference data inventory in Data Advantage Group MetaCenter.

Agree on the Master List of Values for Each Code Table

The next step is to create a master list of values for each code table. In Figure 8.2, Collibra Data Governance Center contains a master list of values for U.S. states based on the ISO 3166-2:US standard.

■	Name	Code
☐	Alabama	AL ✕
☐	Alaska	AK ✕
☐	American Samoa	AS ✕
☐	Arizona	AZ ✕
☐	Arkansas	AR ✕
☐	California	CA ✕
☐	Colorado	CO ✕
☐	Connecticut	CT ✕
☐	Delaware	DE ✕
☐	District of Columbia	DC ✕
☐	Florida	FL ✕
☐	Georgia	GA ✕
☐	Guam	GU ✕
☐	Hawaii	HI ✕
☐	Idaho	ID ✕

Figure 8.2: A master list of code values for U.S. states based on the ISO 3166-2:US standard.

Build Simple Mappings Between Master Values and Related Code Tables

The reference data hub should maintain simple mappings between master values and related code tables. As shown in Table 8.4, the ISO 3166-1 alpha-2 country codes are inconsistent with the Bank of England Two Letter codes for United States territories. For example, Puerto Rico is listed as "PR" in the first code list, but "US" in the second. As a result, a bank needs to use different codes when submitting regulatory reports to the United States Federal Reserve and to the Bank of England.

Table 8.4: Inconsistencies Between ISO 3166-1 Alpha-2 and Bank of England Two Letter Codes		
Country	ISO 3166-1 alpha-2	Bank of England Two Letter Code
50 states and District of Columbia	US	US
American Samoa	AS	US
Guam	GU	US
Midway Islands	UM	US
Puerto Rico	PR	US
Wake Islands	UM	US
Northern Mariana Islands	MP	US

Figure 8.3 shows a simple mapping between the two code tables for Puerto Rico in Collibra Data Governance Center.

Code						
Name	Description	Effective Date	Domain			
PR			Country Codes			
US			Bank of England Country Codes			

Figure 8.3: A mapping of Puerto Rico country codes in Collibra Data Governance Center.

Build Complex Mappings Between Code Values

Data governance tools should also support complex mappings between code values. Figure 8.4 shows how individual code values for regions, sales territories, and offices are mapped within Data Advantage Group MetaCenter. The Illinois sales territory contains two offices with the codes 033 and 034. We created a custom relationship called "Contains" to manage this association. Similarly, the Illinois sales territory is part of the Central region. Once again, we created a custom relation called "Is Part Of" to associate the Sales Territories and Regions code tables. As a result, the sales territory Illinois contains office codes 033 and 034 and is part of the Central region.

Figure 8.4: A mapping of the Illinois sales territory to office codes and to the Central region in Data Advantage Group MetaCenter.

Figure 8.5 shows another example of a complex mapping between code tables in Data Advantage Group MetaCenter. Certain U.S. states permit insurance companies to offer uninsured motorist coverage. The first code table includes "Y" or "N" as allowable values for uninsured motorist coverage. The second code table contains a list of U.S. states. MetaCenter allows the mapping of the uninsured motorist coverage indicator with a subset of states using the "Applies to" relationship. In other words, insurance companies can only offer uninsured motorist coverage in certain states.

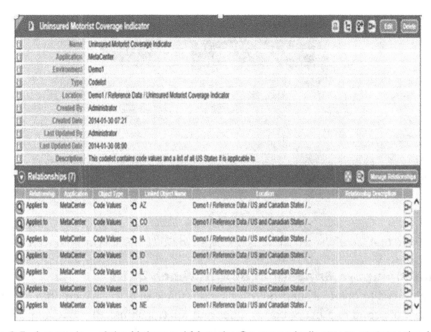

Figure 8.5: A mapping of the Uninsured Motorist Coverage indicator to state codes in Data Advantage Group MetaCenter.

Manage Hierarchies of Code Values

The reference data hub should also support the creation of hierarchies of code values. In Figure 8.6, Collibra contains a code value called "Vehicle" that groups three other code values: 2 Wheeler, 3 Wheeler, and 4 Wheeler. Each of these code values groups other code values. For example, 2 Wheeler groups Cycle and Motorcycle.

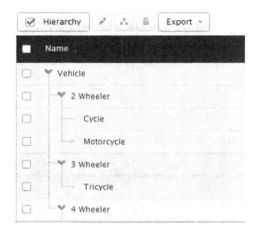

Figure 8.6: A hierarchy of vehicle code values in Collibra Data Governance Center.

Build and Compare Snapshots of Reference Data

Users might need to create a snapshot of their reference data at a given point in time. These snapshots contain a list of code values and relationships, allowing administrators to go back in time to see how the data might have looked then. Snapshots also allow administrators to roll back any changes. The reference data hub should also allow users to compare versions of snapshots of reference data. In Figure 8.7, the user is working with reference data relating to the 2012 version of the North American Industry Classification System (NAICS) codes. The user has created two snapshots on July 29, 2013 and July 30, 2013 in Collibra Data Governance Center. The user has the ability to filter on items that have been added, changed, removed, or other.

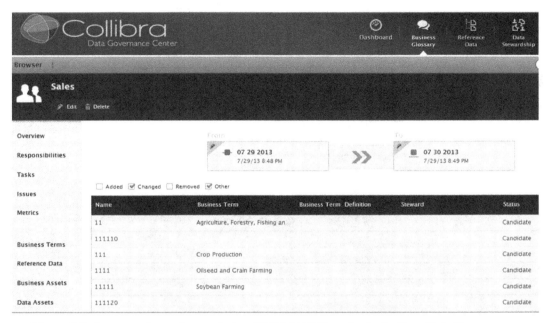

Figure 8.7: A comparison of snapshots of 2012 NAICS codes in Collibra Data Governance Center.

Visualize Inter-Temporal Crosswalks Between Reference Data Snapshots

The reference data hub should also support the visualization of inter-temporal crosswalks between reference data snapshots. In other words, because reference data sets are subject to revision over time, the reference data hub needs to map changes to reference data sets for comparison purposes.

In Figure 8.8, Orchestra Networks EBX compares the snapshots of NAICS industry codes between 2007 and 2012. EBX highlights that "Industry 22111 – Electric Power Generation" has changed between 2007 and 2012.

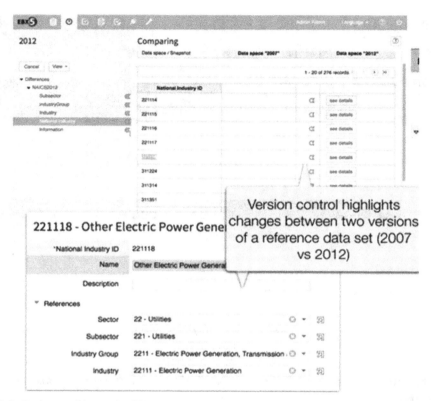

Figure 8.8: Orchestra Networks EBX highlights changes to NAICS data between 2007 and 2012.

In Figure 8.9, we can see that a firm classified in 2007 as NAICS code 221119 is classified in 2012 as 221114, 221115, 221116, 221117, or 221118.

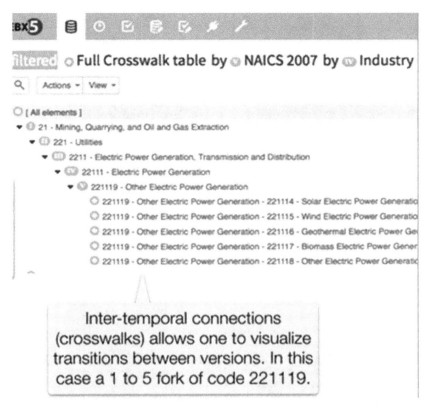

Figure 8.9: Orchestra Networks EBX visualizes changes to NAICS code 221119 between 2007 and 2012.

Summary

In this chapter, we learned that reference data hubs need to support critical functionality such as code table inventories, simple and complex mappings, hierarchy management, snapshots, and inter-temporal crosswalks.

CHAPTER 9

INFORMATION POLICY MANAGEMENT

Many large institutions, especially those in the financial services industry, are subject to intense scrutiny from regulators regarding their data management practices. These institutions need to demonstrate that they have the appropriate practices to improve the trustworthiness of their data. A best practice is for these institutions to use Internal Audit as the "first line of defense" with the regulators. The data governance teams should document information policies and then request Internal Audit to report on the adherence to these policies.

Organizations have their own nomenclature for information policies. One approach is to maintain a hierarchy of information policies, standards, and processes as follows:

- *Information policies*—These provide a broad framework for how decisions will be made regarding data.
- *Information standards*—These provide detailed information on how information policies will be implemented by the organization. Each information policy relates to one or more information standards.
- *Information processes*—These provide detailed information on the procedures to implement information standards. Each information standard relates to one or more information processes.

Figure 9.1 shows a sample information policy hierarchy. At the highest level, the organization has an information policy relating to data ownership. At the next level, the organization has an information standard relating to data roles, such as stewards. At the lowest level, the organization has an information process relating to data stewardship meetings.

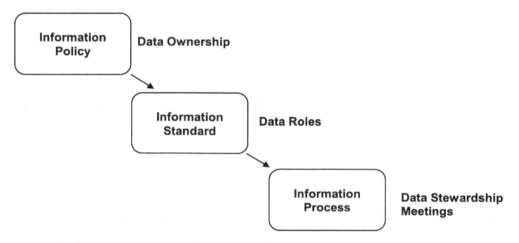

Figure 9.1: A hierarchy of information policies, standards, and processes.

Information policies, standards, and processes need to be reviewed and approved by the data governance council. There are several approaches to manage these artifacts:

1. *Artifacts are stored on file shares.*
   Information policies, standards, and processes may be documented in Microsoft Word or PDF format and stored in Microsoft SharePoint. This is the most cost-effective approach, but there is limited governance over these artifacts.
2. *Artifacts are stored in GRC tools.*
   Information policies, standards, and processes may be maintained within Governance, Risk, and Compliance (GRC) tools, such as EMC RSA Archer GRC or IBM OpenPages GRC. The challenge is that GRC tools do not provide the granularity required for information artifacts.
3. *Artifacts are stored natively in the business glossary.*
   Several business glossary vendors have added support for information policies. These business glossaries allow users to link the policies, standards, and processes with the underlying data artifacts.

4. *Artifacts are stored externally but hyperlinked from the business glossary.*
    Some organizations choose to manage their data artifacts in Microsoft
    SharePoint or other custom tools. However, they add a hyperlink from the business
    glossary to the location of these artifacts.

This chapter will focus on the third option.

Manage Information Policies, Standards, and Processes Within the Business Glossary

Business glossaries should allow users to govern information policies, standards, and
processes. For example, Figure 9.2 shows the "Metadata" policy in IBM InfoSphere
Business Glossary. This policy is associated with a number of standards, such as
"Audit Trail" and "Business Glossary." Each standard provides additional detail on
the overall policy.

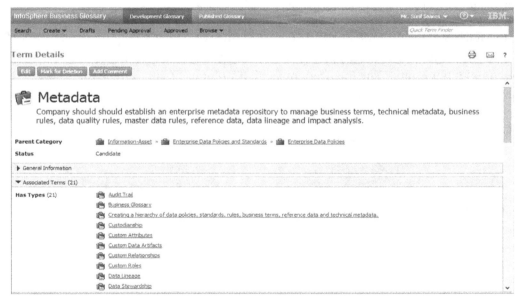

Figure 9.2: The Metadata policy has a number of standards in IBM InfoSphere Business Glossary.

Manage Business Rules

Data governance tools should also manage business rules, especially for critical data
elements. In Figure 9.3, the Data Validation Advisor in SAP Information Steward
contains the following business rules:

- There are specific allowed values for AddressType.
- The U.S. postal code must be nine digits.
- Customer address information must be entered. (It cannot be null or blank.)
- The Customer_PostalCode must be valid.
- The state or province abbreviation pattern must be checked.

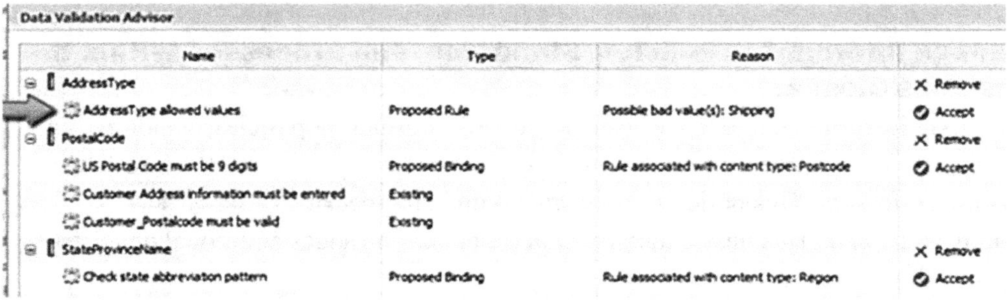

Figure 9.3: SAP Information Steward's Data Validation Advisor contains a list of business rules.

In Figure 9.4, we drill into the Rule Editor for the rule about U.S. postal codes in SAP Information Steward. The rule states that the U.S. postal code must be nine digits and in the 99999-9999 format. The financial impact is $50 for each failure. The rule is bound to the US_Postal_Code field, which is of the VARCHAR data type.

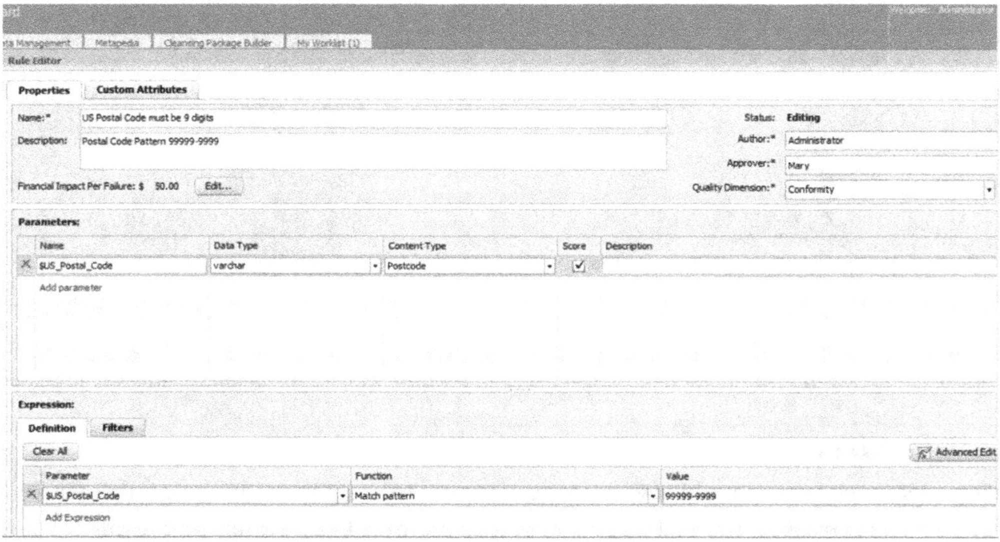

Figure 9.4: The Rule Editor in SAP Information Steward for the U.S. postal code rule.

Leverage Data Governance Tools to Monitor and Report on Compliance

Data governance tools should also allow teams to monitor and report on compliance with information policies. For example, a key information policy relates to data ownership of applications, data repositories, schemas, code tables, business terms, categories, and other data artifacts. Data governance tools should support the formalization of this data ownership.

Figure 9.5 shows an example of a data ownership matrix in Data Advantage Group MetaCenter. The organization has established a policy that every data repository needs to have a Data Executive, Managing Data Steward, and Data Steward. The administrator has created these custom roles in MetaCenter. The administrator has also imported a list of data repositories into MetaCenter and has produced a view showing the roles for each system. This makes it easy for Internal Audit to monitor the adherence to the overall data ownership policy.

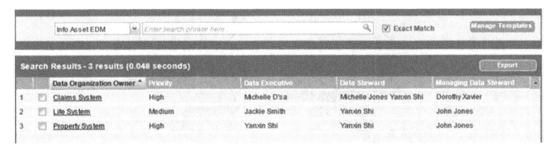

Figure 9.5: Data ownership of enterprise applications in Data Advantage Group MetaCenter.

Manage Data Issues

Data governance tools should provide capabilities to document, assign, reassign, track, close out, and report on data issues. Data governance tools should also support OOTB and custom workflows to deal with data issues. Several data governance tools have built-in issue resolution capabilities. In addition, some organizations have repurposed general-purpose issue management tools like BMC Remedy, HP Quality Center, and JIRA to handle data issues.

Let's walk through a detailed issue management workflow using Collibra Data Governance Center. In Figure 9.6, an auto insurer has two applications. Application A has a field called AGE, and Application B has a field called Youthful_Driver. The data governance team uses IBM InfoSphere Discovery to infer a hidden business rule that the

AGE field in Application A, which shows the age of drivers in an insurance application, is related by the CASE statement to the Youthful_Driver field in Application B.

The business rule is that a driver is flagged as Youthful_Driver if his or her age is less than or equal to 25. However, not all rows of data follow this business rule. In the example, an 83-year-old driver has a "Y" in the Youthful_Driver field. This row of data is automatically flagged as not following the discovered rule. Someone identifies this data issue, and the entire data issue resolution process kicks off.

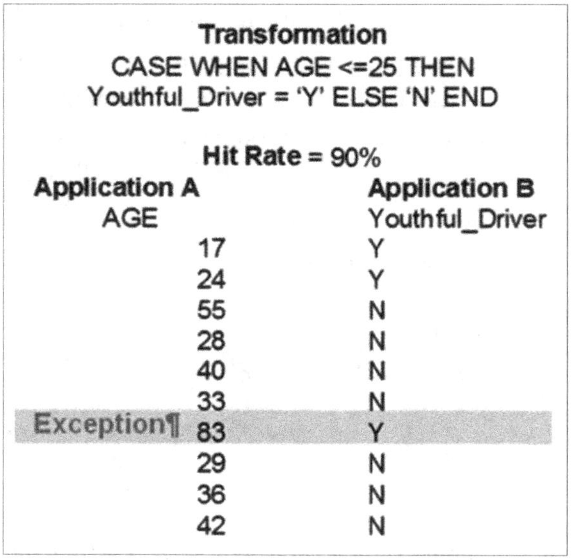

Figure 9.6: IBM InfoSphere Discovery discovers anomalies in customer data at an insurance carrier. (Image courtesy of IBM.)

John Smith is the user who discovered the data issue. As shown in Figure 9.7, John Smith clicks the **Log Issue** button on the home page of Collibra Data Governance Center.

Figure 9.7: John Smith clicks "Log Issue" in Collibra Data Governance Center.

As shown in Figure 9.8, John Smith now populates the Log Issue form in Collibra Data Governance Center. He types "Non-Youthful Drivers" in the title box. In the description box, he types, "An 83 year old is listed as a Youthful Driver in Application A." In the Priority box, he selects "Normal." In the Responsible Community box, he types "Underwriting Dept." In the Relevant Data Assets box, he types "date of birth." In the Issue Classification box, he selects "Accuracy Issue." This information allows Collibra to create and log the issue within the system.

Figure 9.8: John Smith fills out an issue form in Collibra Data Governance Center.

In Figure 9.9, the administrator can now view the Non-Youthful Drivers data issue that was requested by John Smith.

Figure 9.9: The administrator views the list of open issues in Collibra Data Governance Center.

The administrator then needs to accept, reject, or reassign the data issue. As shown in Figure 9.10, the administrator formally accepts the issue and assigns it to Jane Smith in Collibra Data Governance Center.

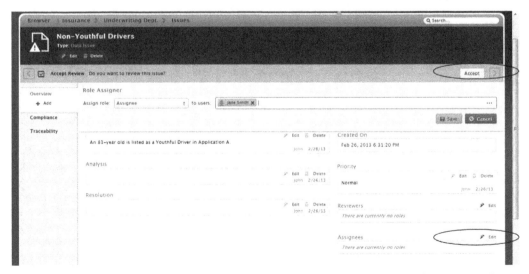

Figure 9.10: The administrator accepts and assigns the issue in Collibra Data Governance Center.

As shown in Figure 9.11, Jane Smith can view her list of data issues, along with the Assignee, Requester, and Reviewer roles.

Figure 9.11: Jane Smith views her list of open issues in Collibra Data Governance Center.

As shown in Figure 9.12, Jane Smith clicks the Non-Youthful Drivers data issue. She then types in her analysis: "The Youthful_Driver flag is incorrectly set to 'Y' in Application B." She also enters her resolution: "I changed the Youthful_Driver flag to 'N' in Application B."

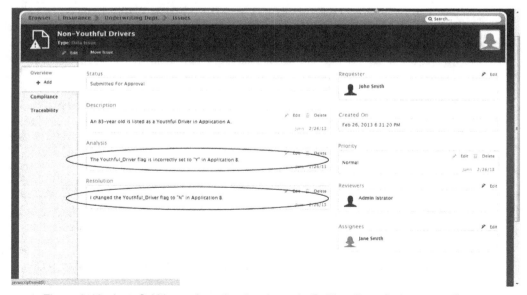

Figure 9.12: Jane Smith resolves the data issue in Collibra Data Governance Center.

As shown in Figure 9.13, the administrator clicks the **Approve/Reject** button to approve the resolution of the issue in Collibra Data Governance Center.

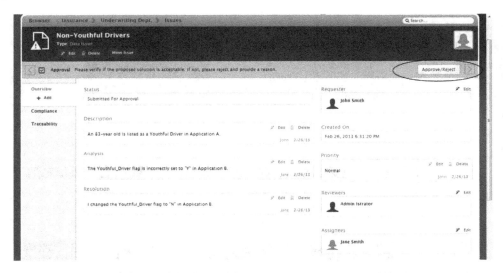

Figure 9.13: An administrator approves the resolution of the data issue in Collibra Data Governance Center.

As shown in Figure 9.14, the administrator also enters the rationale for the decision to mark the issue as resolved.

Figure 9.14: An administrator documents the rationale for approving the resolution of the data issue in Collibra Data Governance Center.

As shown in Figure 9.15, the administrator then navigates to the list of data issues, and confirms that the status of the Non-Youthful Driver data issue has been set to "resolved."

Figure 9.15: An administrator views the status of the resolved issue in Collibra Data Governance Center.

As shown in Figure 9.16, Collibra auto-generates an email to notify stakeholders that the workflow has completed, and the Non-Youthful Drivers data issue has been resolved. Each step in the workflow can be supported with an auto-generated email.

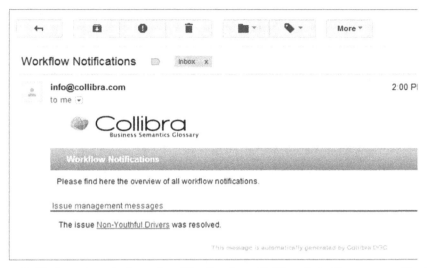

Figure 9.16: An automated email notification from Collibra Data Governance Center.

Summary

In this chapter, we learned that data governance tools can support information policies, standards, processes, and rules. The business glossary should also support the monitoring and enforcement of information policies. Finally, we reviewed a structured process to manage data issues.

PART THREE

THE INTEGRATION BETWEEN ENTERPRISE DATA MANAGEMENT AND DATA GOVERNANCE TOOLS

CHAPTER **10**

DATA MODELING

Data modeling is a critical exercise to develop an understanding of an organization's data artifacts. A data model is a wayfinding tool for both business and IT professionals, which uses a set of symbols and text to precisely explain a subset of real information to improve communication within the organization and thereby lead to a more flexible and stable application environment.[1]

According to the American National Standards Institute, there are three types of data models:

1. *Conceptual data model*—This type of data model describes the semantics of a domain. It is used to communicate core data concepts, rules, and definitions to a business user as part of an overall application development or enterprise initiative. The number of objects should be very small and focused on key concepts.[2]

2. *Logical data model*—This type of data model shows a detailed representation of some or all of an organization's data, independent of any particular data management technology, and described in business language.[3]

---

1   Hoberman, Steve. *Data Modeling Made Simple 2nd Edition.* Technics Publications LLC, 2009.

2   Hoberman, Steve, Donna Burbank, and Chris Bradley. *Data Modeling for the Business.* Technics Publications LLC, 2009.

3   http://en.wikipedia.org/wiki/Logical_data_model.

3. *Physical data model*—This type of data model is a representation of a data design that takes into account the facilities and constraints of a given database management system.[4]

Data models start at a high level of abstraction with conceptual models, and become more granular with logical and physical models. Data modeling and data governance tools have a strong affinity, which we will discuss in this chapter.

Integrate the Logical and Physical Data Models with the Metadata Repository

In chapter 2, we discuss the importance of ingesting logical and physical data models into the metadata repository. That topic is reiterated in this section. In Figure 10.1, SAP PowerDesigner contains a business glossary in the far left panel, and a logical data model for Customer in the bottom left panel. The business glossary and the logical data model are interrelated. For example, the business glossary contains the definition for the term "Customer" that is the subject of the logical data model.

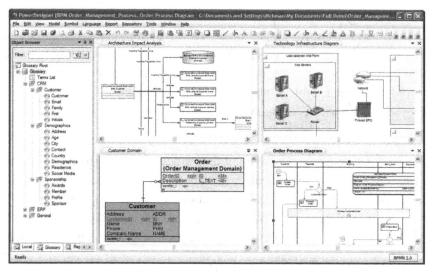

Figure 10.1: SAP PowerDesigner contains a business glossary (far left panel) and logical model (bottom left panel).

---

4   http://en.wikipedia.org/wiki/Physical_data_model.

Expose Ontologies in the Metadata Repository

In computer science and information science, an *ontology* formally represents knowledge as a hierarchy of concepts within a domain, using a shared vocabulary to denote the types, properties, and interrelationships of those concepts. Ontologies are used in library science, systems engineering, biomedical science, and data architecture as a form of knowledge representation about the world or some part of it. Figure 10.2 shows the Global IDs scanner for the Financial Industry Business Ontology (FIBO), which includes business terms and definitions for the financial industry.

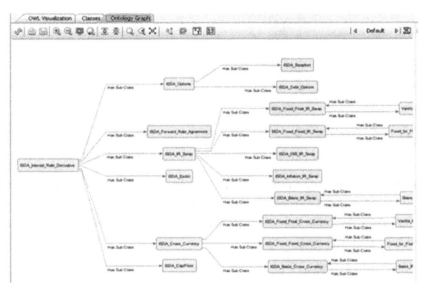

Figure 10.2: The Financial Industry Business Ontology (FIBO) scanner from Global IDs.

Prototype a Unified Schema Across Data Domains Using Data Discovery Tools

Data discovery tools can also prototype a unified schema across data domains. Unified schema prototyping is an important step to prepare for data consolidation and migration projects. It is important to prototype what the data will look like before actually moving it. In Figure 10.3, we pick up from the discussion about overlapping columns in chapter 5. IBM InfoSphere Discovery discovers overlapping columns across the Community, Region, and CRM data sources.

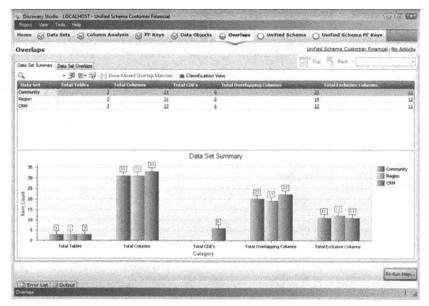

Figure 10.3: IBM InfoSphere Discovery discovers overlapping columns.

The first step is to define a unified schema across the source data sets. Figure 10.4 shows a unified schema for Customer across the three data sets. The unified schema includes a number of columns, including FIRST_NAME, MIDDLE_NAME, LAST_NAME, PHONE, and TAX_ID.

App...	#	Column Name	Classification	Data Type	Length	Precision	Scale	Note
		1 FIRST_NAME		Varchar	12	0	0	
		2 MIDDLE_NAME		Varchar	11	0	0	
		3 LAST_NAME		Varchar	12	0	0	
		4 PHONE		Varchar	15	0	0	
		5 TAX_ID		Varchar	12	0	0	
		6 GENDER		Varchar	2	0	0	
		7 BIRTH_DATE		DateTime	25	0	0	
		8 ADDRESS_LINE_1		Varchar	32	0	0	
		9 CITY		Varchar	21	0	0	
		10 STATE		Varchar	3	0	0	
		11 POSTAL_CODE		Decimal	0	31	0	
		12 COUNTRY		Varchar	14	0	0	

Figure 10.4: Defining a unified schema for Customer in IBM InfoSphere Discovery.

The next step is to map the sources to the target, as shown in Figure 10.5. For example, COMMUNITY_BRCH.F_NAME is the source and Customer.FIRST_NAME is the target.

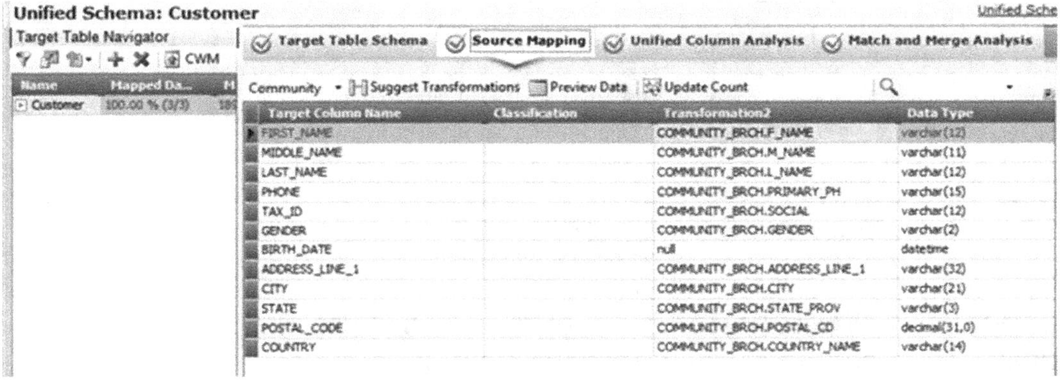

Figure 10.5: Mapping sources to target column names in IBM InfoSphere Discovery.

Figure 10.6 shows a column analysis of the unified schema for Customer in IBM InfoSphere Discovery.

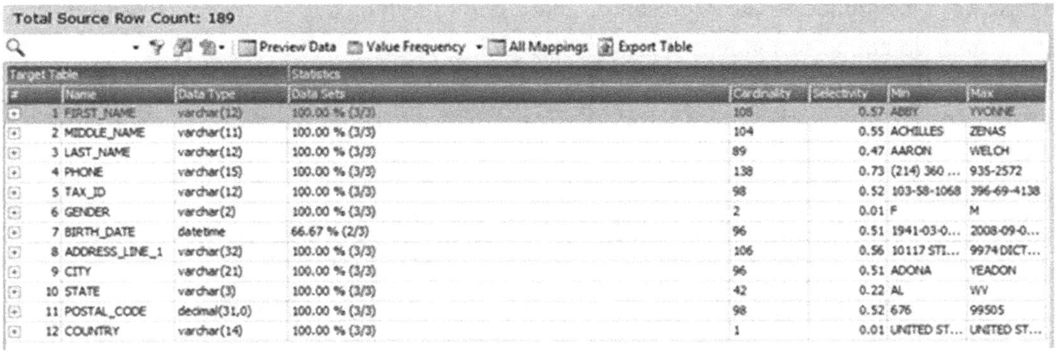

Figure 10.6: Column analysis of the unified schema for Customer in IBM InfoSphere Discovery.

Finally, Figure 10.7 shows a match and merge analysis for Customer.ADDRESS_LINE_1 for the merged entity against the COMMUNITY, CRM, and REGION data sources. At the bottom of the screen, we can view the details for Libby Hopkins in the merged entity, as well as in the three data sources.

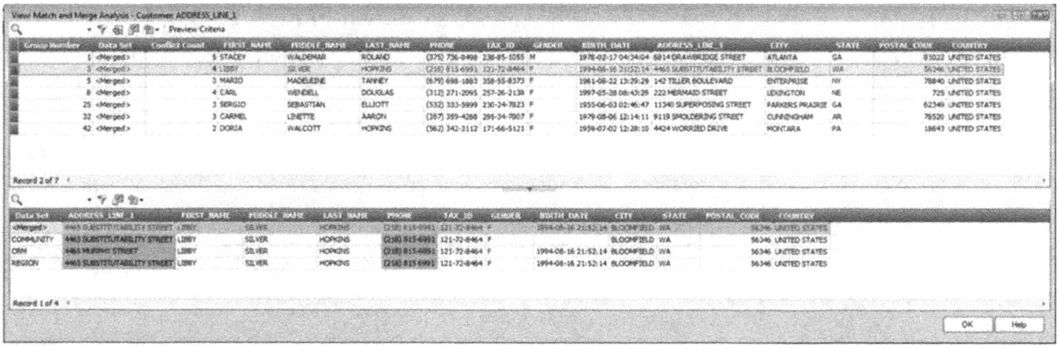

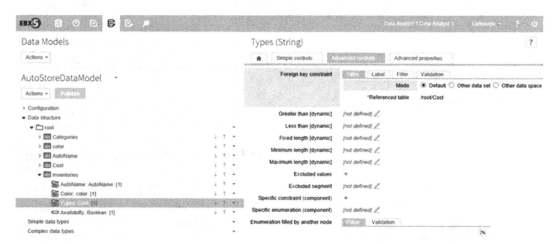

Figure 10.7: Match-and-merge analysis for the merged entity against the data sources in IBM InfoSphere Discovery.

Establish a Data Model to Support Master Data Management

Best-in-class master data management (MDM) hubs are model-driven to support rapid development and time to value. In Figure 10.8, a simple data model has been set up in Orchestra Networks EBX. The data model supports the MDM implementation of a store that sells automobiles. The data model includes tables for Categories, Color, AutoName, Cost, and Inventories. The table contains three foreign keys: AutoName, Color, and Types. These keys are linked to the AutoName, Color, and Cost tables respectively. In addition, a Boolean field called Availability has also been defined.

Figure 10.8: AutoStoreDataModel in Orchestra Networks EBX.

As shown in Figure 10.9, Orchestra Networks EBX automatically generates the data authoring user interface from the data model. In this instance, EBX generates the data authoring user interface so that Human Resources can on-board a new employee.

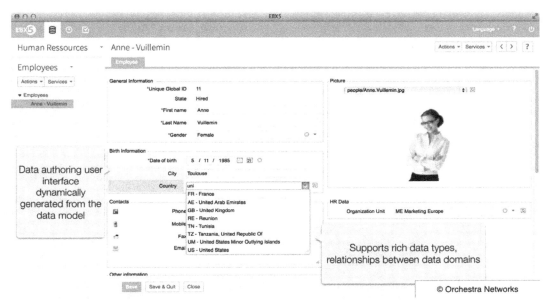

Figure 10.9: Orchestra Networks EBX automatically generates the data authoring user interface from the data model.

Summary

In this chapter, we learned that data modeling tools have a crucial role with respect to data governance. Metadata repositories need to integrate logical and physical data models as well as ontologies. Data discovery tools can also support the creation of a unified schema for data consolidation and migration. Finally, data modeling is critical to MDM.

11

DATA INTEGRATION

D ata integration technologies fall into three different categories: bulk data movement, data replication, and data virtualization.

- *Bulk data movement*—Bulk data movement includes technologies such as Extract, Transform, and Load (ETL) to extract data from one or more data sources, transform the data, and load the data into a target database. There are several variations, such as Extract, Load, and Transform (ELT), which extracts data from one or more data sources, loads the data into a target database, and transforms the data in the target database.
- *Data replication*—According to *Information Management Magazine*, data replication is "the process of copying a portion of a database from one environment to another and keeping the subsequent copies of the data in sync with the original source. Changes made to the original source are propagated to the copies of the data in other environments."

  Replication technologies such as Change Data Capture (CDC) allow the capture of only change data and the transfer of that data from publisher to subscriber systems. Rather than performing queries directly against the database, CDC tools improve system performance by capturing inserts, updates, and deletes directly from the database transaction (redo) logs. As a result, CDC technology can capture big data such as utility smart-meter readings in near real-time, with minimal impact to system performance. Replication tools include IBM InfoSphere Data Replication, Oracle GoldenGate, Informatica Fast Clone, and Informatica Data Replication.

- *Data Virtualization*—Data virtualization is also known as *data federation*. According to *Information Management* magazine, data federation is "a method of linking data from two or more physically different locations and making the access/linkage appear transparent, as if the data were co-located. This approach is in contrast to the data warehouse method of housing data in one place and accessing data from that single location."

  Data virtualization allows an application to issue SQL queries against a virtual view of data in heterogeneous sources such as in relational databases, XML documents, and on the mainframe. Offerings include IBM InfoSphere Federation Server, Informatica Data Services, and Denodo.

Data integration tools have a few key points of integration with data governance. We discuss each of these in detail in this chapter.

Deploy Data Quality Jobs in an Integrated Manner with Data Integration

Several tools, including IBM InfoSphere, Informatica PowerCenter, and Talend Data Integration, have integrated their data integration and data quality offerings into a single environment for ease-of-use and ease-of-development. In Figure 11.1, Talend provides a unified process to load customer master data with de-duplication, survivorship rules, address standardization, and data enrichment with geographical information.

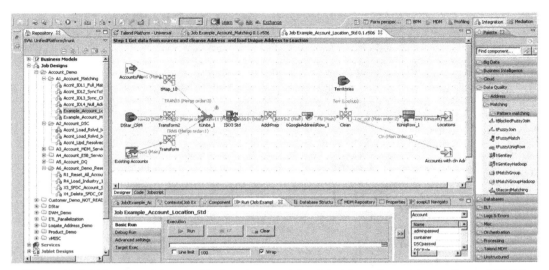

Figure 11.1: Talend provides a unified environment for data integration, data quality, and MDM.

Figure 11.2 shows an IBM InfoSphere DataStage job with the Rule Stage. The developer can create data rules in IBM InfoSphere Information Analyzer and access those rules within the IBM InfoSphere DataStage and QualityStage Designer. The developer can see how many rows have been analyzed and how many of the rows are valid and invalid. The developer can then choose to process the invalid records differently than the valid records for reporting or automated remediation. Publishing a data rule to the shared repository from IBM InfoSphere DataStage or from IBM InfoSphere Information Analyzer makes the rule available for use across jobs or modules. For example, the developer might execute the IBM Information Analyzer rule first in the data warehouse. If bad data causes disruptions of the business, the same rule can be embedded in a DataStage job to ensure that only clean data gets loaded into the data warehouse.

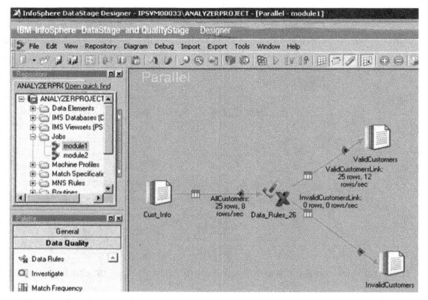

Figure 11.2: IBM InfoSphere DataStage job with the Rule Stage from IBM InfoSphere Information Analyzer.[1]

Move Data Between the MDM or Reference Data Hub and the Source Systems

Data integration tools are critical to extract data from an MDM or reference data hub and load it into downstream systems. Conversely, data integration tools should also extract data from one or more source systems and load it into an MDM or reference data hub. For example, IBM InfoSphere DataStage includes pre-built jobs to support data extraction from IBM InfoSphere Master Data Management.

Figure 11.3 shows the IBM InfoSphere DataStage and QualityStage Designer client. The user interface includes stages to retrieve data from IBM InfoSphere Master Data Management. In Figure 11.3, the DB2_Retrieve_Entrecno stage retrieves records from the DB2 MDM tables based on the enterprise ID (Entrecno). The Memget_multiple_OutFiles stage then creates multiple output files, including Name_SSN, All-Segments, and Address_Birthdt.

---

1   From the IBM Redbook *Metadata Management with IBM InfoSphere Information Server*, October 2011, Jackie Zhu et al.

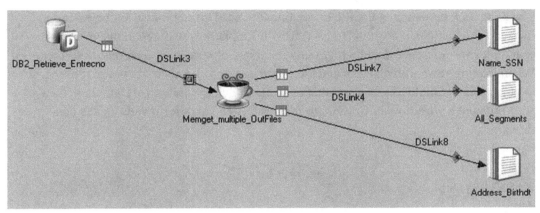

Figure 11.3: IBM InfoSphere DataStage and QualityStage Designer client includes stages to retrieve data from IBM InfoSphere Master Data Management.

Leverage Reference Data for Use by the Data Integration Tool

The data integration tool should re-use data that is governed within the reference data hub. Figure 11.4 shows a snippet of the reference data pertaining to country codes.

Name	Description
AD	ANDORRA
AE	UNITED ARAB...
AF	AFGHANISTAN
AG	ANTIGUA AN...
AI	ANGUILLA
AL	ALBANIA
AM	ARMENIA
AO	ANGOLA
AQ	ANTARCTICA
AR	ARGENTINA
AS	AMERICAN S...
AT	AUSTRIA
AU	AUSTRALIA
AW	ARUBA
AX	ALAND ISLAN...
AZ	AZERBAIJAN
BA	BOSNIA AND...
BB	BARBADOS
BD	BANGLADESH
BE	BELGIUM
BF	BURKINA FASO

Figure 11.4: A snippet of reference data for country codes.

These country codes can then be used as part of data integration jobs. For example, Figure 11.5 shows a mapping in Informatica PowerCenter where CountryCodesLookup is used to look up data in a flat file or relational table. This approach can be extended further. For example, a health plan used IBM InfoSphere DataStage to discover new candidates for reference data that was governed in Collibra Data Governance Center. When loading rows, if the DataStage job found a code value that was not part of the lookup table, it would "soft insert" that row into the data warehouse. DataStage then auto-initiated a workflow in Collibra to route the code value for review by the data steward.

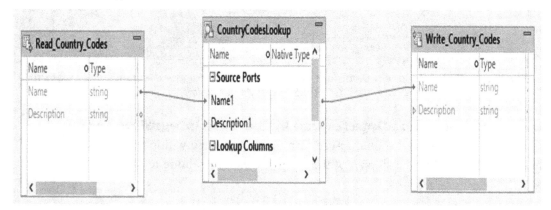

Figure 11.5: Informatica PowerCenter mapping includes a lookup for country codes.

Integrate Data Integration Tools into the Metadata Repository

Metadata repositories need to include scanners for data integration tools to support end-to-end data lineage and impact analysis. This topic is covered in detail in chapter 4, on metadata management.

Automate the Production of Data Integration Jobs by Leveraging the Metadata Repository

Data analysts spend a lot of time building mapping specifications in Excel. These mapping specifications show the source columns, the target columns, and the transformations. Data integration tools can automate this process by leveraging content from the metadata repository. Figure 11.6 shows IBM InfoSphere FastTrack. At the bottom of the screen, we can see the source columns on the left and the target columns on the right. The data analyst selects these columns from a list of candidates that are automatically populated from IBM InfoSphere Metadata Workbench, which is the shared metadata repository that underlies IBM InfoSphere Information Server. Data analysts can also re-use business terms from IBM InfoSphere Business Glossary. This process eliminates the need to manually re-type column and table names and reduces the potential for errors.

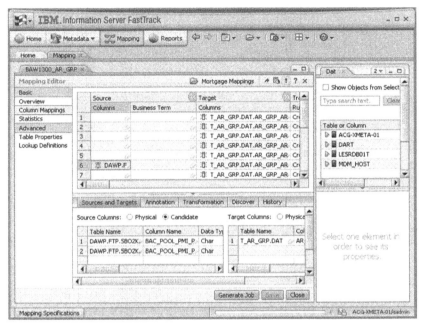

Figure 11.6: IBM InfoSphere FastTrack.

Summary

In this chapter, we discussed the alignment between data integration and data governance tools. We learned that data quality and data integration jobs can be integrated. We also reviewed how reference data and master data can move around using data integration tools. We learned the importance of reference data to provide lookups for data integration tools. Further, we learned that metadata hubs need to integrate with data integration tools, Finally, we covered the automated creation of data integration jobs based on metadata.

CHAPTER **12**

ANALYTICS AND REPORTING

At the end of the day, organizations need to analyze their data to make business decisions. A number of open-source and proprietary tools can support data analytics and reporting. These tools include SAS Business Intelligence, SAS Analytics, IBM Cognos, IBM SPSS, SAP BusinessObjects, Tableau, QlikView, R, and Pentaho. There are three key points of integration between analytics/reporting and data governance tools:

- Export data profiling results to a reporting tool for further visual analysis.
- Export data artifacts to a reporting tool for visualization of data governance metrics.
- Integrate analytics and reporting tools with the business glossary for semantic context.

This chapter covers each of these integration points.

Export Data Profiling Results to a Reporting Tool for Further Visual Analysis

Several organizations combine the power of their data profiling and reporting tools. In the example in Figure 12.1, the data governance team profiles the data using Trillium

TS Discovery. The team then exports the data into Tableau to produce a data assurance dashboard with eye-catching visualization capabilities.

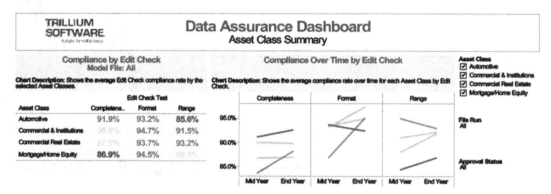

Figure 12.1: Trillium's data assurance dashboard, exposed in Tableau.

Export Data Artifacts to a Reporting Tool for the Visualization of Data Governance Metrics

Data governance teams can also use reporting tools to visualize key data governance metrics. In the example in Figure 12.2, the data administrator exports business glossary terms into a spreadsheet. The administrator then imports those terms into Tableau to visualize the level of progress across the different teams. As we can see, the "HCPCS Glossary" has the most terms, followed by the "NAICS Terms" glossary.

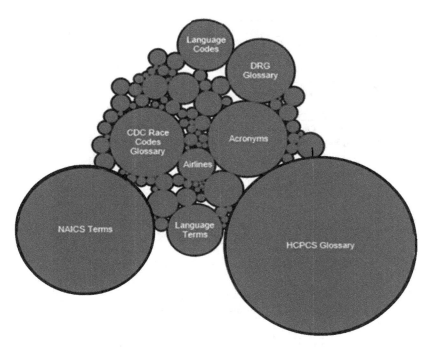

Figure 12.2: Visualizing business glossary categories in Tableau.

Integrate Analytics and Reporting Tools with the Business Glossary for Semantic Context

Many business glossary tools ship with a client widget so that users can access the definitions of key terms directly from the business intelligence environment. For example, a user views a term called "risk" in a reporting tool such as SAP BusinessObjects. The enterprise already has a business glossary within ASG-metaGlossary. The user's desktop contains a small widget called ASG-MyInfoAssist. Depending on the configuration, the user highlights the term in SAP BusinessObjects, presses Shift+F5, and pulls up the definition in ASG-MyInfoAssist, as shown in Figure 12.3.

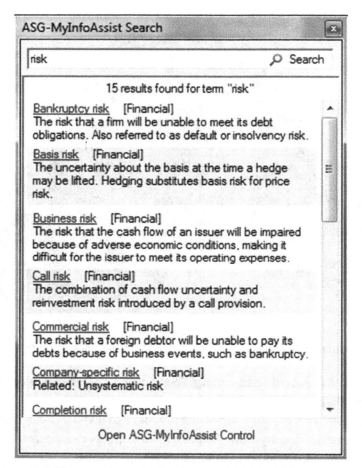

Figure 12.3: The search results for the term "risk" in ASG-MyInfoAssist.

Summary

In this chapter, we learned about the symbiotic nature of analytics/reporting and data governance tools. Data analysts can export data profiling results to a reporting tool for further visual analysis. Data stewards can export data artifacts to a reporting tool for visualization of data governance metrics. Finally, business glossaries can integrate with analytics and reporting tools for semantic context.

CHAPTER **13**

BUSINESS PROCESS MANAGEMENT

Business process management (BPM) is a holistic management approach to aligning an organization's business processes with the wants and needs of clients.[1] Business process management tools include IBM Business Process Manager, Pega Business Process Management, and Talend BPM. In addition, the Eclipse open-source framework includes a plug-in for Business Process Model and Notation (BPMN). There are three key integration points between BPM and data governance tools that we will discuss in this chapter.

Data Governance Workflows Should Leverage BPM Capabilities

Data governance tools should leverage BPM capabilities to enforce data governance workflows. As part of these workflows, specific roles may be involved in changes to data governance artifacts, including business terms, data policies, business rules, and code values. Let's consider a simple example of a multinational corporation that wants to do business in Kosovo. The EDM department has a list of approved country codes in the reference data repository. However, Kosovo is not on the list of ISO 3166-1 alpha-2 country codes. EDM adopts the following workflow to approve a new business term called "Kosovo" with country code "KO":

---

1   http://en.wikipedia.org/wiki/Business_process_management.

1. The European finance steward proposes the change.
2. The Global finance steward approves the change.
3. EDM adds the new entry to the code table for Country.

The code tables are already maintained in Collibra Data Governance Center. As shown in Figure 13.1, EDM uses the OOTB approval workflow in Collibra Data Governance Center. The workflow is based on BPMN and can be customized using the Activiti plug-in to the Eclipse Integrated Development Environment (IDE) for Java. For the sake of simplicity, we map the three swim lanes in the workflow to the key actors in the approval process:

1. Subject matter expert (European finance)
2. Stakeholder (global finance)
3. Steward (EDM)

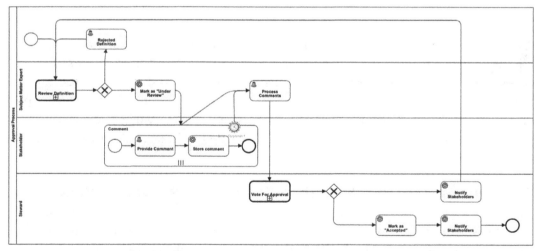

Figure 13.1: The OOTB approval workflow in Collibra Data Governance Center.

As shown in Figure 13.2, "Kosovo" is a business term with the status set to "Candidate." The administrator clicks the Approval button to initiate the workflow in Collibra Data Governance Center.

Figure 13.2: The administrator initiates the Approval workflow in Collibra Data Governance Center.

As shown in Figure 13.3, the subject matter expert clicks the **Approve/Reject** button to approve the business term.

Figure 13.3: The subject matter expert approves the business term in Collibra Data Governance Center.

In Figure 13.4, the stakeholder clicks the **Comment** button in Collibra Data Governance Center. The status is changed to "Under Review."

Figure 13.4: The stakeholder clicks the Comment button in Collibra Data Governance Center.

In Figure 13.5, the subject matter expert processes the comments and clicks **Done** at the top of the screen.

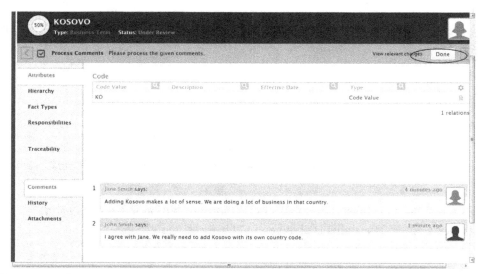

Figure 13.5: The subject matter expert processes the comments in Collibra Data Governance Center.

The next step in the approval process is for the steward to vote for approval. In Figure 13.6, the steward reviews the comments from the subject matter expert and stakeholder at the bottom of the screen. The steward then votes to approve or reject the business term.

Figure 13.6: The steward votes for the business term in Collibra Data Governance Center.

If all the processes are approved, the status of the business term "Kosovo" changes to "Accepted," as shown in Figure 13.7.

Figure 13.7: The status of the business term changes to "Accepted" in Collibra Data Governance Center.

Master Data Workflows Should Leverage BPM Capabilities

MDM projects typically involve a number of repetitive tasks, such as duplicate suspect processing, that should be chained together in a workflow. The MDM hub should have built-in BPM capabilities to automate these repetitive tasks.

In Figure 13.8, the Talend BPM solution enables collaborative stewardship. In this example, the data steward does not have the permissions to change Account Company Name in the MDM hub. The data steward launches an Account Company Name Request form that is routed for approval to the manager and then to the operations manager via BPM. Authorized users then receive the form and can process the request.

Figure 13.9 shows further details on the BPM workflow in Talend.

Figure 13.8: The Talend BPM solution enables collaborative stewardship.

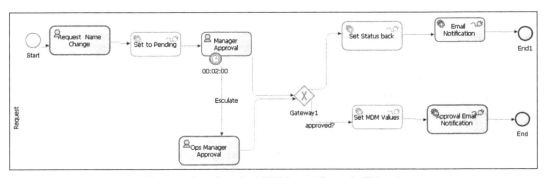

Figure 13.9: Detailed BPM workflows in Talend.

Data Governance Tools Should Map to BPM Tools

BPM tools support business processes, but they also need to be integrated with data governance processes. Put another way, data governance tools should map data policies and standards to key activities and milestones in BPM tools.

Figure 13.10 shows a simple map for the Know Your Customer (KYC) business process at a bank. The business process is reflected in Diaku Axon. The business process consists of seven activities:

1. Initiate KYC
2. Due diligence

3. KYC risk classification
4. Decision
5. Enhanced due diligence (EDD)/monitor
6. Activate customer
7. Escalate

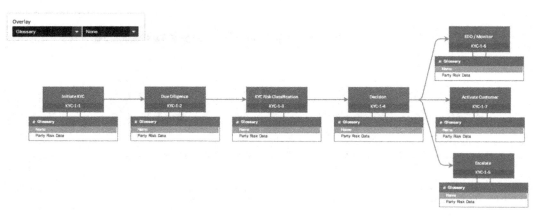

Figure 13.10: The KYC business process for a bank in Diaku Axon.

In Figure 13.11, we can see further details on each activity. For example, the Initiate KYC activity involves sourcing required information according to the type of customer and the products requested. Diaku Axon then maps each activity to the associated business glossary "Party Risk Data." The glossary contains definitions of business terms, as well as data policies and standards associated with the related activity in the KYC business process.

Ref. Number	Process	Description	Parent	Status	Predecessor	Type	
∨ KYC-1-1	Initiate KYC	Sourcing KYC required information according to the type of customer and the products requested.	Know Your Client (KYC) Process	Active		Step	◉
∨ KYC-1-2	Due Diligence	Verification of information for new or existing accounts along with checks against PEP watch lists.	Know Your Client (KYC) Process	Active	KYC-1-1	Step	◉

Figure 13.11: The KYC activities are mapped to a business glossary in Diaku Axon.

Summary

In this chapter, we reviewed the integration points between BPM and data governance tools. Data governance workflows should leverage BPM capabilities. In addition, master data workflows should leverage BPM capabilities. Finally, data governance tools should map data policies and standards to key activities and milestones in BPM tools.

14

DATA SECURITY AND PRIVACY

O rganizations need to safeguard the security and privacy of critical data relating to their customers, employees, financials, and trade secrets. Before proceeding any further, here is some background on key concepts that will be discussed in this chapter:

- *Data masking*—The process of systematically transforming sensitive information into realistic, but fictionalized, values.[1]
- *Data encryption*—The process of rendering sensitive data unreadable so that an attacker cannot gain unauthorized access to it.
- *Data tokenization*—The process of substituting a sensitive data element with a non-sensitive equivalent, referred to as a *token*, that has no extrinsic or exploitable meaning or value. The token is a reference that maps back to the sensitive data through a tokenization system. The mapping from original data to a token uses methods which render tokens infeasible to reverse in the absence of the tokenization system, for example using tokens created from random numbers.[2]
- *Database monitoring*—A form of security technology that monitors the activities of the database but operates independently of the database itself. Database monitoring

1   Soares, Sunil. *The IBM Data Governance Unified Process*. MC Press, 2010.

2   http://en.wikipedia.org/wiki/Tokenization_(data_security).

technologies typically have a limited impact on the performance of the database system because they do not monitor database logs.

A number of integration points exist between these products and data governance tools. These will be discussed in the rest of this chapter.

Determine Privacy Obligations

Privacy and data protection laws vary greatly by industry, state, province, and country. An essential step in compliance is understanding what laws apply to which information sources and categories. The big data governance program requires tools that can catalog privacy laws and associate requirements and procedures to specific data sources and data categories. Tools in this space include IBM Global Retention Policy and Schedule Management.

Discover Sensitive Data Using Data Discovery Tools

Once sensitive data has been defined, data discovery tools should discover hidden sensitive data. For example, Social Security numbers may be hidden in a field called EMP_NUM. Figure 14.1 shows the Column Classifications view in IBM InfoSphere Discovery, which lists available sensitive data discovery patterns. Examples of sensitive data discovery patterns include phone number, email address, Social Security number, and credit card number.

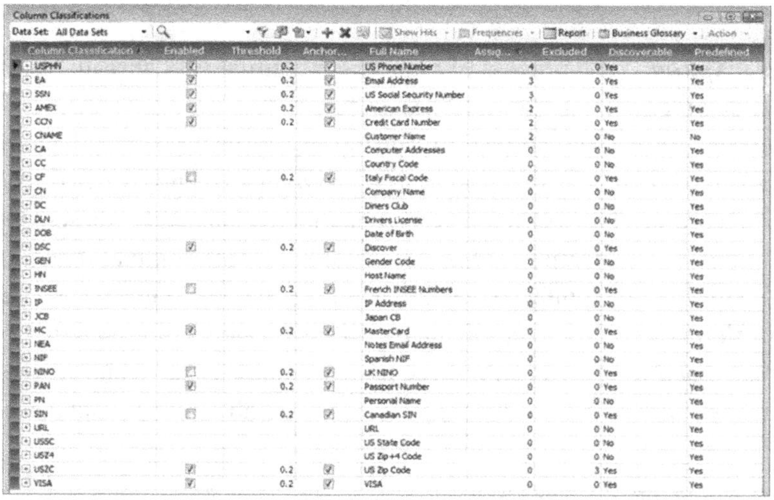

Figure 14.1: Sensitive data classifications in IBM InfoSphere Discovery.

In Figure 14.2, we can drill down into CCN, credit card number, and view the complex pattern that has been set up in the Administration Console of IBM InfoSphere Discovery.

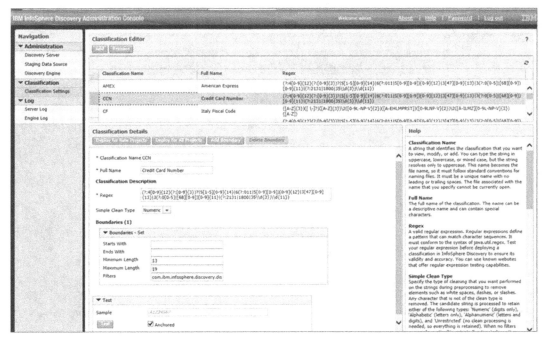

Figure 14.2: The pattern for credit card number in IBM InfoSphere Discovery.

Finally, we can view the Column Analysis view with sensitive data classifications for several columns of the OPTIM_CUSTOMERS table in Figure 14.3. For example, CUSTNAME has been classified as customer name (CNAME), EMAIL_ADDRESS as email address (EA), PHONE_NUMBER as U.S. phone number (USPHN), and NATIONAL_ID as U.S. Social Security number (SSN).

Flag Sensitive Data in the Metadata Repository

Once the data governance team has identified sensitive data, it needs to flag all such instances in the metadata repository. In Figure 14.4, the data steward has flagged the business term "Social Security Number" as sensitive data by setting the custom attribute called "Sensitive Data" to true.

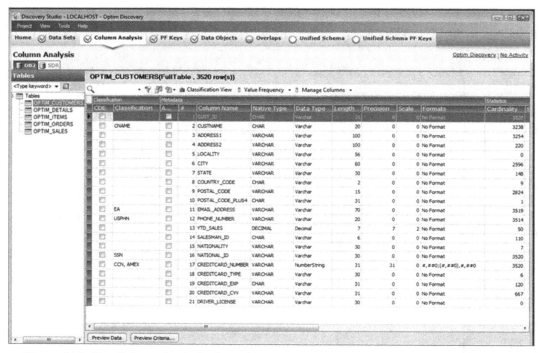

Figure 14.3: The Column Analysis view with sensitive data classifications in IBM InfoSphere Discovery.

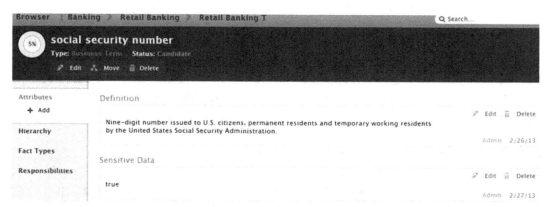

Figure 14.4: Social Security number is flagged as sensitive data in Collibra Data Governance Center.

Mask Sensitive Data in Production Environments

Data masking tools need to mask sensitive data in production environments. This sensitive information includes birth dates, bank account numbers, street addresses, and national identifiers such as U.S. Social Security numbers, Canadian Social Insurance numbers, and Italian Codice Fiscale. In Figure 14.5, Oracle, DB2, MySQL, SAP Sybase, and other databases contain sensitive data such as Social Security numbers. If an outsourced database administrator or unauthorized user issues a SQL command against the database, he or she will only be able to view the last four digits of the Social Security number. This is accomplished by dynamic data masking with IBM InfoSphere Guardium.

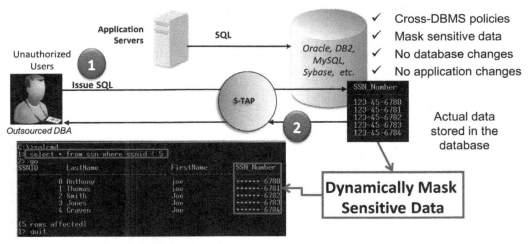

Figure 14.5: IBM InfoSphere Guardium masks Social Security numbers in production databases.

Mask Sensitive Data in Non-Production Environments

Data masking tools also need to mask sensitive data in non-production environments. Tools in this space include IBM InfoSphere Optim Data Masking Solution and Informatica Data Masking solutions. In Figure 14.6, the customer contact database is a non-production application. The contact database contains an Office Phone field with sensitive data.

Figure 14.6: A customer contact database contains office phone numbers that are considered sensitive data.

In Figure 14.7, IBM InfoSphere Optim Data Masking Solution masks the data in the Office Phone field.

Figure 14.7: IBM InfoSphere Optim Data Masking Solution masks office phone numbers.

Monitor Database Access by Privileged Users

Database monitoring tools enforce the separation of duties; all audit data must be stored in a secure, tamper-proof repository, external to monitored databases. The database monitoring functionality has a minimal impact on database performance, so it should not require any changes to databases or applications. Vendors include IBM InfoSphere Guardium Data Activity Monitor and Imperva Database Activity Monitoring.

Document Information Policies Implemented by Data Masking and Database Monitoring Tools

The business glossary needs to contain information policies that are executed by data masking and database monitoring tools. In this section, we will use the governance of utility smart meter data as the underlying example.[3]

Since the inception of electricity deregulation and market-driven pricing, utilities have been looking for ways to match consumption with generation. Traditional electricity and gas meters were only read monthly or quarterly. These meters measured only gross consumption and gave no insight into when the energy was consumed. Several North American utilities either have rolled out, or are in the process of rolling out, smart meters. These smart meters typically capture usage data every 15 to 60 minutes for residential and commercial customers and communicate that information on a daily basis to the utility for billing and analytics.

These smart meters enable utilities to offer differentiated billing to customers, such as lower rates during off-peak hours and higher rates during peak hours. As a result, utilities are able to offer pricing plans that encourage customers to reduce usage during peak hours. Utilities can reduce generation capacity if they are able to appropriately manage customer peak demand, avoiding the need to build expensive power generation capacity that might be used for only a few days in a year. In fact, some utilities believe they can avoid building one or two expensive power plants altogether as a direct result of the smart meter program.

From a data management perspective, utilities have to deal with reams of real-time interval data from smart meters that are brought into their data warehouses. Customers need to access this data from the web to understand how electricity use affects their monthly bills. The utility itself can leverage this data to understand customer usage patterns. The data governance program needs to establish policies around the following:

- *Data archiving*—The data governance program needs to set policies around data archiving to avoid runaway storage costs from the explosion of data from smart meters. For example, one utility decided to maintain meter interval data for a rolling period of 42 months. Any data beyond that period was moved to secondary storage to reduce costs.
- *Data access*—The data governance program needs to set policies around who within the organization is authorized to access what data. In a purely hypothetical

---

3 Adapted from *Selling Information Governance to the Business*, Sunil Soares (MC Press, 2011).

example, would celebrities want their excessive home energy consumption to get into the public domain? The answer is probably no, especially if a celebrity has been a vocal opponent of the harmful impact of carbon emissions. In several instances, utilities are now implementing solutions to monitor access by privileged users to smart meter data.

There have been several newspaper reports of the potential privacy threats posed by smart meters. For example, smart meter data could possibly tell an observer everything subscribers do in the home, down to how often they wash their towels, or even what brand of washer they wash them in.[4] As smart meters become more mainstream, regulators such as the state Public Utility Commissions (PUCs) in the United States will become more assertive about protecting consumers' privacy rights.

Figure 14.8 shows a number of data governance policies related to smart meters in IBM InfoSphere Business Glossary.

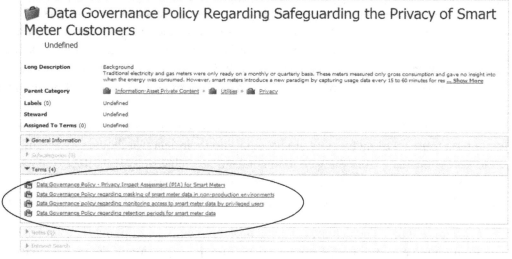

Figure 14.8: Smart meter data governance policies in IBM InfoSphere Business Glossary.

---

4   "Smart Meters Raise Privacy Concerns." *Smart Money Magazine*, June 3, 2010.

First, IBM InfoSphere Business Glossary contains a parent policy called "Safeguarding the Privacy of Smart Meter Customers." This has four child policies:

1. Data governance policy regarding a Privacy Impact Assessment (PIA) for smart meters
2. Data governance policy regarding masking of smart meter data in non-production environments
3. Data governance policy regarding monitoring access to smart meter data by privileged users
4. Data governance policy regarding retention periods for smart meter data

In Figure 14.9, we drill down into the policy regarding the masking of smart meter data in non-production environments. This policy would need to go into detail on the specific fields that need to be masked. The policy is also linked to IBM InfoSphere Optim Data Masking Solution via IBM InfoSphere Metadata Workbench. Note that this linkage is for illustrative purposes only and was not supported in the IBM InfoSphere tooling as of the publication of this book. However, we anticipate that IBM and other vendors will introduce tighter policy-based integration between their metadata and data masking tools.

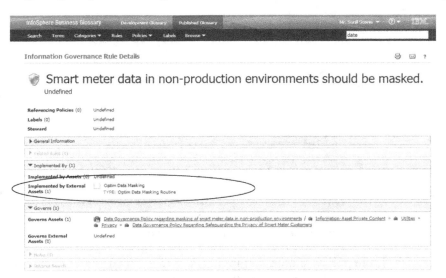

Figure 14.9: A smart meter data governance policy in IBM InfoSphere Business Glossary theoretically integrated with IBM InfoSphere Optim Data Masking Solution.

As of the publication of this book, IBM had introduced limited policy-based integration between IBM InfoSphere Business Glossary and IBM InfoSphere Optim Data Masking Solution. Figure 14.10 illustrates the following integration elements:

- *Classifications*—In the left panel in Figure 14.10, we can view a list of data classifications using the Business Glossary viewer in IBM InfoSphere Optim Designer. One such classification is "Email Address."
- *Bindings*—This classification applies to the DB2.PRD.OPTIM_CUSTOMERS.EMAIL_ ADDRESS column in the middle pane.
- *Data masking policies*—The far right panel shows a drop-down list of the actual data masking policies in IBM InfoSphere Optim Designer, including one for Email Address.
- *Data masking routines*—The bottom right panel shows the data masking routine for NATIONALID in IBM InfoSphere Optim Designer.

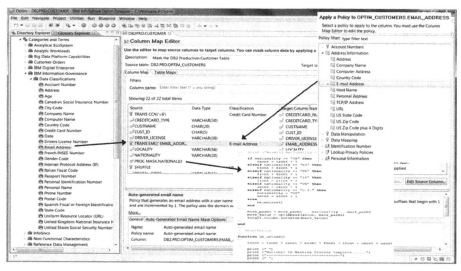

Figure 14.10: Policy-based integration between IBM InfoSphere Business Glossary and IBM InfoSphere Optim Data Masking Solution.

In Figure 14.11, the policy relating to monitoring access to customer names is documented in IBM InfoSphere Business Glossary. This policy flags customer last name as sensitive data in the metadata repository. It should also state that any database access requests by privileged users such as database administrators should be sent to a third party. The policy is implemented in IBM InfoSphere Guardium Data Activity Monitor.

As in Figure 14.9, the linkage shown in Figure 14.11 between IBM InfoSphere Business Glossary and IBM InfoSphere Guardium Data Activity Monitor is only theoretical; it has not been actually implemented in the tools. However, we anticipate that IBM and other vendors will introduce tighter policy-based integration between their metadata and database activity monitoring tools.

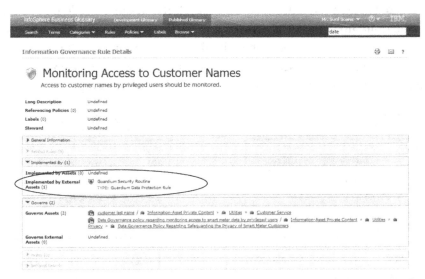

Figure 14.11: Smart meter data governance policy in IBM InfoSphere Business Glossary theoretically integrated with IBM InfoSphere Guardium Data Activity Monitor.

Create a Complete Business Object Using Data Discovery Tools That Can Be Acted Upon by Data Masking Tools

Complete business objects are simply lists of tables and the relationships between those tables. In terms of data masking, understanding and modeling the relationships in the complete business object allows developers to propagate sensitive data through the data model if that sensitive data acts as a key. Data masking represents a simple concept, but it is technically challenging to execute. Developers need the capability to propagate masked data elements to all related tables in the database, and across databases, to maintain referential integrity. For example, if a masked data element such as a telephone number is a primary or foreign key in a database table relationship, this newly masked data value must be propagated to all related tables in the database, or across data sources. If the data is a portion of another row's data, it must be updated with the same data as well. Without an understanding of the business object and its relationships, masking data would create orphans, which again would make the application fail unintentionally.[5]

In Figure 14.12, the Customers.Cust_ID column is the primary key and Orders.Cust_ID is the foreign key. The tables on the left contain original data, and those on the right contain masked data. On the left, we see that Elliot Flynn, Cust_ID 27645, has placed two orders. On the right, his Cust_ID has changed to 10002, and his name to Pablo Picasso. However, referential integrity has been maintained by changing the Cust_ID in the Orders table to 10002, as well. Data discovery tools like IBM InfoSphere Discovery can uncover these primary key-foreign key relationships to support data masking.[6]

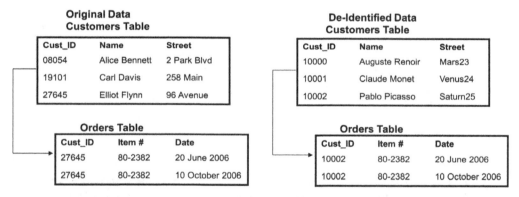

Figure 14.12: Masked data needs to be propagated based on primary key-foreign key relationships.

Summary

In this chapter, we learned about the key integration points between security/privacy and data integration tools. Data discovery tools should discover sensitive data, which should be flagged in the metadata repository. Sensitive data should be masked in production and non-production environments. Data governance teams should establish capabilities to monitor database access by privileged users. In addition, data stewards should document key security and privacy policies in the business glossary. Finally, data discovery tools should identify complete business objects that can be acted upon by data masking tools.

---

5   "InfoSphere Optim and the complete business object Part 1: Understanding the complete business object." http://www.ibm.com/developerworks/data/library/techarticle/dm-1110optimobjectpart1/.

6   Soares, Sunil. *The IBM Data Governance Unified Process*. (IBM, 2010.)

CHAPTER 15

INFORMATION LIFECYCLE MANAGEMENT[1]

Information lifecycle management (ILM) is a process and methodology for managing information throughout its lifecycle, from creation through disposal, including compliance with legal, regulatory, and privacy requirements. ILM encompasses business processes and policies across legal, records, and IT. ILM programs should enable the efficient disposition of information at the end of its usefulness to the business, in accordance with legal and regulatory obligations.

The components of an ILM platform are as follows:

- *Information archiving*—As data volumes grow, production systems become overburdened with information that is less frequently accessed or no longer needed by business users. Organizations need solutions that enable efficient and timely archiving of structured and unstructured information while enabling its discovery for legal requirements and its timely disposition when no longer needed by business, legal, or records stakeholders.

    Content repositories include Microsoft Exchange, IBM Notes and Domino, Microsoft SharePoint, Oracle, IBM DB2, and SAP. IBM InfoSphere Optim Data Growth Solution and Informatica Data Archive enable organizations to move structured data to less expensive storage for later retrieval. This approach reduces

---

1 This chapter includes content from *Big Data Governance*, Sunil Soares (MC Press, 2012).

storage costs and improves application performance. OpenText offers solutions for archiving SAP data. Vendor offerings such as Symantec Enterprise Vault, HP Consolidated Archive, IBM Value-Based Archiving Solutions, and EMC SourceOne also offer unified archives for a variety of data types.

- *Records and retention management*—Every ILM program must maintain a catalog of laws and regulations that apply to information in the jurisdictions in which the business operates. These laws, regulations, and business needs drive the need for a retention schedule that determines how long documents should be kept. Records management solutions enforce a business process around document retention. Vendor tools include IBM Enterprise Records, EMC Documentum Records Manager, HP Records Manager, and OpenText Records Management.

- *Legal holds and evidence collection (eDiscovery)*—Most corporations and entities are subject to litigation and governmental investigations that require them to preserve potential evidence. Large entities might have hundreds or thousands of open legal matters with varying obligations for data. A typical legal matter lasts three years, and many last five or more years.

  According to the *Information Lifecycle Governance Leader Reference Guide* by Deidre Paknad and Rani Hublou, legal eDiscovery costs are largely a function of information volume. The guide notes that 97 percent of all matters settle before trial, and of the three percent that go to trial, 1.5 percent settle before the trial concludes. Because of these dynamics, improvements in the eDiscovery process increase transparency, enable the defensible disposal of unnecessary data, and considerably reduce outside legal fees.

  The legal department needs to define evidence obligations; coordinate with IT, records, and business teams; search large volumes of documents; and gather evidence. Data sources include email messages, instant messages, Excel spreadsheets, PDF documents, audio, video, and social media. Vendor tools include Symantec Enterprise Vault, HP eDiscovery, IBM eDiscovery Manager, Recommind Axcelerate eDiscovery Suite, Nuix eDiscovery, ZyLAB eDiscovery and Production System, and Guidance Software EnCase eDiscovery.

- *Test data management*—The data governance program needs tools to streamline the creation and management of test environments, subset and migrate data to build realistic and right-sized test databases, mask sensitive data, automate test result comparisons, and eliminate the expense and effort of maintaining multiple database clones. IBM InfoSphere Optim Test Data Management and Informatica Data Subset streamline the creation and management of test environments.

Figure 15.1 shows IBM InfoSphere Optim Test Data Management. The panel in the top right shows statistics for key tables before and after the test data subsetting process. Source 1 is for post-subset tables, and Source 2 is for pre-subset tables. We can see that DB2.PRD.OPTIM_SALES has 14 rows before and after the subsetting process. However, these rows are different, which means that the subsetting process changed or masked the values. Similarly, DB2.PRD.OPTIM_CUSTOMERS has nine rows that were also all changed. On the other hand, the other tables remained unchanged during the subsetting process. In the bottom right panel, a developer can also test that the values have been masked appropriately. For example, the values of EMAIL_ADDRESS, PHONE_NUMBER, NATIONAL_ID, and CREDITCARD_NUMBER have been changed, as expected.

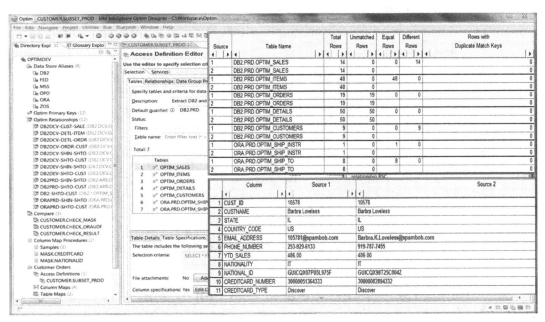

Figure 15.1: IBM InfoSphere Optim Test Data Management.

There are a few intersection points between data governance and ILM tools, discussed in the rest of this chapter.

Document Information Policies in the Business Glossary That Are Implemented by ILM Tools

Business glossaries should document information policies that are implemented by ILM tools. We continue with the example from the previous chapter, relating to the governance of smart meter data in utilities. In Figure 15.2, IBM InfoSphere Business Glossary contains an information governance policy relating to the retention rules for smart meter data. The policy states that smart meter interval data may be retained in detailed form for a period of 13 months. This policy is then implemented by IBM InfoSphere Optim Data Growth Solution. This integration is for illustrative purposes only and is not supported in the tool as of the publication of this book. However, we anticipate that IBM and other vendors will continue to pursue policy-based integration between their metadata and ILM tools.

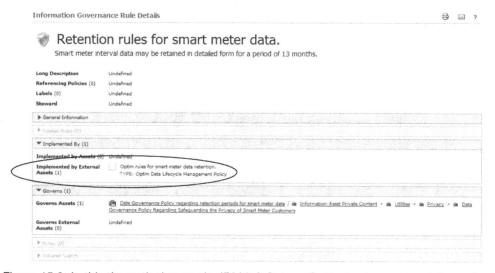

Figure 15.2: In this theoretical example, IBM InfoSphere Optim implements an Information Governance Policy in IBM InfoSphere Business Glossary.

Discover Complete Business Objects That Can Be Acted on Efficiently by ILM Tools[2]

As discussed earlier, complete business objects are simply lists of tables and the relationships between those tables. For data extraction through a data archiving tool like IBM InfoSphere Optim Data Growth Solution, the complete business object is used to create an immutable historical snapshot of the data at a point in time. The transactional

---

2   http://www.ibm.com/developerworks/data/library/techarticle/dm-1110optimobjectpart1/.

data is archived, along with the reference data that gives it context. This context is crucial in order to give the transactional data meaning when the data in the archives is recalled and reported on later.

The primary purpose of complete business objects in test data management is to create relationally intact subsets of data. These subsets allow users to create test databases that are only as large as they need to be for their particular testing purposes. Figure 15.3 shows the creation of a complete business object, called a Data Object in IBM InfoSphere Discovery, for OPTIM_ORDERS that also include data from the OPTIM_SALES, OPTIM_ DETAILS, OPTIM_CUSTOMERS, and OPTIM_ITEMS tables.

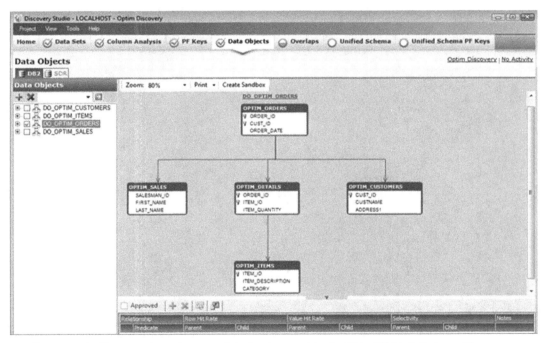

Figure 15.3: The creation of a complete business object within IBM InfoSphere Discovery.

Summary

In this chapter, we discussed the different components of an ILM platform, including archiving, records and retention management, eDiscovery, and test data management. We discussed how business glossaries may document information policies that are implemented by ILM tools. We also reviewed how data discovery tools can identify a complete business object to support ILM.

PART FOUR

BIG DATA GOVERNANCE TOOLS

CHAPTER 16

HADOOP AND NOSQL

Apache Hadoop is an open source software library that supports the distributed processing of large data sets across thousands of computers based on commodity hardware. The Apache Hadoop project grew out of pioneering work at Yahoo! and Google, where researchers worked with huge volumes of data across large clusters of computers. These technologies are gradually making their way into government and commercial applications and have unleashed the big data revolution.

Because it consists of a bewildering array of technologies with their own release schedules, Hadoop can be somewhat intimidating to the novice user. As with other open source software, Apache Hadoop does not come with product support for things like bug fixes. To address these shortcomings, a number of vendors have released their own distributions of Apache Hadoop that have undergone release testing. These vendors bundle product support and offer training for an additional fee. Most enterprises that have deployed Hadoop for commercial use have selected one of the Hadoop distributions. Standalone vendors who offer Hadoop distributions include Cloudera, MapR, and Hortonworks. In addition, IBM offers a Hadoop distribution called InfoSphere BigInsights. Amazon Web Services offers a Hadoop framework that is part of a hosted web service called Amazon Elastic MapReduce (EMR), which distributes workloads over a cluster of Amazon Elastic Compute Cloud (EC2) instances. EMC Pivotal offers a Hadoop distribution called Greenplum HD.

Figure 16.1 shows the landing page for Apache Hadoop User Experience (Hue) in Cloudera.

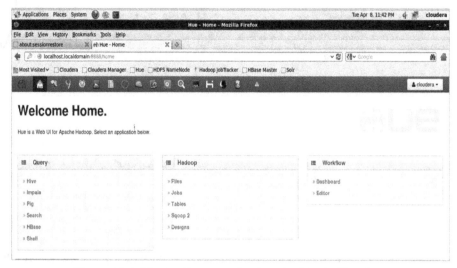

Figure 16.1: The landing page for Apache Hue in Cloudera.

The following are a few basic Hadoop technologies:

- *Hadoop Distributed File System (HDFS)*—Hadoop Distributed File System (HDFS) is a distributed file system that is designed to be highly fault tolerant and to run on low-cost hardware.
- *MapReduce*—MapReduce applications can process vast amounts (multiple terabytes) of data in parallel on large clusters in a reliable, fault-tolerant manner. MapReduce is a computational paradigm in which an application is divided into self-contained units of work. Each of these units of work can be executed on any node in the cluster. A MapReduce job splits the input data set into independent "chunks" that are processed by map tasks in parallel. Although the Hadoop framework is implemented in Java, MapReduce applications do not have to be written in Java.[1]
- *Hive*—Apache Hive is a data warehousing infrastructure that sits on top of Hadoop. Hive provides a SQL-like interface called HiveQL to query large volumes of data

---

1 http://publib.boulder.ibm.com/infocenter/bigins/v1r1/topic/com.ibm.swg.im.infosphere.biginsights. welcome.doc/doc/welcome.html.

in Hadoop. Because Hive insulates users from having to learn the intricacies of MapReduce programming in Java, it is a great transition for relational database programmers who are looking to work with Hadoop.

- *Impala*—Cloudera Impala allows users to issue SQL (Structured Query Language) queries against data stored in HDFS and Apache HBase.
- *Pig*—Apache Pig is a platform for analyzing large semi-structured data sets in Hadoop. It uses a procedural language called Pig Latin that insulates users from learning the intricacies of MapReduce programming in Java. Hive and Pig evolved as separate Apache projects for the analysis of large datasets. Hive is better suited to users who are familiar with SQL. Pig, on the other hand, is ideal for users who are familiar with procedural programs like Microsoft Visual Basic and Python.
- *HBase*—Apache HBase is a column-oriented database that sits on top of HDFS. It is designed to store large tables, with billions of rows and millions of columns. HBase is not a relational database and does not support SQL.
- *Oozie*—Apache Oozie is a workflow scheduler to manage Hadoop jobs.
- *HCatalog*—HCatalog is a table and storage management layer for Hadoop that enables users with different data processing tools (such as Pig and MapReduce) to more easily read and write data on the grid.[2]
- *Sqoop*—Apache Sqoop is a tool that supports the movement of massive volumes of data between Apache Hadoop and structured data stores such as relational databases. Many ETL vendors also support similar functionality.

In the rest of this chapter, we discuss the intersection between Hadoop and data governance tools.

Conduct an Inventory of Data in Hadoop

Many big data teams start by creating a "data lake" in Hadoop to act as a landing zone for data across the organization and for big data analytics. Left unchecked, these data lakes can quickly become unmanageable for data scientists who might have to deal with multiple copies of the same data set.

Because you cannot govern what you do not know exists, the first step to governing big data is to build an inventory. In Figure 16.2, we show the Hadoop data inventory file browser in Waterline Data Science. The data scientist views the search results for Customer. In the left panel, the data scientist can also view the faceted search with results

---

2 https://cwiki.apache.org/confluence/display/Hive/HCatalog+UsingHCat.

classified by categories. For example, there are seven results classified by SAP and three results in the Northeast.

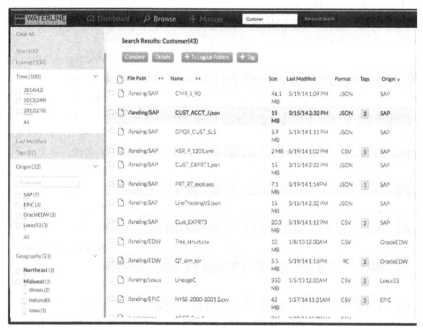

Figure 16.2: The Hadoop Data Inventory file browser in Waterline Data Science.

Assign Ownership for Data in Hadoop

Data governance programs need to assign the ownership of data, whether or not it resides in Hadoop. As shown in Figure 16.3, a retailer uses Data Advantage Group MetaCenter to manage data ownership for all types of data. For example, the Finance Reporting application and Data Mart 1 are owned by Finance and Merchandising, respectively. On the other hand, big data in the form of Twitter and Facebook are primarily managed in Hadoop and are under the ownership of Marketing. Finally, Supply Chain owns radio-frequency identification (RFID) data. MetaCenter also contains the names of the data executive, managing data steward, and data steward for each application or data type.

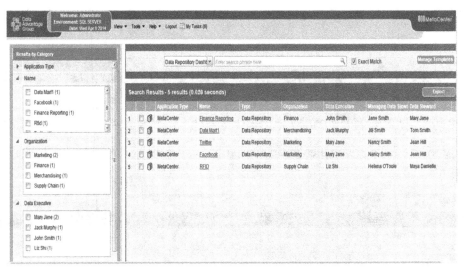

Figure 16.3: Data ownership in Data Advantage Group MetaCenter.

Provision a Semantic Layer for Analytics in Hadoop

Although Hadoop is a powerful analytics platform, it is meaningless without the appropriate semantic layer to provide meaning to key business terms. In the next few screenshots, we explore a simple MapReduce word-count program that executes within Cloudera. The business definitions for the key terms are available in Collibra Data Governance Center. Figure 16.4 shows a list with comma separated values (CSV) of banking terms related to the Dodd-Frank legislation in the United States.

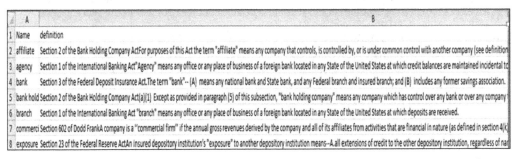

Figure 16.4: Banking business terms relating to the Dodd-Frank legislation in the United States.

In Figure 16.5, we compile the WordCount.java file using the command-line interface in Cloudera.

Figure 16.5: Compiling the WordCount.java file using the command-line interface in Cloudera.

In Figure 16.6, we create the wordcount.jar file using the command-line interface in Cloudera.

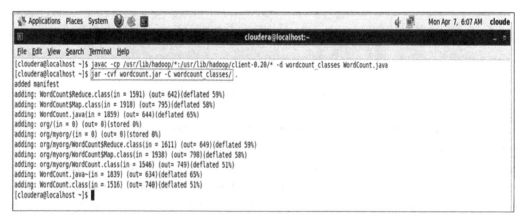

Figure 16.6: Creating the wordcount.jar file using the command-line interface in Cloudera.

In Figure 16.7, we execute the MapReduce code on the .csv file with the Dodd-Frank terms.

In Figure 16.8, we view the results of the MapReduce word-count program in Cloudera. The words "affiliate" and "bank" appear once each.

Figure 16.7: Executing MapReduce code on the .csv file with Dodd-Frank business terms.

Figure 16.8: Viewing the results of the MapReduce word-count program in Cloudera.

Finally, we can view the business definitions of these terms in Collibra Data Governance Center, as shown in Figure 16.9. In this way, Collibra provides the semantic layer for Hadoop analytics in Cloudera.

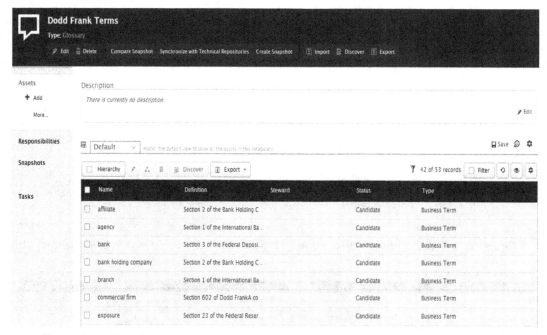

Figure 16.9: Viewing definitions of business terms in Collibra Data Governance Center.

View the Lineage of Data In and Out of Hadoop

As Hadoop becomes more mainstream, organizations will use the platform for mission-critical applications. This means that data governance teams will need to include Hadoop within their data lineage views. In Figure 16.10, ASG-Rochade displays the metadata relating to the EMP_EXPENSE_FACT table, which resides within the Oracle system, the XE database, and the GOSALESDW schema. We can see that EMP_EXPENSE_FACT "contains expense details of employees working for the Great Outdoors Company."

Figure 16.10: The EMP_EXPENSE_FACT Oracle table in ASG-Rochade.

In Figure 16.11, ASG-Rochade shows the high-level forward lineage of the EMP_
EXPENSE_FACT table to the emp_expense_fact table in Hive.

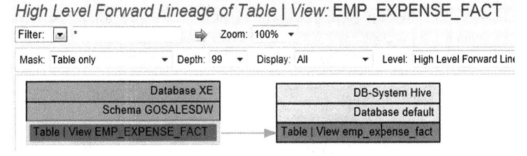

Figure 16.11: The high-level forward lineage of the EMP_EXPENSE_FACT table in ASG-Rochade.

In Figure 16.12, ASG-Rochade shows the detailed forward lineage of the EMP_
EXPENSE_FACT table. The lineage report shows the emp-expense-fact Hive table, as well
as two sets of Sqoop ETL jobs.

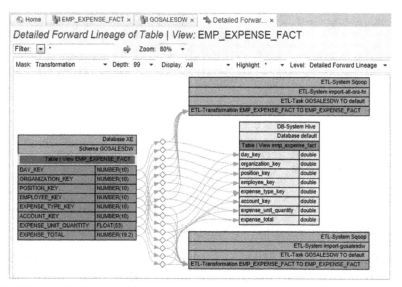

Figure 16.12: The detailed forward lineage of the EMP_EXPENSE_FACT table in ASG-Rochade.

In Figure 16.13, ASG-Rochade displays the detailed forward lineage of the EMPLOYEE-KEY column in the EMP_EXPENSE_FACT table. The data goes through two Sqoop jobs before landing in the employee-key column in the emp_expense_fact Hive table.

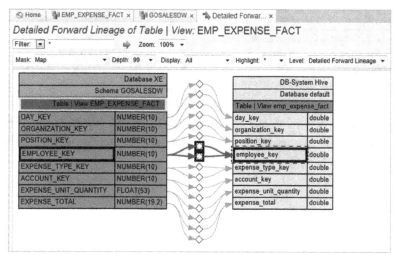

Figure 16.13: The detailed forward lineage of the EMP_EXPENSE_FACT table in ASG-Rochade, with EMPLOYEE_KEY highlighted.

Manage Reference Data for Hadoop

Hadoop implementations also need high-quality reference data. In Figure 16.14, the GDP_Test.csv file contains the Gross Domestic Product (GDP) in millions of U.S. dollars by country. This data is in an unsorted format and will be used as the input file for a Pig script.

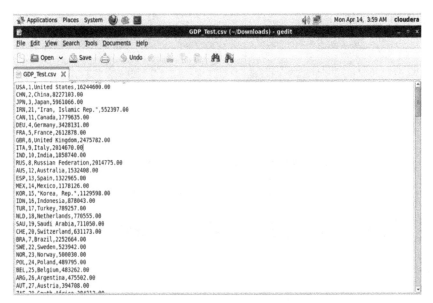

Figure 16.14: The GDP_Test.csv file contains GDP by country.

In Figure 16.15, we have created a Pig script to sort the countries in descending order of GDP. The script runs in Cloudera and takes the GDP_Test.csv file as an input file. The script places the result in a file called "output."

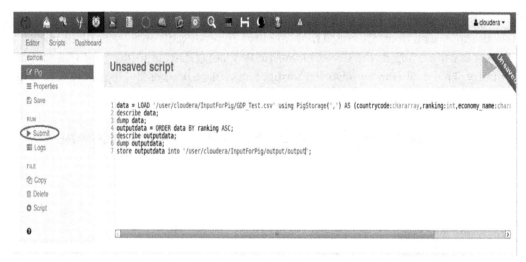

Figure 16.15: A Pig script to sort countries in descending order of GDP.

Figure 16.16 shows the results of the Pig script in sorted format.

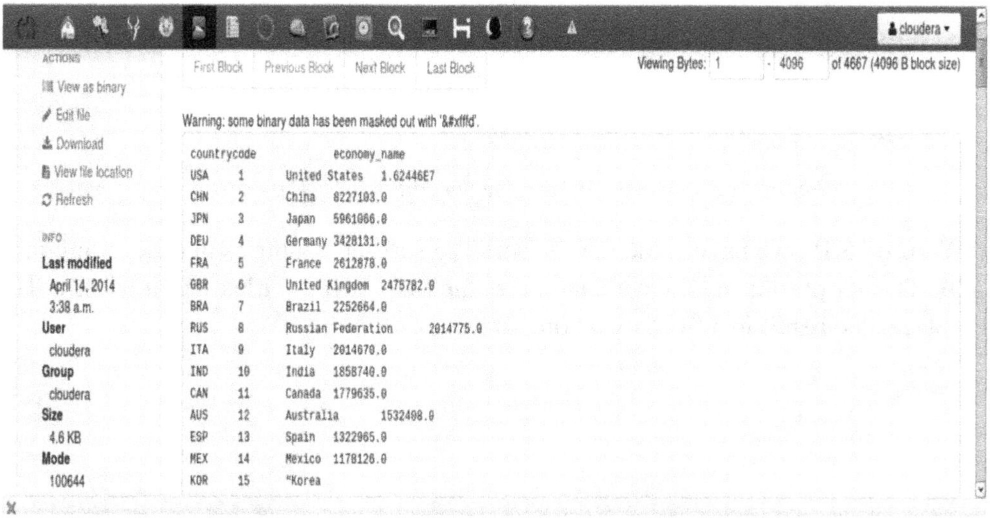

Figure 16.16: The output of the Pig script shows a sorted list of countries in descending order of GDP.

Figure 16.17 shows the reference data for country codes in Data Advantage Group MetaCenter. The left panel shows a list of country codes. In the Description field of the right panel, you can see that "FR" represents France.

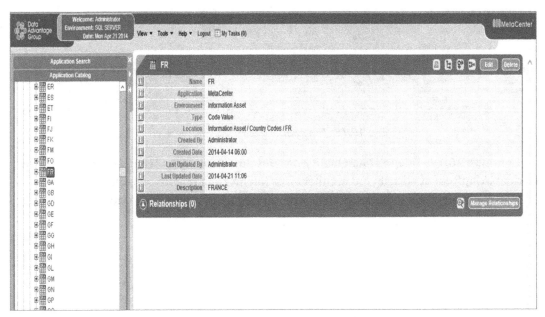

Figure 16.17: Data Advantage Group MetaCenter contains country codes relating to the GDP Pig script.

Profile Data Natively in Hadoop

Organizations also need to profile data natively in Hadoop without moving large volumes into structured data stores. Figure 16.18 shows the Global IDs HDFS File Profiler. The screenshot shows a column analysis for the product data in semi-structured format in the Inventory.txt file. The profiler has uncovered 49 columns, including FAMILY, PRODUCTGROUP, COMMODITYGROUPID, PRODUCT_TYPE, and SELL_SWAP_INDICATOR.

Name	Documented Datatype	Inferred Datatype	Description	Primary Key	% Uniques	Profiled On
FAMILY	VARCHAR	Text		☐	14.7	2013 10 21, 16:45:15
PRODUCTGROUP	VARCHAR	Text		☐	5.73	2013 10 21, 16:45:14
COMMODITYGROUPID	VARCHAR	Text		☐	87.81	2013 10 21, 16:45:12
PRODUCT_TYPE	VARCHAR	Text		☐	75.99	2013 10 21, 16:45:12
SELL_SWAP_INDICATOR	VARCHAR	Text		☐	8.96	2013 10 21, 16:45:15
ITEM_PRODUCT	VARCHAR	Text		☐	8.96	2013 10 21, 16:45:13
CREATEUSER	VARCHAR	Unknown		☐	0.0	2013 10 21, 16:45:15
MODIFYDATE	VARCHAR	Unknown		☐	0.0	2013 10 21, 16:45:14
MODIFYUSER	VARCHAR	Unknown		☐	0.0	2013 10 21, 16:45:15
STATUS	VARCHAR	Text		☐	0.36	2013 10 21, 16:45:15
PROGRAM	VARCHAR	Text		☐	3.23	2013 10 21, 16:45:16
SUPPLIER	VARCHAR	Unknown		☐	0.0	2013 10 21, 16:45:15
VENDOR	VARCHAR	Unknown		☐	0.0	2013 10 21, 16:45:15
SITEID	VARCHAR	Text		☐	3.23	2013 10 21, 16:45:15
WAREHOUSELOCATION	VARCHAR	Text		☐	3.73	2013 10 21, 16:45:17

#Columns: 49 #Profiled Columns: 49

Figure 16.18: The Global IDs HDFS File Profiler.

In Figure 16.19, Talend Data Quality profiles data natively in Hive. By leveraging the Hadoop MapReduce distributed architecture, Talend Data Quality can cleanse, match, and de-duplicate large volumes of data without having to move it prior to processing.

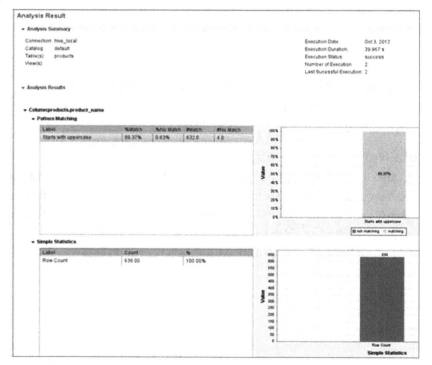

Figure 16.19: Talend Data Quality profiles data natively in Hive.

Discover Data Natively in Hadoop

Data profiling tools should also natively discover hidden data in Hadoop. Figure 16.20 shows how Informatica PowerCenter Big Data Edition can be set up to discover IPAddress and StockSymbol data within a WebLogs Logical Data Object in Apache Hive.

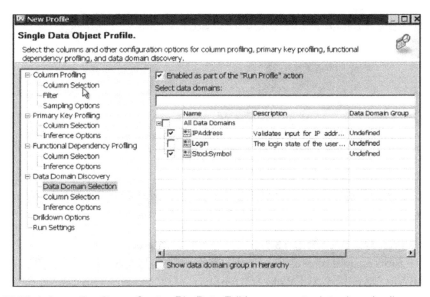

Figure 16.20: Informatica PowerCenter Big Data Edition supports data domain discovery within Apache Hive.

In Figure 16.21, Informatica PowerCenter Big Data Edition shows the results of the data domain discovery for the WebLogs Logical Data Object. We can see that 100 percent of the values in the IP_Address column conform to the IPAddress pattern. The same holds true for the Stock_Symbol column relative to the StockSymbol pattern.

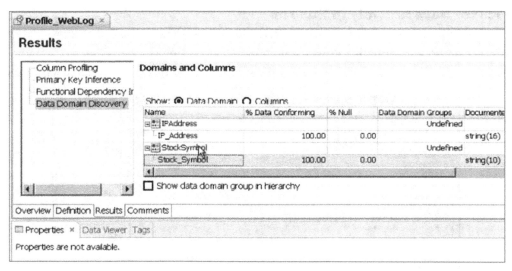

Figure 16.21: Informatica PowerCenter Big Data Edition shows the results of the data domain discovery exercise.

Execute Data Quality Rules Natively in Hadoop

Data quality tools should also execute rules natively in Hadoop. Figure 16.22 shows a sample web log file called DailyWebLogDump.txt.

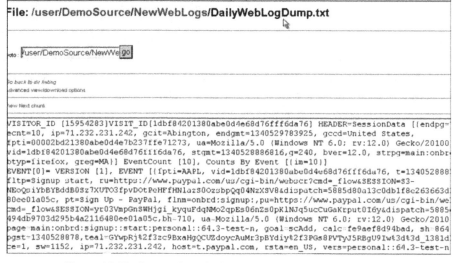

Figure 16.22: A sample web log file in semi-structured format.

Figure 16.23 shows the mappings in Informatica PowerCenter Big Data Edition. The DailyWebLogDump.txt is read as a binary source file in the Read mapping on the left. The file is then parsed in the POC_Session transformation in the middle, and the results are passed to the Joiner mapping on the right.

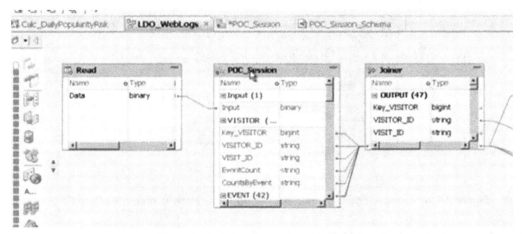

Figure 16.23: Mappings in Informatica PowerCenter Big Data Edition.

Figure 16.24 provides further detail on how the binary file is parsed in Informatica PowerCenter Big Data Edition. The parser conducts a text search for Visitor_id. It then populates any associated text found in parentheses in the VISITOR_ID element in the VISITOR object in a pre-defined schema.

Figure 16.24: Complex data parsing with Informatica PowerCenter Big Data Edition.

Integrate Hadoop with Master Data Management

MDM hubs generally contain a lot of information about internal data relating to customers, materials, equipment, and vendors. However, there is a huge volume and variety of external data, such as Twitter, Facebook, and blogs, that can enrich internal master data. Hadoop can parse this external data, as well as match it with the internal master data.

As shown in Figure 16.25, IBM InfoSphere BigInsights Hadoop distribution uses advanced text analytics techniques and business rules to derive insight from unstructured information relating to a hypothetical individual named Jane Doe. It uses the location on her Twitter account to discern that she is a football fan and lives in Tampa, FL. Jane Doe's Tweet indicates that she is interested in yoga and that Tony C. is part of her network. Since the blog contained a reference to her Twitter handle, IBM InfoSphere BigInsights was also able to figure out that Jane Doe blogs about food-related topics.

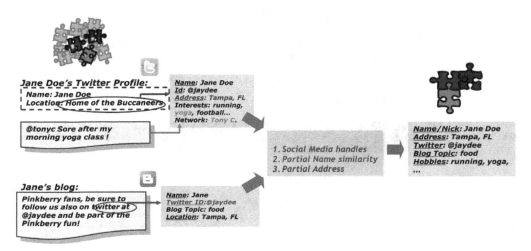

Figure 16.25: The creation of an unstructured entity from social media with IBM InfoSphere BigInsights.

As shown in Figure 16.26, IBM InfoSphere BigInsights extracts entities from social media. These entities are then fed into IBM InfoSphere Master Data Management, where they are linked with existing customer master data records using probabilistic matching techniques.

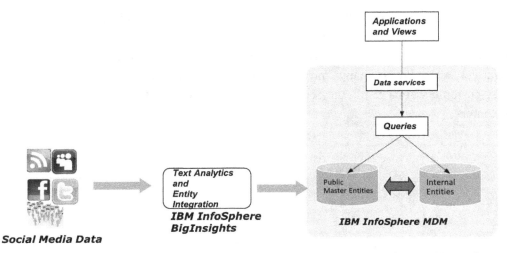

Figure 16.26: The integration of IBM InfoSphere BigInsights and IBM InfoSphere Master Data Management.

As shown in Figure 16.27, the data steward can view a customer's profile and social media feedback in IBM InfoSphere Master Data Management. The data steward can view the customer's name, Twitter handle, and Tweets relating to key products like camping and golf equipment. The steward can see that the customer was disappointed with the Mapreader product, as well as the Course Pro golf bag.

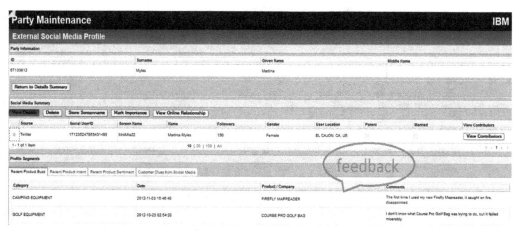

Figure 16.27: The data stewardship console in IBM InfoSphere Master Data Management displays the customer's social profile and feedback.

As shown in Figure 16.28, the data steward can also drill down to view the customer's Twitter followers and follows. The steward can see that the customer follows Jacob Hitt and Emily Keller, both of whom are also customers. If the customer is Tweeting negatively about the company's products, it might adversely affect the sentiment of these customers. As a result, the company might want to proactively reach out to these customers.

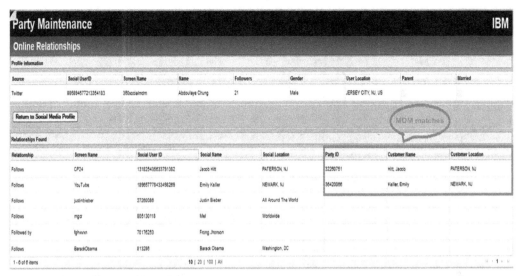

Figure 16.28: The data stewardship console in IBM InfoSphere Master Data Management displays the customer's followers and follows, and locates additional master data matches.

Port Data Governance Tools to Hadoop for Improved Performance

Organizations can leverage the power of Hadoop to turbo-charge their data governance platforms. For example, marketing organizations often need to match lists of prospects against internal records to remove any customers who have made do-not-call elections. These large datasets push the limits of existing computational resources when IT needs to match 200 million prospects against a database of 100 million customers and turn around the results to marketing in 24 hours. The largest bulk entity resolution on the IBM InfoSphere Master Data Management platform was approximately one billion records. However, this exercise typically required manual partitioning of the data across several large machines and took multiple days to process.

As shown in Figure 16.29, IBM has implemented the IBM InfoSphere Master Data Management probabilistic matching engine within the IBM InfoSphere BigInsights platform. This offering is also known as "Big Match." This has helped organizations implement probabilistic matching on ultra-large datasets in hours, rather than days or weeks.

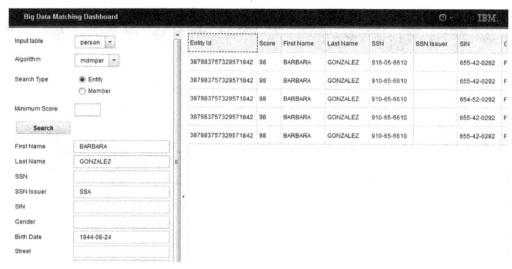

Figure 16.29: The probabilistic matching engine in IBM InfoSphere BigInsights ("Big Match").

In a similar vein, Figure 16.30 shows fuzzy matching with Informatica Master Data Management in a Hadoop MapReduce cluster.

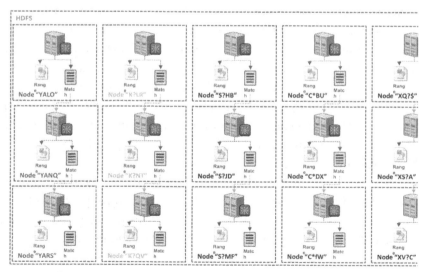

Figure 16.30: Fuzzy matching with Informatica Master Data Management in a Hadoop MapReduce cluster.

Govern Data in NoSQL Databases

NoSQL ("Not Only SQL") databases are a category of database management systems that do not use SQL as their primary query language. These databases might not require fixed table schemas, and they do not support join operations. These databases are optimized for highly scalable read-write operations rather than for consistency. Apache HBase is a type of NoSQL. Other NoSQL databases include Apache Cassandra, MongoDB, Apache CouchDB, Couchbase, and Riak, as well as Amazon DynamoDB, which forms part of the Amazon Web Services software as a service platform.

NoSQL databases are slowly becoming a viable alternative to relational databases for certain applications. For example, Cassandra is in use at organizations such as Netflix, Twitter, Constant Contact, and Cisco, with the largest known cluster having over 300 terabytes of data across over 400 machines.[3]

Because these databases contain data that is starting to become mission critical, data governance tools need to support data ownership, semantics, data lineage, reference data, data profiling and data quality for NoSQL data as well. Figure 16.31 shows the Global IDs Graph Database Profiler. A graph database is a type of NoSQL database that uses graph structures with nodes, edges, and properties to represent and store data.[4]

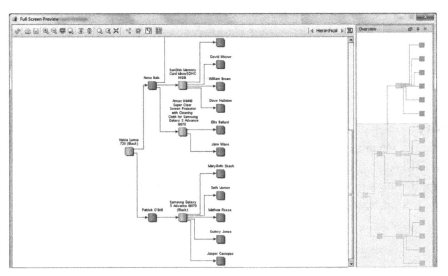

Figure 16.31: The Global IDs Graph Database Profiler.

---

3   http://cassandra.apache.org/.

4   http://en.wikipedia.org/wiki/Graph_database.

Mask Sensitive Data in Hadoop

Big data teams also need to mask sensitive data within their Hadoop data lakes. Many vendors such as IBM and Informatica support data masking functionality in Hadoop. Figure 16.32 shows the batch interface on HDFS that uses IBM InfoSphere Optim Data Privacy Solution to mask sensitive data.

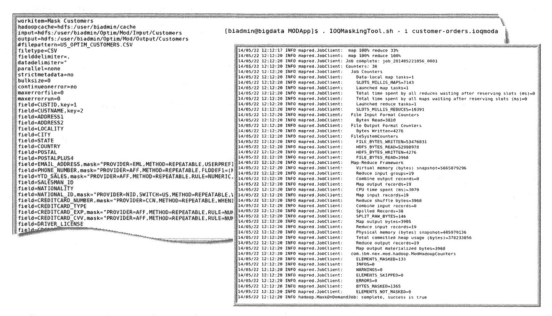

Figure 16.32: IBM InfoSphere Optim Data Privacy Solution masks sensitive data in Hadoop.

Summary

In this chapter, we emphasized that Hadoop and NoSQL also need data governance discipline. This discipline can be enforced by data governance tools that support data ownership, business glossaries, data lineage, reference data, data profiling, data quality, MDM integration, and data privacy.

CHAPTER

17

STREAM COMPUTING

A s discussed in the previous chapter, Hadoop is well suited to handle large volumes of data at rest. However, big data also involves high-velocity data in motion. *Stream computing* refers to a class of technologies that leverage massively parallel processing capabilities to analyze data in motion, as opposed to landing large volumes of structured, unstructured, and semi-structured data on disk. Incorporating stream computing into a big data solution can support low latency responses (such as alerts) based on the receipt of new data, as well as filtering, correlating, and enriching data before it is stored on disk.

A related term is *complex event processing* (*CEP*), which combines data from multiple sources to infer events or patterns that suggest more complicated circumstances. The goal of CEP is to identify meaningful events (such as opportunities or threats) and respond to them as quickly as possible.[1] CEP applications include surveillance, homeland security, intelligence services, and financial services algorithmic trading.

There are a number of different open source and vendor-proprietary tools in this space. For example, Apache Flume uses streaming data flows to collect, aggregate, and move large volumes of data into HDFS. IBM offers a tool called InfoSphere Streams, shown in Figure 17.1, which grew out of early work with the United States government. TIBCO StreamBase and SAP Sybase Event Stream Processor also offer CEP platforms.

---

1   http://en.wikipedia.org/wiki/Complex_event_processing.

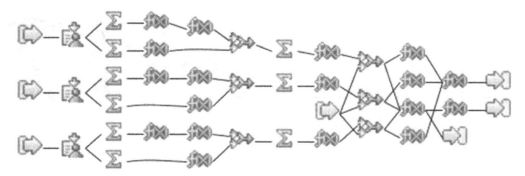

Figure 17.1: A streaming application flow graph in IBM InfoSphere Streams. [2]

Data governance tools can support multiple aspects of stream computing applications, as discussed in the following sections.

Use Data Profiling Tools to Understand a Sample Set of Input Data

Stream computing applications need to consider two aspects relating to the underlying data:

- *Sources*—This refers to data available as input to the stream computing application. This data could be from a socket connection, database query, Java Message Service (JMS) topic/queue, or file. A schema can usually define each source, although the transport medium may vary.
- *Sinks or destinations*—This refers to data produced by a stream computing application and sent or written to a socket connection, database table, JMS topic/queue, file, or web service.

Before building a stream computing application, big data teams need to understand the characteristics of the source data. If Marketing wants to analyze Twitter feeds, for example, the big data team would use the Twitter API to download a sample set of Tweets for further analysis. The profiling of a sample set of stream data is similar to traditional data quality projects. It may leverage tools such as IBM InfoSphere Information Analyzer, Informatica Data Quality, and Trillium TS Discovery. Both types of projects need to understand the characteristics of the underlying data, such as the frequency of

---

2   http://www.ibm.com/developerworks/data/tutorials/dm-1004infospherestreamscluster/index.html?ca=dat, "IBM—Installing and configuring InfoSphere Streams on a virtual machine," by Edward J. Pring.

null values. However, the profiling of stream data also needs to consider two additional aspects of the source data:

- *Temporal alignment*—Stream computing applications need to discover the temporal offset when joining, correlating, and matching data from different sources. For example, a stream computing application that needs to combine data from two sensors needs to know that one sensor generates events every second, while the other generates events every three seconds.
- *Rate of arrival*—Stream computing applications also need to understand the rate of arrival of the source data:
  - Does the data arrive continuously?
  - Are there bursts in the data?
  - Are there gaps in the arrival of data?

Govern Reference Data to Be Used by the Stream Computing Application

The stream computing application also needs high quality reference data that can be managed in tools such as Collibra Data Governance Center, Orchestra Networks EBX, and IBM InfoSphere Master Data Management Reference Data Management Hub. For example, consider a bank that uses real-time feeds of hundreds of data sources, including stock prices, currency rates, commodity prices, and weather reports, to make split-second buy-sell decisions on stocks. The bank builds complex algorithms using a stream computing application. The stream computing application needs consistent reference data on the allowable values for stock ticker symbols and commodities.

As another example, consider the data quality and reference data management considerations associated with a stream computing application that monitors sensor data in a school building. A simple stream computing application correlates data from motion and temperature sensors in a school building. The big data team has profiled the data to understand its characteristics. Data from the motion sensors arrives every 30 seconds, while data from the temperature sensors arrives every 60 seconds. The stream computing application uses this information to conduct a temporal alignment of the motion and temperature sensor data that arrive at different intervals. It accomplishes this by creating a window during which it holds both types of sensor events in memory, so that it can match the two streams of data.

The stream computing application also uses reference data that room A is a classroom and room B is the boiler room. The stream computing application stores temperature data every 10 minutes in Hadoop. The analytics team has used Hadoop to build a normalized model over several months, indicating that the average temperature readings of the boiler room and classroom are 65 degrees at 3:00 a.m. and 75 degrees at 9:00 a.m., respectively.

Finally, the stream computing application will use the available data to generate alerts, such as when sensor data does not arrive for five minutes, the temperature of the boiler room rises to 75 degrees at 3:00 a.m., or the motion sensor detects movement in the classroom at 5 a.m.

Govern Business Terms to Be Used by the Stream Computing Application

The stream computing application also needs high quality business terms that can be managed in tools such as Collibra Data Governance Center, IBM InfoSphere Business Glossary, and Informatica Metadata Manager. Figure 17.2 shows a composite flow graph called "POS_TxHandling" in IBM InfoSphere Streams to handle point-of-sale (POS) transactions. The bottom of the screenshot shows how the Streams Processing Language sets up the graph. The key elements of the graph are as follows:

- *TCP-Source*—We define two source-type operators to get data from the outside world by means of a Transmission Control Protocol (TCP) link. These operators fetch POS_Transactions and Deliveries data, respectively. Both POS_Transactions and Deliveries should be defined in IBM InfoSphere Business Glossary to ensure the appropriate semantic context for the stream computing application.
- *Operator 1*—This operator produces the stream Sales, which should also be defined in IBM InfoSphere Business Glossary.
- *Operator 2*—This operator produces TaxableSales while consuming Sales. The term "TaxableSales" should also be defined in IBM InfoSphere Business Glossary.
- *Operator 3*—This operator produces TaxesDue, which should be defined in IBM InfoSphere Business Glossary.
- *Operator 4*—This operator produces Inventory, which should be defined in IBM InfoSphere Business Glossary.
- *Operator 5*—This operator produces Reorders, which should be defined in IBM InfoSphere Business Glossary.
- *TCP-Sink*—This is a sink-type operator, which has no output stream but sends data to the outside world via the TCP link.

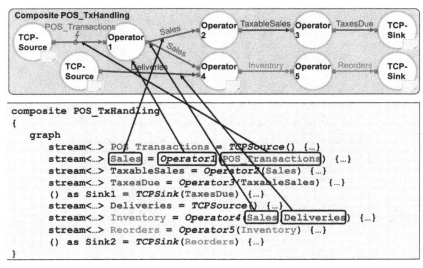

Figure 17.2: A composite flow graph to handle POS transactions with IBM InfoSphere Streams.

Summary

In this chapter, we reviewed the importance of data governance tools for stream computing projects. We discussed the applicability of data profiling, reference data, and business glossaries.

CHAPTER 18

TEXT ANALYTICS

O rganizations increasingly need to derive insights from large volumes of unstructured content within call center agents' notes, social media, IT logs, and medical records. Text analytics is a method for extracting usable knowledge from unstructured text data through the identification of core concepts, sentiments, and trends and then using this knowledge to support decision-making. Text analytics results can then be incorporated into models used for predictive analytics. Offerings include SAS Text Miner, Oracle Endeca Information Discovery, IBM text analytics solutions, and Clarabridge. Figure 18.1 shows a screenshot of Oracle Endeca Information Discovery.

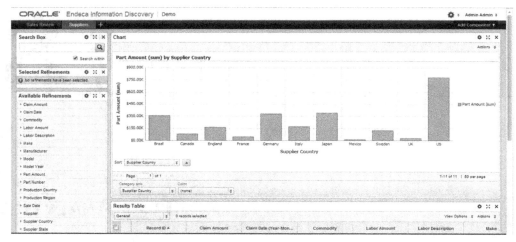

Figure 18.1: Oracle Endeca Information Discovery.

This chapter is devoted to analyzing the data governance issues relating to text analytics at a large hospital system. The details of this example have been disguised.

Big Data Governance to Reduce the Readmission Rate for Patients with Congestive Heart Failure[1]

A hospital system consisting of 15 facilities offered a broad range of services, including emergency care. A significant portion of its patient population was indigent. The hospital implemented a pilot program to leverage big data analytics using IBM SPSS, aimed at reducing the readmission rate of patients with congestive heart failure.

The study had two objectives:

1. *Reduce costs not reimbursed by insurance.*

    The United States Medicare and Medicaid programs were moving to approaches that would reduce or eliminate payments for care of patients who were readmitted for the same disease.

2. *Increase the quality of patient care by proactively implementing early intervention to prevent the progression of disease.*

    Because the hospital system had limited funds for programs such as smoking cessation and home health care, it wanted these programs to be targeted at patients who were more likely to be readmitted within 30 days. For example, if

---

1   Modified from *Big Data Governance*, Sunil Soares (MC Press, 2012).

smoking was a key predictor of patients who were readmitted within 30 days, then the hospital system wanted to target those individuals with smoking cessation programs.

The analytics department built a predictive model based on 150 variables and 20,000 patient encounters over five years. This data was sourced from a variety of applications, including electronic medical records, the admissions system, and the cost accounting database.

The analytics team implemented data governance in a number of different areas. The team adopted manual processes rather than using data governance tools. These processes are discussed in the remaining sections of this chapter.

Leverage Unstructured Data to Improve the Quality of Sparsely Populated Structured Data

The hospital system's analytics team determined that a number of variables were significant predictors of a patient's readmission rate, including smoking status and drug or alcohol abuse.

Smoking status is a significant factor associated with heart disease. Surprisingly, the hospital did not have a complete history of patient smoking status, including years of smoking and frequency. At the outset, only 25 percent of the structured data around smoking status was populated with binary yes/no answers. However, the analytics team was able to increase the population rate for smoking status to 85 percent by using content analytics. The content analytics team was also able to unlock additional information, such as smoking duration and frequency.

There were a number of reasons for this discrepancy. For example, some patients indicated that they were non-smokers, but text analytics revealed the following from the doctors' notes:

- "Patient is restless and asked for a smoking break."
- "Patient quit smoking yesterday."
- "Quit."

The clinical team also knew from experience that drug and alcohol abuse were significant predictors of hospital readmission rates. Only 20 percent of the patients checked off the box at admission to indicate whether they were addicted to drugs and alcohol. However, the analytics team used unstructured data sources to expand the population of the data to 76 percent of the encounters.

Extract Additional Relevant Predictive Variables Not Available in Structured Data

The analytics team discovered clinical factors such as assisted living and pharmacology that were not available in a structured format. By adopting natural-language processing technology, important clinical factors were unlocked and available for clinical and reporting purposes.

For example, the clinical team knew from experience that patients in assisted living facilities were more likely to take their medications than patients who lived alone. However, the hospital system was not capturing this information in a formalized manner. The business intelligence team analyzed the text in discharge summaries, echocardiograms, patient histories, doctors' notes, and physicals to find that 25 percent of the patients were in assisted living facilities. The analysis confirmed that residence in an assisted living facility did indeed reduce the likelihood that a patient would be readmitted within 30 days.

Information on pharmacology compliance was also critical to clinicians and case managers because it indicated the degree to which patients were taking their medications as part of their treatment plans. The business intelligence team analyzed doctors' notes and electronic medical records to populate this data.

Define Consistent Definitions for Key Business Terms

The analytics team had to drive for consistent definitions of key business terms. For example, the term "readmission" had at least three different definitions:

1. *Clinical perspective: 30 days, all causes*
    A patient was readmitted to the hospital whether or not the condition related to congestive heart failure.
2. *Clinical perspective: 30 days, same diagnosis*
    A patient was readmitted to the hospital where the dominant ICD-9 diagnosis code was related to heart failure.
3. *Finance perspective: quarterly and annually*
    Finance had definitions of readmissions that were based on longer periods, including three to 12 months.

Ensure Consistency in Patient Master Data Across Facilities

The information technology department also struggled with the lack of consistent patient data within the hospital system, which was caused by the proliferation of identification numbers for each patient. The hospital personnel were not able to track medical events for the same patient across different facilities. As a workaround, the hospital system instituted a lengthy manual process to reconcile the medical events that related to the same patient. As a result, the team lost significant time in retrieving a patient's medical history when he or she was readmitted to another hospital in the same system within a very short period. This had the potential to adversely affect the medical personnel's decision on treatment plans and clinical outcomes.

Adhere to Privacy Requirements

Adhering to privacy requirements is key to successful data governance in healthcare. The medical research and analytics departments wanted to analyze clinical data to improve patient care and improve outcomes. However, this data constituted protected health information (PHI) governed by United States HIPAA regulations.

In a specific instance, the analytics department wanted to optimize the use of expensive paramedic services. The goal was to identify patients who could use a complimentary pick-up service to the hospital instead of expensive paramedic services. However, the analytics team had to address privacy issues because the patient's address constituted PHI. The hospital adhered to the privacy requirements by obtaining patient approvals before using the address in research.

Manage Reference Data

ICD-9 reference data is a well-defined database with great granularity. For example, ICD-9 assigns code 428 for heart failure. There are different ICD-9 codes that describe details of heart failure conditions, such as 428.1 for left heart failure and 428.2 for systolic heart failure. Medical researchers tried to analyze comorbidity—the presence of one or more diseases or disorders—associated with congestive heart failure using ICD-9 data. Being able to categorize ICD-9 codes into similar diseases helped to manage the results more effectively. The analytics team collaborated with clinicians to categorize over 21,000 ICD-9 codes into 20 disease groups. Based on this exercise, the analytics team was able to minimize the noise in their analysis and yield better clinical insights.

Summary

In this chapter, we reviewed an example relating to the use of text analytics in an advanced analytics project in healthcare. In this context, we discussed the applicability of the core data governance disciplines, including semantics, master data, reference data, data quality, and privacy.

EVALUATION CRITERIA AND THE VENDOR LANDSCAPE

CHAPTER 19

THE EVALUATION CRITERIA FOR DATA GOVERNANCE PLATFORMS

P arts 2, 3, and 4 of this book include evaluation criteria relating to specific categories of data governance tools. For example, the chapter on MDM in Part 2 includes evaluation criteria that are specific to those tools. The chapter on data modeling in Part 3 includes evaluation criteria relating to the integration of those tools with data governance. Finally, Part 4 includes evaluation criteria relating to big data governance. However, there are additional criteria that pertain to the entire data governance platform. This chapter includes a comprehensive set of evaluation criteria for data governance platforms.

The Total Cost of Ownership

Organizations should consider the following cost categories when evaluating data governance tools:

- The software license cost
- The upfront cost to implement the tool
- The ongoing cost to maintain the tool, including the cost of labor and the annual software maintenance expense

- The ongoing cost to use the tool, including time allocation from data stewards and business analysts

Data Stewardship

Data governance tools should support stewardship over data artifacts. This means that administrators should be able to add and delete data stewards. Data stewards should also be able to manage categories, business terms, code lists, code values, data policies, data standards, data quality rules, data quality metrics, data issues, master data rules, and other data artifacts. Figure 19.1 shows the data stewardship interface in Orchestra Networks EBX.

Figure 19.1: The data stewardship interface in Orchestra Networks EBX.

Approval Workflows

Data governance tools should support OOTB and custom workflows for different processes, such as adding a business term, adding a code value, resolving a data issue, updating master data, and adding a business rule. Figure 19.2 shows a Simple Approval Workflow in Collibra Data Governance Center. The workflow has three roles: Start User, Steward, and Stakeholder. These roles perform a number of tasks, as defined by the workflow.

Every Collibra user is assigned a role within the tool. A workflow developer creates this workflow in BPMN format using an open source tool such as Activiti. The administrator then imports this workflow into Collibra and configures it for specific activities such as Add New Business Term, Modify Code Value, and Add Business Rule.

Whenever a new business term is added in Collibra, the relevant users will perform their tasks based on the workflow configuration. For example, if John Smith is the steward for risk terms, he will receive an email to vote for approval for any business terms that are added to that category.

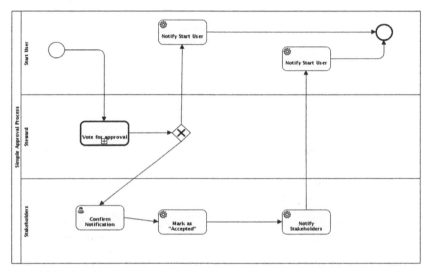

Figure 19.2: The Simple Approval Workflow in Collibra Data Governance Center.

The Hierarchy of Data Artifacts

Data governance tools need to support a hierarchy of data artifacts. In the example in Figure 19.3, a data policy addresses the data quality process for rating attributes at an insurance carrier. A rating attribute is a data attribute that can affect insurance premiums. Examples of rating attributes might include date of birth, gender, smoking status, and city of residence.

A child policy deals specifically with data quality for National Change of Address (NCOA). An associated data rule validates the state against a list of states based on the ISO 3166-2:US standard. The data rule relates to the business term "State." Finally, the business term "State" links to the Address table and to the ISO 3166-2:US code table. The data governance tool should support the management of this hierarchy of data artifacts.

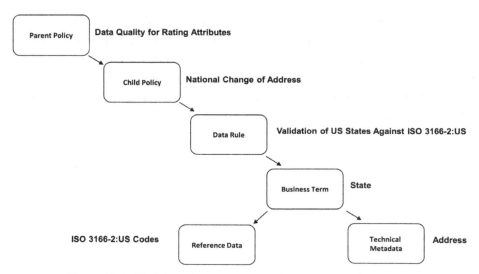

Figure 19.3: The hierarchy of data artifacts at an insurance carrier.

Now, let's implement these data artifact hierarchies in a data governance tool. In Figure 19.4, an insurance carrier has documented a data policy in IBM InfoSphere Business Glossary. In this section, we will use the terms "data policy" and "information governance policy" synonymously. Similarly, we will use the terms "data rule," "business rule," and "information governance rule" synonymously. The data policy states that IT cannot change rating attributes without approval from the underwriting department. In practical terms, even if IT discovers data quality issues with these attributes, it needs to consult the underwriting department before making any changes.

- Rating Attributes drive insurance premiums

- Examples may include Address, Date of Birth and Gender

- Data Policy may state that IT cannot change Rating Attributes without approval from Underwriting

Figure 19.4: IBM InfoSphere Business Glossary contains a data policy relating to data quality for rating attributes.

In Figure 19.5, the insurance carrier has documented an information governance policy relating to NCOA in IBM InfoSphere Business Glossary. The insurance carrier has implemented NCOA software to identify all customers whose addresses have changed. NCOA is a registry of address changes maintained by the United States Postal Service. Organizations use NCOA to maintain their bulk mailing discounts from the Postal Service.

The data policy states that the carrier cannot just change the addresses on policies without further validation from the customer. This is because the customer address is a rating attribute that drives the premium on an insurance policy, especially for homes. For example, a customer whose address changes from Illinois to a coastal area of Florida might see his or her homeowner's premium increase dramatically due to increased risk of loss from hurricane damage.

The data policy includes a list of steps that must be followed as part of the NCOA process:

1. IT strips off addresses from insurance policies and marketing lists on a monthly basis.
2. IT runs these addresses through the NCOA software.
3. IT receives a list of customers whose addresses have changed.

4.   A customer service representative (CSR) calls the customer to verify the address change.

5.   If the customer confirms the address change, the CSR forwards the record to the Underwriting department to deal with premium adjustments.

6.   In cases where the customer might be going through a divorce or separation and might not know his or her future address, the CSR creates a reminder to contact the customer in a few months, when circumstances have firmed up.

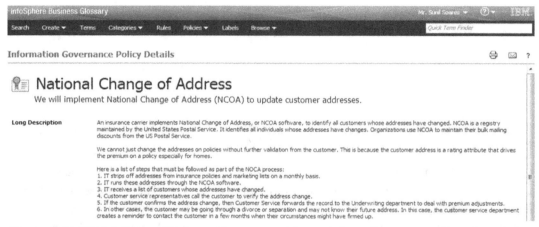

Figure 19.5: IBM InfoSphere Business Glossary contains an information governance policy relating to National Change of Address.

In Figure 19.6, the insurance carrier documents an information governance rule in IBM InfoSphere Business Glossary. The rule states that the U.S. State Code is a two-letter abbreviation for 50 states, the District of Columbia, and six outlying areas of the United States based on the ISO 3166-2:US standard.

Figure 19.6: IBM InfoSphere Business Glossary contains a data validation rule for U.S. State.

In Figure 19.7, the insurance carrier then links the child policy for NCOA with its parent policy for data quality for rating attributes and to the information governance rule relating to data validation for U.S. State.

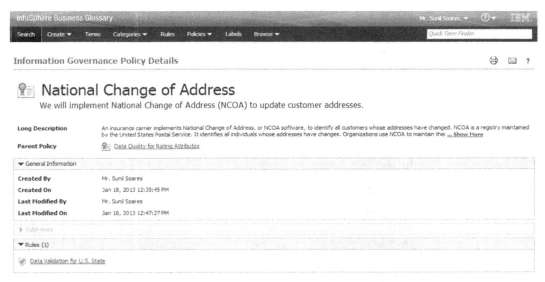

Figure 19.7: The NCOA data policy in IBM InfoSphere Business Glossary.

In Figure 19.8, the insurance carrier then links the "State" business term with the information governance rule relating to the data validation for U.S. State.

Figure 19.8: The "State" business term is linked to the information governance rule for data validation for U.S. State in IBM InfoSphere Business Glossary.

Next, the insurance carrier needs to link the business term to the code table for U.S. State. An extract from the code table for U.S. State is shown in Figure 19.9.

Alabama	AL
Alaska	AK
Arizona	AZ
Arkansas	AR
California	CA
Colorado	CO
Connecticut	CT
Delaware	DE
Florida	FL
Georgia	GA
Hawaii	HI
Idaho	ID
Illinois	IL
Indiana	IN
Iowa	IA
Kansas	KS
Kentucky	KY
Louisiana	LA
Maine	ME
Maryland	MD
Massachussetts	MA
Michigan	MI
Minnesota	MN
Mississippi	MS

Figure 19.9: An extract of the U.S. State code table.

In Figure 19.10, the information governance rule for data validation for U.S. State is implemented by the U.S. State code table in IBM InfoSphere Master Data Management Reference Data Management Hub. This governs the business term called "State" in IBM InfoSphere Business Glossary. At the time of publication of this book, IBM did not provide a direct linkage between IBM InfoSphere Master Data Management Reference Data Management Hub and IBM InfoSphere Business Glossary using the "implemented by" relation. Rather, this linkage is attained by linking the business term in IBM InfoSphere Business Glossary with the URL for the code table in IBM InfoSphere Master Data Management Reference Data Management Hub.

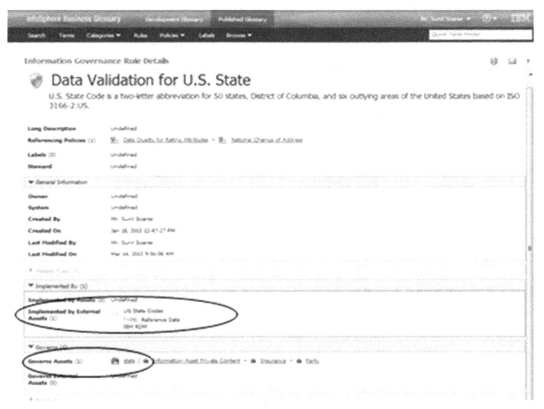

Figure 19.10: The information governance rule for data validation for U.S. State.

Finally, in Figure 19.11, the insurance carrier is able to link all the way back to the Address column in the database based on technical metadata in IBM InfoSphere Metadata Workbench.

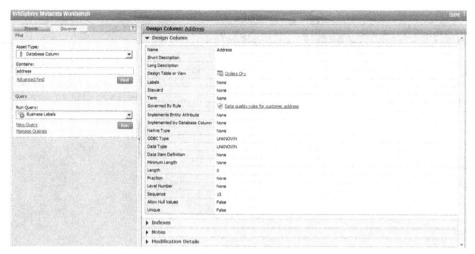

Figure 19.11: IBM InfoSphere Metadata Workbench contains the technical metadata for Address.

Data Governance Metrics

Data governance teams need to establish metrics to monitor the ongoing performance of the program. Data governance tools should provide the following metrics on an overall basis and for different views, including by data steward, data owner, data repository, application, CDE, and data domain:

- *Business glossary*—The number of candidate terms, the number pending approval, and the number approved.
- *Reference data*—The number of candidate code values, the number pending approval, and the number approved.
- *Data issues*—The number of outstanding data issues and the number resolved in the previous period.
- *Data quality scorecard*—The data quality score by application, CDE, or other dimension.
- *Master data*—The number of outstanding tasks, the number of duplicates, and the average number of days for workflow execution.

Figure 19.12 shows a data governance dashboard in Collibra Data Governance Center. The dashboard shows the number of open tasks, new issues, open issues, domains, reference data domains, all assets, approved assets, business terms, code values, applications, processes, data assets, policies and rules, and key performance indicators (KPIs).

Figure 19.12: The dashboard in Collibra Data Governance Center.

In Figure 19.13, Orchestra Networks EBX provides key master data metrics. In the top panel, EBX provides a filter into master data quality metrics relating to Employees. In the bottom panel, EBX provides a view into the trends relating to the cycle time to complete workflows. When this cycle time is combined with participant compensation per hour, we can generate key metrics relating to the human cost associated with key workflows.

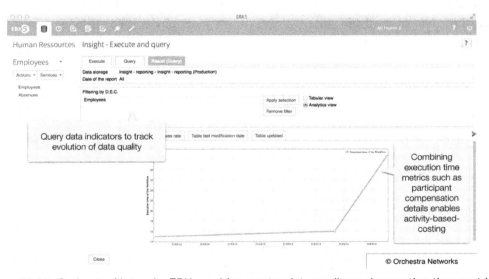

Figure 19.13: Orchestra Networks EBX provides master data quality and execution time metrics.

The Cloud

Organizations are turning to the cloud because of perceived flexibility, faster time-to-deployment, and reduced capital expenditure requirements. A number of vendors offer data governance platforms in the cloud, including the following:

- Data brokers such as Acxiom, Reed Elsevier, Thomson Reuters, and literally thousands of others that specialize by dataset or industry. These companies offer many types of data enrichment and validation services to organizations.
- Collibra Data Governance Center includes Business Glossary, Reference Data Accelerator, and Data Stewardship Manager as a cloud offering with a monthly fee.
- Harte-Hanks Trillium Software TS Quality on Demand provides data validation, cleansing, and enrichment of names, email addresses, and street addresses as a service.
- Informatica Cloud provides data loading, synchronization, profiling, and quality services for Salesforce and other cloud applications.

Summary

In the earlier chapters of the book, we learned about the evaluation criteria for specific data governance categories, such as business glossaries and data profiling. In this chapter, we reviewed the evaluation criteria for data governance platforms that are not covered within individual chapters earlier in the book. These criteria include the total cost of ownership, data stewardship, approval workflows, hierarchy of data artifacts, data governance metrics, and cloud.

20

ASG

ASG has a strong footprint and is a market leader in metadata management. ASG's data governance tools fall into three categories:

- ASG-metaGlossary
- ASG-Rochade
- ASG-becubic

ASG-metaGlossary

ASG-metaGlossary is the company's business glossary, as shown in Figure 20.1.

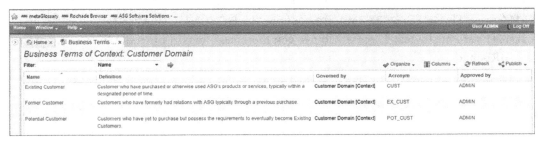

Figure 20.1: ASG-metaGlossary.

ASG-Rochade

ASG-Rochade is a market-leading metadata repository, with a number of scanners and a rich set of reporting capabilities. Figure 20.2 shows a detailed forward lineage report for the CUSTOMERS table in ASG-Rochade.

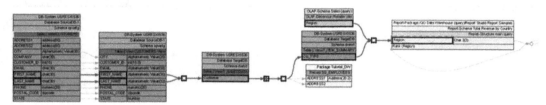

Figure 20.2: A detailed forward lineage report for the CUSTOMERS table in ASG-Rochade.

ASG-becubic

ASG-becubic extends the power of ASG-Rochade by recognizing transformations in custom code and legacy applications. ASG-becubic is an application discovery and understanding solution specifically designed to address the complex issues associated with custom applications. It identifies the primary composition and structure of core applications, their complexity, code redundancies, and duplications.

ASG-becubic identifies problems in the code base, reducing operational risk at runtime and minimizing the downtime for an application. It recognizes over 125 application components, including programming languages, script languages, control languages, monitors, screen generators, middleware, database management systems, and schedulers. These include COBOL, MFS, CICS, JCL, MQSeries, DB2 Stored Procedures, AS/400 RPF, Java, PHP, ASP, ASP.NET, Visual Basic, and Oracle PL/SQL.

Figure 20.3 shows how ASG-becubic is able to discover data within a Visual Basic form. The Visual Basic project CALENDAR.VBP contains the MAIN.FRM and CALENDAR. FRM forms. The CALENDAR.FRM form contains the PICMONTH, LBLMONTH, LBLPREV, and LBLNEXT data attributes. These attributes can then become part of a data lineage report in ASG-Rochade.

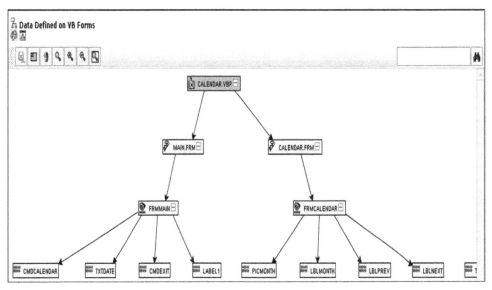

Figure 20.3: ASG-becubic discovers data elements in a Visual Basic form.

CHAPTER **21**

COLLIBRA

C ollibra is a high-growth startup focused exclusively on data governance. Collibra Data Governance Center has a slick user interface that is targeted at business users. The capabilities that Collibra offers, either directly or via integrations with third parties, are discussed in this chapter.

Business Glossary

Collibra Business Glossary offers a highly customizable approach to semantic modeling for business terms, policies, rules, and other data artifacts. It is shown in Figure 21.1.

Figure 21.1: Collibra Business Glossary.

Reference Data Management

As shown in Figure 21.2, Collibra Reference Data Accelerator manages code values, code mappings, and snapshots.

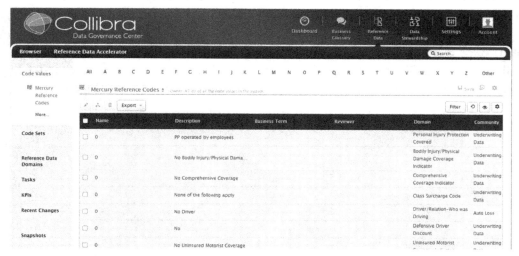

Figure 21.2: Collibra Reference Data Accelerator.

Data Stewardship

As shown in Figure 21.3, Collibra Data Stewardship Manager supports the assignment and management of data issues and tasks.

Figure 21.3: Collibra Data Stewardship Manager.

Workflows

Collibra Data Governance Center ships with OOTB workflows that can be customized using BPMN.

Metadata

As of the publication of this book, Collibra does not ship with a metadata repository. However, the company is developing integrations with key metadata repositories. For example, consider a large financial institution that allows users to author business terms in Collibra. Collibra then invokes the Representational State Transfer (REST) API to move the terms into a third-party metadata repository.

Data Profiling

Collibra does not ship with a data profiling tool. However, Collibra and Harte-Hanks Trillium have developed an integration so that users can run data profiling jobs in Trillium TS Discovery and view the results in Collibra.

CHAPTER 22

GLOBAL IDs

G lobal IDs has established a niche as an "extreme data management" tools vendor that tackles ultra-large implementations. For example, Global IDs has a data profiling program at a large organization that covers 50,000 databases across 2,000 CPUs and 200 servers. Figure 22.1 shows the Global IDs product suite, which includes capabilities for metadata management, data quality, master data management, data governance, and big data.

Objective	Function		Metadata Governance Suite	Master Data Governance Suite	Enterprise Data Governance Suite	Big Data Governance Suite	Deliverables
4 Embed Analytics	Visualize	20				●	Dashboards and Infographics
	Link	19				●	Graph Databases with Linked Data
	Measure	18				●	KPIs and Trend Metrics
	Analyze	17				●	Reporting and Ad-Hoc Analysis
3 Accelerate Integration	Distribute	16			●	●	Data Services for Master Data
	Integrate	15			●	●	Integrated Master Data
	Standardize	14			●	●	Enriched Master Data
	Move	13			●	●	Data Repositories in Relational Databases or Hadoop
2 Improve Quality	Dashboards	12		●	●	●	Master Data Governance Portals
	Stewardship	11		●	●	●	RACI Matrix of Data Stewards
	Validation	10		●	●	●	Data Quality Metrics
	Rules	9		●	●	●	Rules Repository
1 Create Transparency	Monitor	8	●	●	●	●	Change Monitors, Impact Analysis
	Model	7	●	●	●	●	Master Data Models
	Search	6	●	●	●	●	Enterprise Search
	Map	5	●	●	●	●	Business Ontologies
	Classify	4	●	●	●	●	Business Taxonomies
	Profile	3	●	●	●	●	Semantic Metadata Repository
	Ingest	2	●	●	●	●	Inventory of External Data Assets
	Discover	1	●	●	●	●	Comprehensive Data Asset Inventory

Figure 22.1: The Global IDs product suite.

In this chapter, we cover a few of the capabilities of the Global IDs product suite.

Data Profiling

Global IDs can profile a wide variety of data sources in diverse formats, including relational databases, mainframe data, data warehouse appliances, and Hadoop. Figure 22.2 shows the Global IDs Hive Profiler. The Profiler shows the underlying characteristics of the accounts entity, which contains fields including account, stock_code, internal_rating, sector_desc, and market_sector. In the bottom of the screen, we can also view data about the length of the stock_code field.

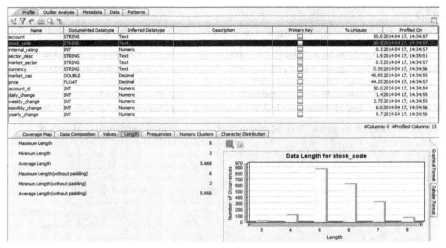

Figure 22.2: The Global IDs Hive Profiler.

Data Quality

Global IDs can also remediate data and produce data quality dashboards. Figure 22.3 shows a data quality scorecard in Global IDs that displays the number of errors by business rule. At the bottom of the screenshot, the Global IDs dashboard has flagged seven data quality errors in the consistency dimension for the MS-SQL@CODD schema relating to the Reference Data Check on USA City business rule.

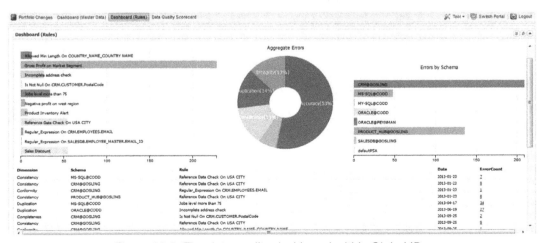

Figure 22.3: The data quality dashboard within Global IDs.

Metadata

Global IDs also has metadata scanners for a wide variety of sources, including relational databases, data warehousing appliances, Hadoop, NoSQL databases, and various ontologies. Figure 22.4 shows the Global IDs Web Ontology Language (OWL) ontology scanner. OWL is a family of knowledge representation languages or ontology languages for authoring ontologies or knowledge bases. OWL has been endorsed by the World Wide Web Consortium and has attracted academic, medical, and commercial interest.[1]

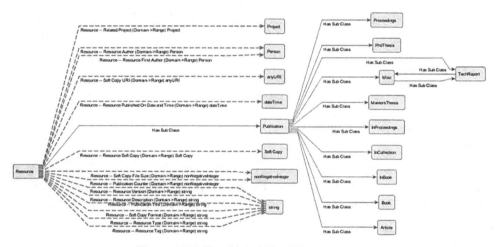

Figure 22.4: The Global IDs OWL scanner.

---

1   http://en.wikipedia.org/wiki/Web_Ontology_Language.

CHAPTER *23*

IBM

I BM has a robust, end-to-end Information Integration and Governance platform, as shown in Figure 23.1. We discuss each component of this platform in this chapter.

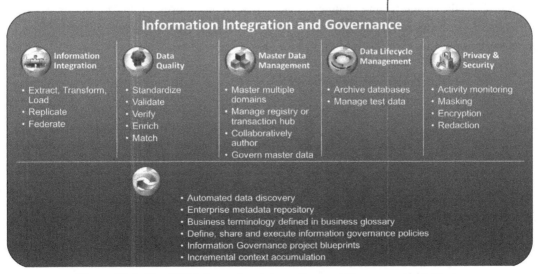

Figure 23.1: The IBM Information Integration and Governance platform.

Metadata

IBM InfoSphere Business Glossary supports a business-driven user interface to govern information policies, rules, and terms. These data artifacts can be linked to technical metadata within IBM InfoSphere Metadata Workbench. IBM InfoSphere Blueprint Director allows IT departments to manage end-to-end blueprints for information projects like data integration, data archiving, test data management, application retirement, and business intelligence. These blueprints serve to align business requirements with the technical implementation and can be linked to data artifacts like terms in IBM InfoSphere Business Glossary.

Information Integration

IBM InfoSphere DataStage is a data integration tool. IBM InfoSphere Data Replication supports data replication, including change data capture. IBM InfoSphere Federation Server supports data virtualization.

Data Quality

IBM InfoSphere Information Analyzer supports data profiling, including the analysis of data at the column, key, source, and cross-domain levels. IBM InfoSphere QualityStage supports data standardization, validation, verification, enrichment, and matching. Figure 23.2 shows a customer data governance dashboard based on IBM Cognos, IBM InfoSphere Information Analyzer, and IBM InfoSphere Business Glossary. The top left corner shows business rules, including the following:

- Emails validated in the previous 30 days
- Null emails
- Null first name
- Null middle name
- Null telephone
- Valid NAICS code
- Valid SIC code

The bottom left corner shows the results of the periodic checks of the Valid_NAICS_ Code business rule. As we can see, the number of failing records has fallen from 28 percent to 10 percent. The pie chart in the top right corner shows the results of the first run of the Valid_NAICS_Code business rule. The table in the bottom right corner shows further details of each run.

From a technical perspective, here are the steps for developing the data quality scorecard:

1. Define business rules in plain English in IBM InfoSphere Business Glossary.
2. Develop data rules in IBM InfoSphere Information Analyzer.
3. Schedule the data profiling job using the built-in scheduler in IBM InfoSphere Information Analyzer.
4. Run the data profiling jobs in IBM InfoSphere Information Analyzer.
5. Store the results in the IBM InfoSphere Information Analyzer Database, which is based on DB2.
6. Expose the results in IBM Cognos using the REST API.

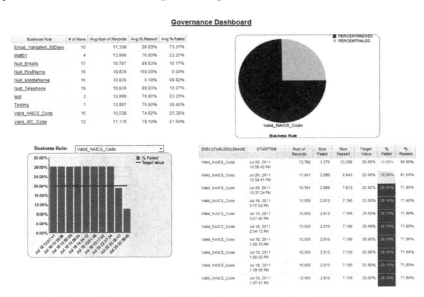

Figure 23.2: This data quality scorecard is based on IBM Cognos, IBM InfoSphere Information Analyzer, and IBM InfoSphere Business Glossary.

Master Data Management

IBM InfoSphere Master Data Management supports multi-domain MDM, including customer, vendor, location, and product, with both transactional and registry styles.

Data Lifecycle Management

IBM InfoSphere Optim Test Data Management supports the creation of right-sized test data sets. IBM InfoSphere Optim Data Growth Solution supports the archiving of data to lower the cost of storage. As shown in Figure 23.3, IBM InfoSphere Optim Test Data Management traverses through the data model to create a subset of data for testing purposes:

1. Extract rows from DB2.PRD.OPTIM_SALES based on selection criteria or statistical controls.
2. Extract rows from DB2.PRD.OPTIM_CUSTOMERS, which are children of rows previously extracted from DB2.PRD.OPTIM_SALES using a DB2 physical constraint called RSC, defined by a database administrator.
3. Extract rows from DB2.PRD.OPTIM_ORDERS, which are children of rows previously extracted from DB2.PRD.OPTIM_CUSTOMERS using a DB2 physical constraint called RCO, defined by a database administrator.

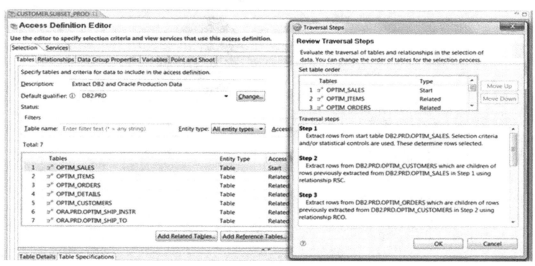

Figure 23.3: IBM InfoSphere Optim Test Data Management.

Privacy and Security

IBM InfoSphere Guardium supports database activity monitoring. IBM InfoSphere Optim Data Privacy Solution supports the masking of non-production data.

CHAPTER 24

INFORMATICA

I nformatica has built a formidable installed base around its PowerCenter data integration platform. With the release of Informatica 9.6, the company has doubled down on a Hadoop migration strategy for the legions of PowerCenter developers in the marketplace. As a result, developers can develop in the PowerCenter environment and then deploy their data integration jobs to Hadoop without having to learn the intricacies of MapReduce, Pig, and Hive. With the release of Informatica 9.6, the company has also made a strong statement of support for data governance, which will be the focus of this chapter.

Data Profiling and Data Quality

Informatica HParser is a data transformation tool optimized for Hadoop. It supports parsing of several unstructured and semi-structured formats, including JSON, XML, EDI, FIX, SWIFT, NACHA, SEPA, ACORD, ASN.1 HL7, and HIPAA.

Informatica Data Quality (IDQ) supports data profiling, data matching, and global address cleansing. These discovery capabilities can also be used by Informatica Data Masking products to discover hidden sensitive data and by Informatica Data Archive to archive complete business objects. Figure 24.1 shows how Informatica PowerCenter Big Data Edition supports data profiling, ETL, and complex data parsing on Hadoop.

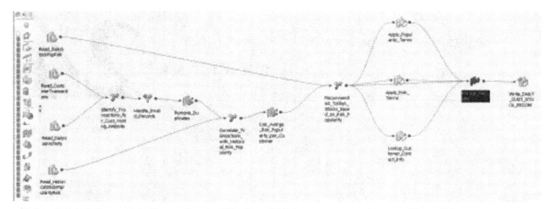

Figure 24.1: Informatica PowerCenter Big Data Edition supports data profiling, ETL, and complex data parsing on Hadoop.

Figure 24.2 shows the WebLogs Logical Data Object in Informatica PowerCenter Big Data Edition. Informatica supports the profiling of this data within an Apache Hive environment.

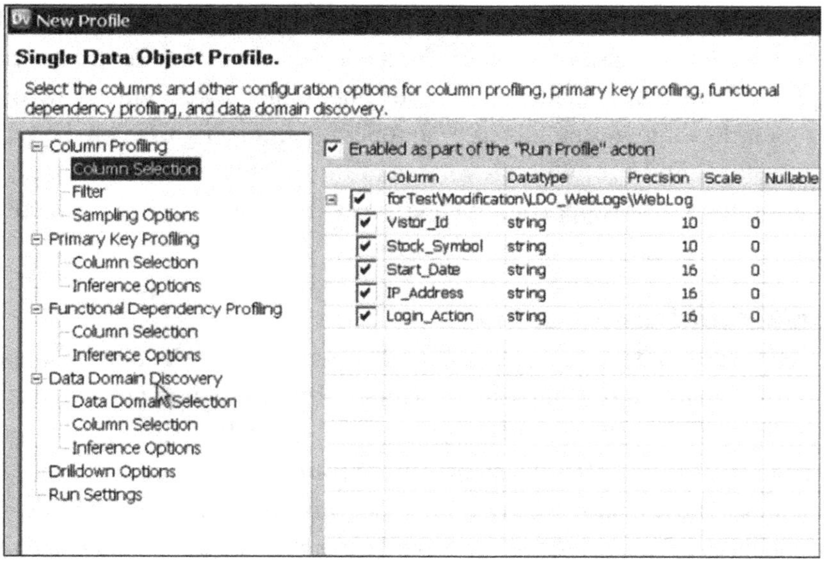

Figure 24.2: Informatica PowerCenter Big Data Edition supports the profiling of the WebLogs Logical Data Object in Apache Hive.

By switching to the Monitoring Console of Informatica PowerCenter Big Data Edition, we can view additional details relating to the Profile_WebLog data profiling job, as shown in Figure 24.3. The job contains the Profile_WebLog_2 mapping, which contains the exec7 Hive script, which in turn contains two Hive queries.

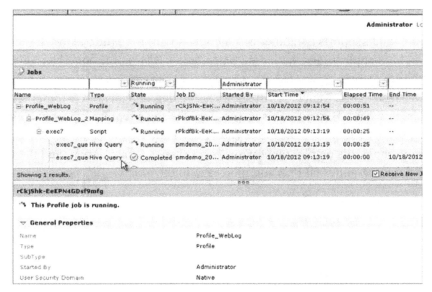

Figure 24.3: The Monitoring Console of Informatica PowerCenter Big Data Edition shows additional details about the profiling job.

Metadata and Business Glossary
Informatica Data Quality, Data Governance Edition includes strong metadata and business glossary capabilities, including a Facebook-style user interface.

Master Data Management
Informatica Master Data Management manages multi-domain implementations, including integration with social media data.

Information Lifecycle Management
Informatica has developed a robust ILM platform for policy-based archiving and test data management. Informatica Data Archive enables organizations to move big data to less expensive storage for later retrieval. Informatica Data Subset enables IT departments to create realistic subsets of data for testing.

Security and Privacy

Informatica Dynamic Data Masking masks sensitive data within production or near-production environments. Informatica Persistent Data Masking masks sensitive data within non-production environments such as testing.

Cloud

Informatica Cloud supports a number of functions to improve the trustworthiness of data within cloud applications, including Salesforce CRM, Force.com, NetSuite, SAP, Oracle CRM On Demand, Oracle EBS, Concur, and Eloqua. As shown in Figure 24.4, Informatica Master Data Management shows a 360 degree view of customer relationships within Salesforce.com. Based on this integration, the sales representative can view an exhaustive profile of John Q. Jones. She can view his transactions, his relationship with the Jones household, his employment with John Q Jones Construction, and the fact that he has purchased a traditional IRA and mortgage in the past.

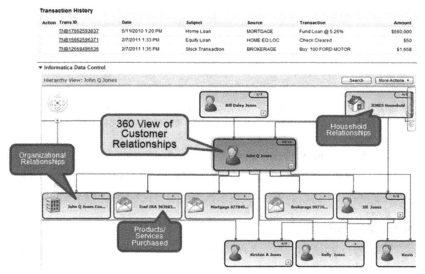

Figure 24.4: Informatica Master Data Management shows a 360 degree view of customer relationships within Salesforce.com.

CHAPTER 25

ORCHESTRA NETWORKS

Orchestra Networks is a fast-growing company with European roots but a growing U.S. presence. The company's EBX platform has a number of loyal customers across multiple industries, including financial services, insurance, retail, oil and gas, and manufacturing. Orchestra Networks EBX includes a number of products that we review in this chapter.

Workflows

In Figure 25.1, the EBX platform supports a workflow that includes a task relating to suspicious records within the Third Parties domain. These suspicious records may be flagged from a fraud or anti-money laundering perspective. The task includes logistical data about the task assignee, when the task was assigned, and the current status.

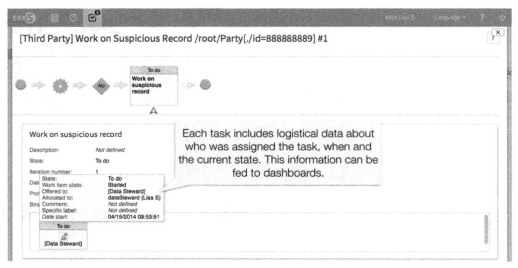

Figure 25.1: The workflow in Orchestra Networks EBX includes task relating to a suspicious record.

Data Modeling

EBX is a model-driven platform for multi-domain MDM and reference data management. A key component of the platform is a data modeling environment. As shown in Figure 25.2, EBX supports a data model for the Third Parties entity. The entity includes a number of attributes, including Identifier, Company Name, and Country.

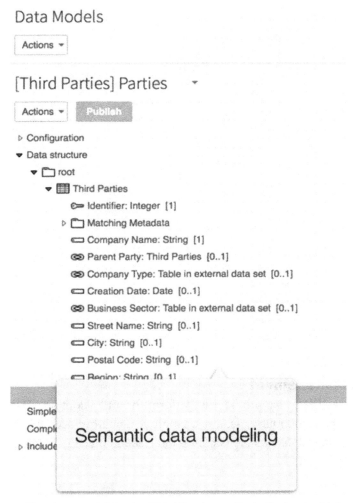

Figure 25.2: The data model for the Third Parties entity in Orchestra Networks EBX.

As shown in Figure 25.3, the Country attribute in the data model links to the reference data for country, specifically the ISO 3166-1 and ISO 3166-2 code sets. The ISO 3166-1 code set includes the names of countries, while ISO 3166-2 includes the names of the states and provinces for each country.

Figure 25.3: The Country attribute in the data model links to reference data in Orchestra Networks EBX.

Master Data Management

Orchestra Networks EBX also provides a platform for multi-domain MDM, including customer, vendor, product, materials, asset, employee, chart of accounts, and cost center. Figure 25.4 shows the EBX data stewardship interface to manage potential duplicates for the Third Parties domain.

	Creation Date	Business Sector	Street Name	City	Postal Code	Region	Country	State
	10/11/2006	Public Administration - 92	Bessingby Road	Bridlington	YO16 4QU	Yorkshire	United Kingdom	Unmatched
	04/27/2003	Transportation and Warehou...	breite strasse	Wernigerode	38855	Saxony-Anhalt	Germany	Golden
	10/01/1986	Transportation and Warehou...	rue oehmichen	Montbéliard	25200	Franche-Comté	France	Golden
	08/17/1992	Administrative and Support ...	Broadway	Gary, Indiana		Indiana	United States	Golden
	06/03/1974	Transportation and Warehou...	Laggan road	Newtonmore	PH20	Inverness-shire	United Kingdom	Golden
	05/14/2001	Construction - 23	Calle caba	Albacete	02001	Castilla - La Mancha	Spain	Golden
	02/09/1960	Manufacturing - 31	Oude Veldstraat	Lochristi	9080	Oost-Vlaanderen	Belgium	Golden

Figure 25.4: The data stewardship interface in Orchestra Networks EBX.

Reference Data Management

EBX also supports reference data management, including code lists, cross-domain mapping, and snapshots. We have covered the EBX solution in the chapter on reference data. The key differentiator is that the EBX platform provides integration from the data model to the business term to the reference data and the master data.

Business Glossary

In Figure 25.5, the data steward is viewing the details for the 50084 LOP Corp Plan in the Cost Centers hierarchy. The data steward can see that this cost center has a value of Communications relative to the Function attribute. The data steward can dynamically look up the definition of Function from the EBX Business Glossary.

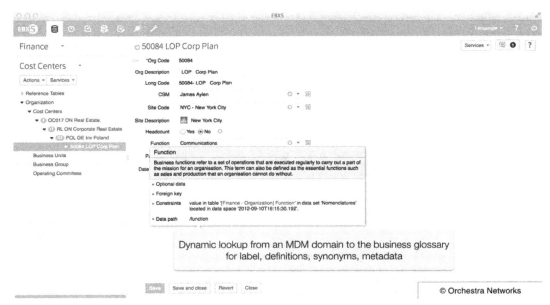

Figure 25.5: Orchestra Networks EBX provides for dynamic lookup from an MDM domain to the business glossary.

SAP

A s shown in Figure 26.1, SAP Solutions for Enterprise Information Management consist of a number of components that we discuss in this chapter.

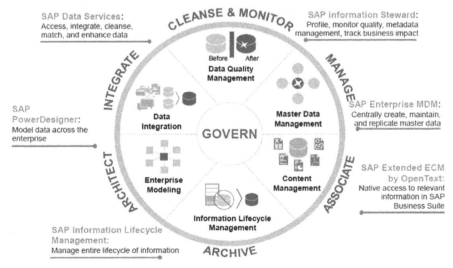

Figure 26.1: SAP Solutions for Enterprise Information Management.

An In-Memory Database

HANA is an in-memory database that is seeing widespread customer interest within the company's large ERP installed base. SAP has positioned HANA as the centerpiece of the company's big data platform.

Data Quality and Metadata Management

As shown in Figure 26.2, SAP Information Steward contains a number of modules:

- Data Insight
- Metadata Management
- Metapedia
- Cleansing Package
- My Worklist

These modules address all aspects of data governance, including data profiling, data quality, business rules, data issue management, business glossary, and metadata management. SAP Information Steward can also push data profiling operations down to HANA for improved performance. SAP Information Steward also collects metadata from HANA, which can be included in an overall data lineage and impact analysis.

Figure 26.2: SAP Information Steward.

Master Data Management

SAP NetWeaver Master Data Management supports a single view of key domains such as customer, materials, and vendor. SAP Master Data Governance enforces MDM policies in the context of business processes. For example, a business user might enter a vendor data change request in an SAP application. The request is then routed through a workflow to a procurement user, who adds payment terms, and then to a finance user, who adds accounting codes to the master data object. The request is then routed to a data steward, who verifies adherence to data management standards, as well as to other users who approve the request.

Content Management

SAP offers an extended set of enterprise content management capabilities for document access and presentment, invoice management, and records management with OpenText.

Information Lifecycle Management

SAP NetWeaver Information Lifecycle Management helps organizations archive data and set retention policies for different types of data, according to business needs and regulatory requirements.

Enterprise Modeling

SAP PowerDesigner supports a role-based user interface for the development of conceptual, logical, physical, requirements, enterprise architecture, business process, XML, and data movement models. SAP PowerDesigner also supports the development of HANA models and the bidirectional sharing of data models with SAP Information Steward.

Data Integration

SAP Data Services provides data connectivity to a long list of data formats and legacy file systems, including relational databases, HANA, Hadoop, SAP Business Suite, COBOL, and ADABAS.

CHAPTER 27

TALEND

Talend has built up a sizeable installed base of customers who like its cost-effective tooling. The Talend Unified Platform consists of two editions: Talend Open Studio, which is open source, and Talend Enterprise, which is subscription-based. Additional platforms provide further enterprise capabilities:

- The data management platform combines data quality and data integration.
- The data services platform adds an enterprise service bus.
- The MDM platform provides a single version of the truth for key master data entities.

As shown in Figure 27.1, the Talend Unified Platform consists of a number of components, discussed in this chapter.

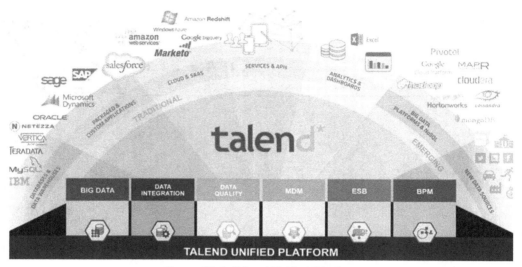

Figure 27.1: Talend Unified Platform

The Extended Ecosystem

The Talend Unified Platform has extended support for a large ecosystem:

- *Databases and data warehouses*—IBM DB2, MySQL, Teradata, HP Vertica, Netezza, and Oracle
- *Packaged applications*—Oracle, SAP, Microsoft Dynamics, Salesforce, and Sage
- *Cloud and Software-as-a-Service*—Amazon Web Services, Marketo, Windows Azure, Amazon Redshift, and Google BigQuery
- Analytics and dashboards
- *Big data platforms and NoSQL*—Pivotal, Google Cloud Platform, MapR, Hadoop, Cloudera, Hortonworks, Cassandra, and MongoDB
- *New data sources*—Facebook, Twitter, telematics, and sensor data

Big Data

Talend provides an easy-to-use graphical environment that allows developers to visually map big data sources and targets without the need to learn and write complicated code. Once a big data connection is configured, the underlying code is automatically generated and can be deployed remotely as a job that runs natively on a HDFS, Pig, HCatalog, HBase, Sqoop, or Hive cluster.

Data Integration

Talend provides the following tools:

- A business modeler, a visual tool for designing business logic for an application
- A job designer, a visual tool for functional diagramming, delineating data development and flow sequencing using components and connectors
- A metadata manager, for storing and managing all project metadata, including contextual data such as database connection details and file paths

Data Quality

Talend Data Quality includes capabilities for data profiling, data standardization, data enrichment, postal validation, data matching, and survivorship for a variety of data sources, including Hadoop.

Master Data Management

Talend MDM supports a single version of the truth across multiple domains, including customer and product. Talend MDM provides a hierarchy browser that lets stewards navigate master data through a hierarchical view. The steward can reassign a record to other nodes in the hierarchy by a simple drag and drop. In In Figure 27.2, the customer data steward is viewing the SHOWBIZ PIZZA PLACE account, which is part of the U.S., in the Midwest region. The data steward can drag and drop the account into the East region, if appropriate.

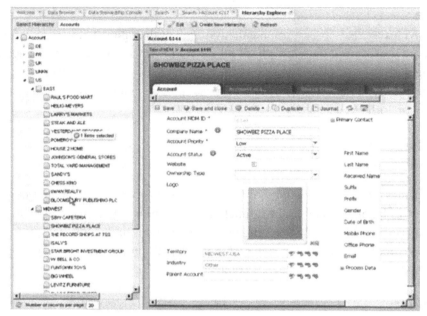

Figure 27.2: Talend MDM allows stewards to navigate customer hierarchies.

Enterprise Service Bus (ESB)

Talend ESB products provide an Eclipse-based tooling environment with messaging, web services, data services, intelligent routing, and data transformation. Talend enables developers to easily build reliable, scalable, and secure REST, web, and data services to integrate heterogeneous IT environments, both on-premise and in the cloud.

Business Process Management (BPM)

Talend BPM includes three solutions: a process modeler, a BPM and workflow engine, and a user interface for the creation of forms.

CHAPTER 28

NOTABLE VENDORS

There are far too many data governance software vendors to be covered exhaustively in this book. In this chapter, we cover a few more vendors with noteworthy offerings.

Adaptive

Adaptive offers the following data governance capabilities:

- *Business glossary*—Adaptive Business Glossary Manager offers a business-oriented user interface to manage data artifacts.
- *Metadata*—Adaptive Metadata Manager supports data lineage and impact analysis.

BackOffice Associates

BackOffice Associates is a company that is almost exclusively focused on data quality and data migration for the SAP platform. The company originally started with a services focus, but has since released products that accelerate data quality and data migration.

Data Advantage Group

Data Advantage Group is a company that focuses exclusively on metadata. Data Advantage Group MetaCenter offers the following capabilities:

- *Business glossary*—MetaCenter ships with a business glossary.
- *Metadata*—MetaCenter has strong ActiveLinx scanner capabilities for metadata integration with many data repositories, including data modeling tools, relational databases, COBOL, ETL, reporting tools, and Hadoop.
- *Reference data*—MetaCenter supports the creation and maintenance of reference data.
- *Workflows*—The latest version of MetaCenter includes support for workflows to manage business terms and reference data.

Diaku

Diaku is a European company focused on data governance, with a specialization in regulatory compliance for financial services. Diaku Axon has integrated capabilities for business semantics, stakeholder analysis, data quality, process mapping, and data lineage. Figure 28.1 shows the business glossary functionality in Diaku Axon.

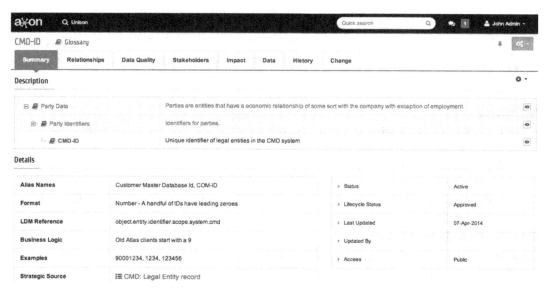

Figure 28.1: The business glossary functionality in Diaku Axon.

Embarcadero Technologies

Embarcadero has a strong footprint in the data modeling community with ER/Studio and its recent acquisition of ERwin from CA. The company recently announced CONNECT, which provides a business glossary with a "Facebook-style" user interface, social enterprise collaboration, and integration with data models.

Global Data Excellence

Global Data Excellence is a European software vendor with a unique approach to data governance. Its Data Excellence Management System connects the dots from business terms and data quality to the business drivers and financial benefits of data governance. Figure 28.2 shows the business glossary functionality within the Data Excellence Management System.

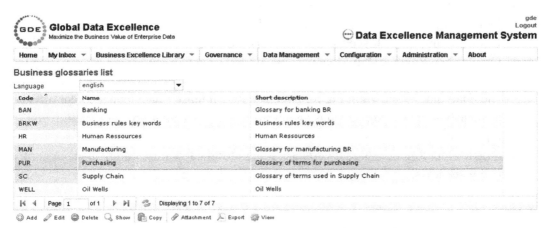

Figure 28.2: The Data Excellence Management System from Global Data Excellence.

Harte-Hanks Trillium

Trillium has a strong heritage in data quality. The company offers the following capabilities, either directly or through third-party integrations:

- *Business glossary and reference data*—Trillium offers these capabilities through integration with Collibra Data Governance Center.
- *Data discovery and profiling*—TS Discovery supports manual and automated data profiling and discovery.
- *Data quality*—TS Quality offers data cleansing and standardization, address verification and correction, and de-duplication.

Oracle

Oracle has a number of capabilities around data governance:

- Oracle Enterprise Data Quality products support profiling, audit and dashboards, data standardization, match and merge, case management, and address verification.
- Oracle Customer Hub provides a single view of the customer.
- Oracle Product Hub provides a single view of the product.
- Oracle Site Hub provides a single view of internal and external sites relating to customers, competitors, and suppliers.
- Oracle Supplier Hub provides a single view of the supplier.
- Oracle Higher Education Constituent Hub provides a single view of students, faculty, alumni, employees, and other constituents.
- Oracle Data Relationship Management supports a single view of chart of accounts, cost centers, profit centers, and legal entities to ensure consistent financial reporting and analytics, as shown in Figure 28.3. Analytical master data management offers a consistent view of dimensions and performance measures, so that departmental reports are consistent with enterprise views.
- Oracle Data Relationship Governance integrates data quality, policy management, and workflows.

SAS

SAS has a very loyal customer base and strong market share in the analytics space. SAS has now fully folded its DataFlux division back into the mother ship. Following this reorganization, SAS has also consolidated its enterprise data management tooling under the SAS Data Management platform. SAS Data Management provides consolidated capabilities for data integration, data profiling, data quality, data monitoring, business glossary, metadata, master data management, reference data management, and entity resolution.

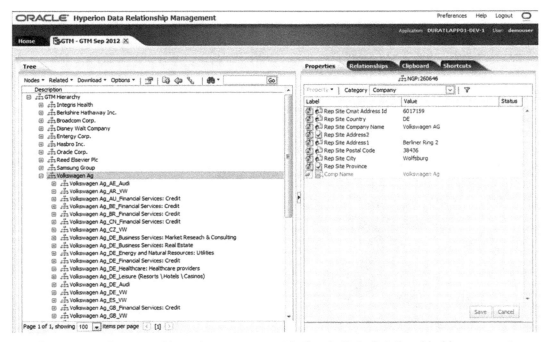

Figure 28.3: Customer hierarchy management in Oracle Data Relationship Management.

LIST OF ACRONYMS

ACORD	Association for Cooperative Operations Research and Development
API	Application Programming Interface
ASN.1	Abstract Syntax Notation One
BPM	Business Process Management
CDE	Critical Data Element
CEP	Complex Event Processing
CPT	Current Procedural Terminology
CSV	Comma-Separated Values
EC2	Amazon Elastic Compute Cloud
EDI	Electronic Data Interchange
EDM	Enterprise Data Management
ELT	Extract, Load, and Transform
EMR	Amazon Elastic MapReduce
ESB	Enterprise Service Bus
ETL	Extract, Transform, and Load
FIX	Financial Information eXchange
HDFS	Hadoop Distributed File System
HIPAA	Health Insurance Portability and Accountability Act
HL7	Health Level 7

HTTP	Hypertext Transfer Protocol
Hue	Hadoop User Experience
ICD-9	International Classification of Diseases—Ninth Revision
ICD-10	International Classification of Diseases—Tenth Revision
ILM	Information Lifecycle Management
JSON	JavaScript Object Notation
JSP	Java Server Page
KPI	Key Performance Indicator
LDO	Logical Data Object
MDM	Master Data Management
NACE	Nomenclature statistique des Activités économiques dans la Communauté Européenne (Statistical Classification of Economic Activities in the European Community)
NAICS	North American Industry Classification System
NCOA	National Change of Address
NoSQL	Not Only SQL
OOTB	Out-of-the-Box
OWL	Web Ontology Language
PIA	Privacy Impact Assessment
PII	Personally Identifiable Information
PUC	Public Utility Commission
RDBMS	Relational Database Management System
REST	Representational State Transfer
SEPA	Single Euro Payments Area
SIC	Standard Industry Classification
SQL	Structured Query Language
SWIFT	Society for Worldwide Interbank Financial Telecommunication
TCP	Transmission Control Protocol
VAT	Value Added Tax
XML	Extensible Markup Language

GLOSSARY

Accuracy

A data quality dimension relating to the degree to which data elements are accurate.

Apache Software Foundation ("Apache")

A not-for-profit organization devoted to supporting the open source Apache software community.

Application Programming Interface (API)

A representation of how computer applications will interface with each other.

Archiving

The process of moving structured and unstructured information to another location for safekeeping or cost reduction. The archive might be in paper or electronic format.

Artifact

Any data object, such as a conceptual data model, a logical data model, a physical data model, an entity, an attribute, a table, a column, a code table, a code value, or a business term.

Attribute

A property of a data entity. In relational database management systems, an entity may be represented by one or more tables, while an attribute may be represented by one or more columns.

Big data

Types of data that are generally referred to in the context of the three *V*s:

Volume (data at rest)—Big data is generally large. Enterprises are awash with data, easily amassing terabytes and even petabytes of information.

Velocity (data in motion)—Often time-sensitive, big data must be used as it is streaming into the enterprise, in order to maximize its value to the business.

Variety (data in many formats)—Big data includes structured data, as well as unstructured data such as text, audio, video, clickstreams, and log files.

Big data governance

Part of a broader data governance program that formulates policy relating to the optimization, privacy, and monetization of big data by aligning the objectives of multiple functions.

Bulk data movement

Includes technologies such as Extract, Transform, and Load (ETL) to extract data from one or more data sources, transform the data, and load it into a target database.

Business glossary

A repository with definitions of key terms that brings together common definitions across business and IT. A business glossary is often distinguished from a data dictionary, which contains the descriptions of key columns and tables.

Business metadata

The definition of business terms along with the relations between these terms, the associated business rules, and reference data.

Business Process Management (BPM)

The discipline that deals with the management of an organization's business processes, such as customer onboarding, procure to pay, and order to cash.

Business rule

A constraint in terms of how an organization goes about its business. For example, a social services agency might have a business rule that minors should have guardians.

Cardinality

The number of unique values in a column.

Change Data Capture (CDC)

A data integration technique that reads the database transaction logs to propagate to the target system only the changes that have been made to the database.

Code list

See *code table*.

Code table

A table containing lookup values for reference data. For example, "U.S. State" is a code table containing the list of acceptable values for states within the United States.

Code value

An individual value in a code table. For example, "NJ" is a code value in the code table U.S. States.

Comma-Separated Values (CSV)

A list of values in tabular format, separated by commas.

Completeness

A data quality dimension relating to the degree to which data elements are populated.

Complex Event Processing (CEP)

See *stream computing*.

Conceptual data model

A data model that describes the semantics of a domain. This model is used to communicate core data concepts, rules, and definitions to a business user as part of an overall application development or enterprise initiative. The number of objects should be very small and focused on key concepts.[1]

---

1   Hoberman, Steve, Donna Burbank, and Chris Bradley. *Data Modeling for the Business*. Technics Publications, LLC, 2009.

Conformity

A data quality dimension relating to the degree to which data elements correspond to expected formats, valid values, or ranges of values.

Consistency

A data quality dimension relating to the degree of relational integrity between data elements and other data elements.

Critical data element

An attribute that has a significant impact on regulatory reporting, operational performance, and business intelligence.

Current Procedural Terminology (CPT)

A uniform set of codes copyrighted by the American Medical Association to describe medical, surgical, and diagnostic services for physicians, patients, accreditation organizations, and healthcare payers for administrative, financial, and analytical purposes. CPT coding is similar to ICD-9 and ICD-10 coding, except that it identifies the services rendered rather than the diagnosis on the claim.

Data broker

A company that offers data enrichment and validation services to organizations.

Data federation

According to *Information Management* magazine, data federation is the method of linking data from two or more physically different locations and making the access/linkage appear transparent, as if the data were co-located. This approach is in contrast to the data warehouse method of housing data in one place and accessing data from that single location. Also referred to as "data virtualization."

Data dictionary

See *business glossary*.

Data discovery

See *data profiling*.

Data domain

A specific category of information, such as customer, product, materials, vendor, or chart of accounts.

Data governance

The formulation of policy to optimize, secure, and leverage information as an enterprise asset by aligning the objectives of multiple functions.

Data governance council

A body consisting of senior business and IT representatives that sets policy regarding information, and acts as the ultimate tiebreaker if lower-level bodies cannot make decisions.

Data governance lead

The operational leader who leads the data governance program on a day-to-day basis.

Data lineage

The audit trail for data movement through integration processes. The result of a data lineage process is the answer to basic questions such as "where did this data come from?", "where does this data go?", and "what happened to it along the way?"

Data masking

The process of systematically transforming confidential data elements such as trade secrets and PII into realistic, but fictionalized, values.

Data model

A wayfinding tool for both business and IT professionals, which uses a set of symbols and text to precisely explain a subset of real information to improve communication within the organization and thereby lead to a more flexible and stable application environment.[2] According to ANSI, there are three types of data models: conceptual, logical, and physical.

Data profiling

The process of understanding the data in a system, where it is located, and how it relates to other systems. This process includes developing a statistical analysis of the data such as data type, null percentages, and uniqueness. Also known as "data discovery."

---

2   Hoberman, Steve. *Data Modeling Made Simple, 2nd Edition.* Technics Publications, LLC, 2009.

Data quality dimension

A recognized term used by data management professionals to describe a characteristic, attribute, or facet of data that can be measured or assessed against defined standards in order to determine the quality of data.[3]

Data quality management

A discipline that includes methods to measure and improve the quality and integrity of an organization's data. While data profiling uncovers issues with the data, data quality actually remediates those issues.

Data steward

A person who ideally reports into the business and, by virtue of his or her deep subject matter expertise, is responsible for improving the trustworthiness and safeguarding the privacy of data as an enterprise asset.

Data tokenization

The process of substituting a sensitive data element with a non-sensitive equivalent, referred to as a "token," that has no extrinsic or exploitable meaning or value. The token is a reference that maps back to the sensitive data through a tokenization system. The mapping from original data to a token uses methods that render tokens infeasible to reverse in the absence of the tokenization system, for example using tokens created from random numbers.[4]

Data virtualization

See *data federation*.

Database monitoring

A form of security technology that monitors the activities of the database, but operates independently of the database itself. Database monitoring technologies typically have a limited impact on the performance of the database system because they do not monitor database logs.

---

3   "The Six Primary Dimensions for Data Quality Assessment." *DAMA UK*, October 2013.

4   http://en.wikipedia.org/wiki/Tokenization_(data_security).

Dodd-Frank

The Dodd-Frank Wall Street Reform and Consumer Protection Act is United States legislation that has wide-reaching consequences for the nation's financial services industry.

Encryption

The process of rendering sensitive data unreadable so that an attacker cannot gain unauthorized access to it.

Enterprise Data Management (EDM)

Enterprise Data Management refers to the ability of an organization to precisely define, easily integrate, and effectively retrieve data for both internal applications and external communication.[5] It includes a number of disciplines, including database management, data integration, metadata management, MDM, reference data management, analytics, reporting, and big data.

Entity

The grouping of objects with similar characteristics, such as customer, employee, asset, and vendor.

Exact match

A matching algorithm that requires two strings to be exactly the same.

Extensible Markup Language (XML)

A markup language that defines a set of rules for encoding documents in a format that is both human-readable and machine-readable.[6]

Extract, Load, and Transform (ELT)

A process used in data warehousing to extract data from one or more data sources, load the data into a target database, and transform the data in the target database.

Extract, Transform, and Load (ETL)

A process used in data warehousing to extract data from one or more data sources, transform the data, and load the data into a target database. ELT conducts

---

5   http://en.wikipedia.org/wiki/Enterprise_data_management.

6   http://en.wikipedia.org/wiki/XML.

transformations in the target database, while ETL conducts these transformations in an intermediate environment before loading into the target database.

Flume

Apache Flume is a service to collect, aggregate, and move large volumes of streaming event data into HDFS.

Gigabyte

One billion (10^9) bytes.

Golden record

A record that is created by merging multiple records in a master data management system.

Governance, Risk, and Compliance (GRC)

An overall term to describe processes related to corporate governance, risk management, and compliance with regulations.

Hadoop

Open source software to enable the distributed processing of large data sets across clusters of computers using a simple programming model.

Hadoop Distributed File System (HDFS)

A distributed file system designed to be highly fault tolerant and to run on low-cost hardware. HDFS provides high throughput access to data and is suitable for applications that have large data sets.

Hadoop User Experience (Hue)

Apache Hue is a web user interface for Hadoop.

HBase

Apache HBase is a column-oriented database that sits on top of HDFS. It is designed to store large tables, with billions of rows and millions of columns. HBase is not a relational database and does not support Structured Query Language (SQL).

HCatalog

HCatalog is a table and storage management layer for Hadoop that enables users with different data processing tools (such as Pig or MapReduce) to more easily read and write data on the grid.[7]

Hive

Apache Hive is a data warehousing infrastructure that sits on top of Hadoop. Hive provides a SQL-like interface called HiveQL to query large volumes of data in Hadoop. Because Hive insulates users from having to learn the intricacies of MapReduce programming in Java, it is a great transition for relational database programmers who are looking to work with Hadoop.

Impact analysis

The ability to understand how a change to one data artifact affects other data artifacts.

Impala

Cloudera Impala allows users to issue SQL queries against data stored in HDFS and Apache HBase.

In-memory database

A database management system that primarily stores data in main memory for faster processing.

Information Lifecycle Management (ILM)

The process and methodology of managing information through its lifecycle, from creation through disposal, including compliance with legal, regulatory, and privacy requirements.

International Classification of Diseases (ICD)

A World Health Organization standard for disease codes that is designed to promote international comparability in the collection, processing, classification, and presentation of mortality statistics. The ninth revision (ICD-9) was published in 1978. The tenth revision (ICD-10) was published in 1999, and significantly increased the number of codes.

---

7 https://cwiki.apache.org/confluence/display/Hive/HCatalog+UsingHCat.

Jaro-Winkler

A measure of similarity between two strings. The higher the Jaro–Winkler distance, the more similar the strings are. The Jaro–Winkler distance metric is designed and best suited for short strings, such as personal names. The score is normalized such that zero equates to no similarity, and one is an exact match.[8]

Key performance indicator (KPI)

An analytical measure used to determine the success of an initiative.

Legal hold

A process to prevent the destruction of paper and electronic documents that might be relevant to a lawsuit.

Levenshtein distance

A string metric to measure the difference between two sequences. The Levenshtein distance between two words is the minimum number of single-character edits (insertions, deletions, or substitutions) required to change one word into the other.[9]

Logical data model

A type of data model showing a detailed representation of some or all of an organization's data, independent of any particular data management technology, and described in business language.[10]

Logical Data Object (LDO)

An Informatica concept that describes a logical entity in an enterprise.

MapReduce

A computational paradigm in which an application is divided into self-contained units of work. MapReduce applications can process vast amounts (multiple terabytes) of data in parallel on large clusters in a reliable, fault-tolerant manner.

Master data management (MDM)

The process of establishing a single version of the truth for an organization's critical data entities, such as customers, products, materials, vendors, and chart of accounts.

---

8   http://en.wikipedia.org/wiki/Jaro-Winkler_distance.

9   http://en.wikipedia.org/wiki/Levenshtein_distance.

10 http://en.wikipedia.org/wiki/Logical_data_model.

Matching attribute

An attribute that is used to match two or more records as duplicates.

Matching function

The specific algorithm that is deployed to match two or more records. Examples include Jaro–Winkler, Levenshtein, or exact.

Metadata

Information that describes the characteristics of any data artifact, such as its name, location, perceived importance, quality, or value to the enterprise, and its relationships to other data artifacts that the enterprise deems worth managing. See also *business metadata* and *technical metadata*.

Metaphone

A phonetic algorithm, published by Lawrence Philips in 1990, for indexing words by their English pronunciation. It fundamentally improves on the Soundex algorithm by using information about variations and inconsistencies in English spelling and pronunciation to produce a more accurate encoding, which does a better job of matching words and names that sound similar.[11]

Monetization

The process of converting an asset such as data into money by selling it to third parties or by using it to develop new services.

National Change of Address (NCOA)

An offering from the United States Postal Service that provides information on individuals, families, and businesses who have submitted change-of-address forms.

Nomenclature statistique des Activités économiques dans la Communauté Européenne (NACE)

European Union industry codes, also known as the Statistical Classification of Economic Activities in the European Community.

---

11 http://en.wikipedia.org/wiki/Metaphone.

North American Industry Classification System (NAICS)

A six-digit standard used by the United States government to classify businesses for statistical purposes. The NAICS is supplanting the Standard Industry Classification (SIC) codes because it covers a broader range of industries.

NoSQL database

A database management system that does not use SQL as its primary query language. The database might not require fixed table schemas, and does not support JOIN operations. NoSQL ("not only SQL") databases include categories such as key-value stores. These databases are optimized for highly scalable read-write operations rather than for consistency.

Oozie

Apache Oozie is a workflow scheduler to manage Hadoop jobs.

Personally identifiable information (PII)

Information that can be used on its own or with other information to identify, contact, or locate a single person, or to identify an individual in context.[12]

Petabyte

A measurement of data equivalent to 1,024 terabytes.

Physical data model

A type of data model that is a representation of a data design which takes into account the facilities and constraints of a given database management system.[13]

Pig

Apache Pig is a platform for analyzing large, semi-structured data sets in Hadoop. It uses a procedural language called Pig Latin that insulates users from learning the intricacies of MapReduce programming in Java. Hive and Pig evolved as separate Apache projects for the analysis of large datasets. Hive is better suited to users who are familiar with SQL. Pig, on the other hand, is ideal for users who are familiar with procedural programs like Microsoft Visual Basic and Python.

---

12 http://en.wikipedia.org/wiki/Personally_identifiable_information.

13 http://en.wikipedia.org/wiki/Physical_data_model.

Policy

The written or unwritten declarations of how people should behave in a given situation.

Precision

The maximum number of digits that can be present in a number.

Privacy

The "right to be left alone," as defined in a *Harvard Law Review* article called "The Right to Privacy" written in 1890 by Louis Brandeis and Samuel Warren. Subsequent regulations and legislation around the world have built on this definition.

Privacy impact assessment (PIA)

An assessment undertaken to determine and minimize the privacy risk associated with a project.

Privileged user

A user such as a database administrator, a call center agent, or a network administrator who, by virtue of his or her job requirements, has read and write privileges that are greater than other users.

Profiling

The process of building a statistical view of the characteristics of data, such as the number of missing fields, number of nulls, and percentage of unique values.

R

An open source package for statistical computing and graphics.

Reference architecture

A technical architecture that includes a standard set of software components that may be implemented on a project within a specific domain (e.g., reference architecture for big data).

Reference data

Static data such as country codes, state or province codes, industry classification codes, and ICD-10 disease codes, which may be placed in lookup tables for reference by other applications across the enterprise.

Representational State Transfer (REST) API

An architectural style developed by the W3C Technical Architecture Group in parallel with HTTP 1.1, based on the existing design of HTTP 1.0. The World Wide Web represents the largest implementation of a system conforming to the REST architectural style.[14]

Retention schedule

A table that includes a classification of documents, the time that those documents should be retained, the legal citation or other reason for the retention period, and the action to be taken after the retention period has expired.

Scale

The maximum number of decimals after the decimal point.

Selectivity

The degree of uniqueness of the values (including nulls) in a column, calculated as Cardinality / (Row Count – Null Count). Selectivity is calculated on each column individually and is not the result of comparison to another column. This value is never greater than one.

Semantics

The study of meaning.

Semi-structured data

Data that is primarily unstructured, although there is some structure within the document. For example, a survey form might be semi-structured data because it includes structured fields such as name, gender, and age, along with multiple fields for free-text comments. See also *structured data* and *unstructured data*.

Sensitive data

Confidential or proprietary data that, if compromised, might cause financial or reputational loss to the person or enterprise that owns it.

---

14 http://en.wikipedia.org/wiki/Representational_state_transfer.

Smart meter

A type of meter that captures usage data every 15 to 60 minutes for residential and commercial customers, and communicates that information on a regular basis to the utility for billing and analytics.

Snapshot

A list of business terms, code values, technical metadata, and other data artifacts, along with their relationships at a given point in time. Snapshots allow administrators to go back in time to see how the data might have looked at that time. Snapshots also allow administrators to roll back any changes.

Soundex

A phonetic algorithm for indexing names by sound, as pronounced in English.[15]

Sqoop

Apache Sqoop is a tool that supports the movement of massive volumes of data between Apache Hadoop and structured data stores such as relational databases. Many ETL vendors also support similar functionality.

Standard Industry Classification (SIC)

A system for classifying industries by a four-digit code. In the United States, the SIC code is being replaced by the NAICS code.

Steward

See *data steward*.

Stream computing

A class of applications that perform high-performance, low-latency processing of large volumes of data leveraging parallel processing capabilities without landing data to disk. Also known as "Complex Event Processing (CEP)."

Structured data

Data with a structured format that is typically stored in a relational database with tables, rows, and columns. See also *unstructured data* and *semi-structured data*.

---

15 http://en.wikipedia.org/wiki/Soundex.

Structured Query Language (SQL)

A programming language used to manipulate data in a relational database management system.

Synchronization

A data quality dimension relating to the degree to which data elements are consistent from one data store to the next.

Synonym

A word with similar meaning.

Technical metadata

Information that describes the assets, models, and process elements used in IT systems.

Terabyte

A measure of data equivalent to 1,024 (10^3) gigabytes.

Test data management

The process of creating datasets that are suitable for testing purposes.

Text analytics

Techniques to derive insight from text.

Timeliness

A data quality dimension relating to the degree to which data is available in a timely manner.

Uniqueness

A data quality dimension relating to the degree to which data elements are unique within a data store.

Unstructured data

Data such as email, video, sound, and images that has no format or organizing principle. See also *structured data* and *semi-structured data*.

Workflow

A chained series of people and system tasks to accomplish a goal. For example, workflows might exist for data issue management, adding a business term, or simple approval.

Zettabyte (ZB)

A measure of data equivalent to one trillion gigabytes (10^{21} bytes).

POTENTIAL DATA GOVERNANCE TASKS TO BE AUTOMATED WITH TOOLS

Business Glossary

1. Bulk load business terms in Excel, CSV or XML format.
2. Create categories of business terms.
3. Facilitate social collaboration features.
4. Automatically hyperlink business terms that are embedded within the definitions of other business terms.
5. Add custom attributes to business terms and other data artifacts.
6. Add custom relationships to business terms and other data artifacts.
7. Add custom roles to the business glossary and other data artifacts.
8. Link business terms and column names to the associated reference data.
9. Link business terms to technical metadata.
10. Support the creation of custom asset types.
11. Flag Critical Data Elements.
12. Provide OOTB and custom workflows to manage business terms and other data artifacts.
13. Review the history of changes to business terms and other data artifacts.

14. Allow business users to link to the glossary directly from reporting tools.
15. Search for business terms.
16. Integrate business terms with associated unstructured data.

Metadata Management

17. Pull logical models from data modeling tools.
18. Pull physical models from data modeling tools.
19. Ingest metadata from relational databases.
20. Pull in metadata from data warehouse appliances.
21. Integrate metadata from legacy data sources.
22. Pull metadata from ETL tools.
23. Pull metadata from reporting tools.
24. Reflect custom code in the metadata tool.
25. Pull metadata from analytics tools.
26. Link business terms with column names.
27. Pull metadata from data quality tools.
28. Pull metadata from big data sources.
29. Provide detailed views on data lineage.
30. Customize data lineage reporting.
31. Manage permissions within the metadata repository.
32. Support the search for assets within the metadata repository.

Data Profiling

33. Conduct column analysis.
34. Discover the values distribution of a column.
35. Discover the patterns distribution of a column.
36. Discover the length frequencies of a column.
37. Discover hidden sensitive data.
38. Discover values with a similar sound within a column.
39. Agree on the data quality dimensions for the data governance program.
40. Develop business rules relating to the data quality dimensions.
41. Profile data relating to the completeness dimension of data quality.
42. Profile data relating to the conformity dimension of data quality.
43. Profile data relating to the consistency dimension of data quality.

44. Profile data relating to the synchronization dimension of data quality.
45. Profile data relating to the uniqueness dimension of data quality.
46. Profile data relating to the timeliness dimension of data quality.
47. Profile data relating to the accuracy dimension of data quality.
48. Discover data overlaps across columns.
49. Discover hidden relationships between columns.
50. Discover dependencies.
51. Discover data transformations.
52. Create virtual joins or logical data objects that can be profiled.

Data Quality Management

53. Transform data into a standardized format.
54. Improve the quality of address data.
55. Match and merge duplicate records.
56. In the Data Quality Scorecard, select the data domain or entity.
57. In the Data Quality Scorecard, define the acceptable thresholds of data quality.
58. In the Data Quality Scorecard, select the data quality dimensions to be measured for the specific data domain or entity.
59. In the Data Quality Scorecard, select the weights for each data quality dimension.
60. In the Data Quality Scorecard, select the business rules for each data quality dimension.
61. In the Data Quality Scorecard, assign weights to each business rule within a given data quality dimension.
62. In the Data Quality Scorecard, bind the business rules to the relevant columns.
63. View the Data Quality Scorecard.
64. Highlight the financial impact associated with poor data quality.
65. Conduct time series analysis.
66. Manage data quality exceptions.

Master Data Management

67. Define business terms that are consumed by the MDM hub.
68. Manage entity relationships.
69. Manage master data enrichment rules.
70. Manage master data validation rules.

71. Manage record matching rules.
72. Manage record consolidation rules.
73. View list of outstanding data stewardship tasks.
74. Manage duplicates.
75. View the data stewardship dashboard.
76. Manage hierarchies.
77. Improve the quality of master data.
78. Integrate social media with MDM.
79. Manage master data workflows.
80. Compare snapshots of master data.
81. Provide a history of changes to master data.
82. Offload MDM tasks to Hadoop for faster processing.

Reference Data Management

83. Build an inventory of code tables.
84. Agree on the master list of values for each code table.
85. Build simple mappings between master values and related code tables.
86. Build complex mappings between code values.
87. Manage hierarchies of code values.
88. Build and compare snapshots of reference data.
89. Visualize inter-temporal crosswalks between reference data snapshots .

Information Policy Management

90. Manage information policies, standards, and processes within the business glossary.
91. Manage business rules.
92. Leverage data governance tools to monitor and report on compliance with information policies.
93. Manage data issues.

Data Modeling

94. Integrate logical and physical data models with the metadata repository.
95. Expose ontologies within the metadata repository.
96. Prototype a unified schema across data domains using data discovery tools.
97. Establish a data model to support MDM.

Data Integration

98. Deploy data quality jobs in an integrated manner with data integration.
99. Move data between the MDM or reference data hub and source systems.
100. Leverage reference data for use by the data integration tool.
101. Integrate data integration tools into the metadata repository.
102. Automate the production of data integration jobs by leveraging the metadata repository.

Analytics and Reporting

103. Export data profiling results to a reporting tool for further visual analysis.
104. Export data artifacts into a reporting tool for visualization of data governance metrics.
105. Integrate analytics and reporting tools with the business glossary for semantic context.

Business Process Management

106. Create data governance workflows to leverage BPM capabilities.
107. Establish master data workflows to leverage BPM capabilities.
108. Map data policies and standards to key activities and milestones in BPM tools.

Data Security and Privacy

109. Determine privacy obligations.
110. Discover sensitive data using data discovery tools.
111. Flag sensitive data in the metadata repository.
112. Mask sensitive data in production environments.
113. Mask sensitive data in non-production environments.
114. Monitor database access by privileged users.
115. Document information policies in the business glossary that are executed by data masking and database monitoring tools.
116. Create a complete business object using data discovery tools that can be acted upon by data masking tools.

Information Lifecycle Management

117. Document information policies in the business glossary that are implemented by ILM tools.
118. Discover complete business objects that can be acted on efficiently by ILM tools.

Hadoop and NoSQL

119. Conduct an inventory of data in Hadoop.
120. Assign ownership for data in Hadoop.
121. Provision a semantic layer for analytics in Hadoop.
122. View the lineage of data in and out of Hadoop.
123. Manage reference data for Hadoop.
124. Profile data natively in Hadoop.
125. Discover data natively in Hadoop.
126. Execute data quality rules natively in Hadoop.
127. Integrate Hadoop with MDM.
128. Port data governance tools to Hadoop for improved performance.
129. Govern data within NoSQL databases.
130. Mask sensitive data in Hadoop.

Stream Computing

131. Use data profiling tools to understand a sample set of input data.
132. Govern reference data to be used by the stream computing application.
133. Govern business terms to be used by the stream computing application.

Text Analytics

134. Leverage unstructured data to improve the quality of sparsely populated structured data.
135. Extract additional relevant predictive variables not available within structured data.
136. Define consistent definitions for key business terms.
137. Ensure consistency in patient master data across facilities.
138. Adhere to privacy requirements.
139. Manage reference data.

INDEX